CIVIL SERVICE EXAMS

OTHER TITLES OF INTEREST FROM
LEARNINGEXPRESS, LLC

Becoming a Police Officer

Becoming a Firefighter

Civil Service Career Starter and Test Prep

Firefighter Exam

Math and Vocabulary for Civil Service Exams

Paramedic Exam

Police Officer Exam

Postal Worker Exam

CIVIL SERVICE EXAMS

Second Edition

LEARNINGEXPRESS®

NEW YORK

Library of Congress Cataloging-in-Publication Data:
Civil service exams.—2nd ed.
   p.cm.
 ISBN-13: 978-1-57685-744-1
 1. Civil service—United States—Examinations. 2. Civil service—United States. I. LearningExpress
(Organization)
 JK716.C466 2010
 352.6'5—dc22

                    2010010697

Printed in the United States of America

9 8 7 6 5 4

Second Edition

For information or to place an order, contact LearningExpress at:
  80 Broad Street
  4th Floor
  New York, NY 10004

Contents

CIVIL
SERVICE
EXAMS

I ▶ THE THREE LEVELS OF CIVIL SERVICE

1 ▶ CIVIL SERVICE

What Is Civil Service?

The term *civil service* refers to any job in the service of government, with the exception of uniformed military positions. Civil servants teach in public schools, staff libraries, maintain public buildings, collect taxes, enforce laws, fight fires, and perform thousands and thousands of other essential functions.

Today, most civil service jobs are filled competitively, either through a combined process of examination and job application or through a systematic vetting system in which each candidate's qualifications are weighted in order to evaluate (and, in many cases, assign a numerical score to) his or her suitability to the job. This wasn't always the case, however. In the early days of our nation, civil service jobs were regarded as prizes to be awarded to political supporters. Civil service employment ran under a *spoils system*, so called to reflect the old axiom "to the victor belong the spoils." As you might expect, civil service was not especially efficient during this period. For one thing, even the most capable appointees rarely stayed at their jobs long enough to master them. Each election cycle brought with it an army of new, and inexperienced, political appointees. Others were simply incompetent. Fortunately, the government was relatively small, so the fact that it was being run by the president's political pals rather than the most qualified candidates did not do too much damage to the nation.

All that changed in 1883, with the passage of the Pendleton Civil Service Act. Political activists had begun campaigning for reform in the 1870s, arguing that the rapid growth of government during the period mandated the creation of a professional civil service. The problems with the situation were greatly magnified by the 1881 assassination of newly elected president John Garfield by Charles Guiteau, a Garfield supporter angered by the new administration's failure to reward him with a comfortable government job. Support for reform grew, and in 1883, the Pendleton Act passed, reclassifying many patronage positions as competitive civil service jobs. Thereafter, applicants were required to take exams and otherwise prove their worthiness to assume government positions. Many jobs were no longer contingent upon who was in power; the office-holder remained a civil servant regardless of whether Democrats or Republicans held the White House. A Civil Service Commission was established to oversee the system and ensure its fairness.

The Private Sector versus the Public Sector

Civil service jobs are **public sector** jobs; they are funded publicly through tarevenues and other sources of government income (e.g., lotteries, license fees, bonds). Public sector employers work from a budget provided by the government, which they must meet; because public sector concerns may not turn a profit, they cannot simply increase prices and fees to generate more revenue. Civil service jobs are typically organized hierarchically by grade. The pay for a civil service job at a particular grade is determined by a matrithat takes into account the officeholder's position, years of service, and other relevant details. Many aspects of the job—including job description, work hours, pay, and benefits—are fixed by law. A civil servant's employer is the government for

which he or she works (federal, state, or local) or a publicly owned corporation (e.g., the Corporation for Public Broadcasting).

The **private sector** employs many more workers than does the public sector (although the federal government is the single largest employer in the United States). The private sector is competitive; Wal-Mart, for example, competes with Target and other discount retailers. In this way, the private sector differs from the public sector; you will not find two competing government agencies trying to provide you with the same service. You will, however, find many of the same jobs in the public sector that you find in the private sector. Again, though, there is a difference. In the private sector, wages and salaries, benefits, hours, and other aspects of the job are typically open to negotiation; they are not fixed by law (if you belong to a union, however, some or all of these may be fixed by your union contract). The private sector includes privately and publicly owned companies, nonpublic universities and hospitals, nonprofit and nongovernmental organizations, and anything else not operated by the government.

The Three Levels of Civil Service

Americans talk about the government as if it were one unified entity, but, in fact, Americans live under several sometimes overlapping, sometimes independent governments. First, there's the national, or federal, government in Washington, D.C.; its chief executive is the president of the United States. It provides for the nation's defense, regulates interstate commerce, polices interstate crimes, polices our coastlines, manages Social Security, Medicaid, and Medicare, and performs a host of other duties. Second is the state's government; its chief executive is the governor. State governments police and prosecute crimes, maintain roads (sometimes with financial assistance from the federal government), develop educational standards for public schools, operate state lotteries, administer various licenses (e.g., driver's licenses, hunting and fishing licenses, etc.), and perform many other jobs. Finally, there is the local government, presided over by a mayor, county executive, or perhaps even a board of commissioners. Local governments also police and prosecute crimes, manage garbage collection, fund and manage public schools, build and maintain sewers and other public works, and perform many other necessary tasks.

In this book, we'll cover the federal system in Chapter 2 and the state and local systems in Chapter 3. Note that because state and local systems vary widely, this book focuses on general principles that apply to most. To learn more specifics about working for your state or local government, visit the appropriate website or drop by a government office and ask for literature on the subject. Contact information for state governments is provided at the end of Chapter 3; nearly all state government websites provide links to local government websites.

Why Get a Job in Civil Service?

There are many compelling reasons to choose a career in the civil service. There are also a few drawbacks; for example, you are unlikely to grow wealthy in civil service. Overall, though, a civil service career is a very good one. Civil servants:

- provide essential services to the public
- enjoy the satisfaction of helping fellow citizens
- earn salaries that range from respectable to comfortable to highly desirable
- typically have opportunities for significant career advancement
- typically receive generous benefits packages
- have fewer worries about being downsized or outsourced than do their counterparts in the private sector
- know that their employer will not go bankrupt, as private employers sometimes do

If you're ready to pursue a career in civil service, read on. This book provides valuable information to guide you through the job search, application, and examination processes.

2 ▶ FEDERAL CIVIL SERVICE

Our country operates under a federal system of government defined by the Constitution of the United States of America. Because it is a federal system, some powers and responsibilities belong exclusively to the national government, headquartered in Washington, D.C.; some powers and responsibilities belong to state and local governments; and some powers are shared.

Although this use of the term *federal* refers to the national, state, and local governments (and their complex interrelations), when we talk about federal civil service, we are referring only to civil service jobs for the national government. To make matters more confusing, many of these jobs are not located in Washington, D.C. Postal workers, FBI agents, Social Security administrators, and a wide range of other federal employees do their work in every state of the nation.

This chapter discusses which jobs fall under the category of federal civil service positions. It describes the different categories of federal civil service jobs and tells you how to apply for these positions. We will discuss these subjects as they relate to state and local civil service positions in Chapter 3.

Mine Safety and Health Inspector, U.S. Department of Labor

Mining can be dangerous work, which is why mining companies must adhere to strict safety standards. The Mine Safety and Health Administration (MSHA), a division of the Department of Labor, regularly inspects mines to ensure that each mine meets federal workplace requirements so that each miner can do his or her job in a safe and healthy environment.

The MSHA offers a number of entry-level positions to inspectors of both metal and nonmetal mines. Successful candidates must score well on preemployment math and writing tests, pass drug screening and medical examinations, and submit to a background check. Those who stick with the job can eventually rise to the GS-12 level.

Applicants for the position are typically required to attend a screening session, at which they take the aforementioned tests. The tests are graded on site; applicants who earn qualifying scores are required to sit for an interview immediately. Those hired are enrolled in a two-year training program that includes extensive on-the-job training supplemented by nearly five months of formal training at the National Mine Health and Safety Academy in Beckley, West Virginia; those who succeed in the program are typically reclassified as permanent employees.

The responsibilities of a mine inspector include conducting on-site inspections of mines (underground and surface) as well as of mills and quarries. During these inspections, inspectors identify and report potential dangerous and/or unhealthy work conditions; inspect equipment to ensure that it is properly used and well maintained; investigate accidents and instruct mining concerns in accident prevention; participate in rescue and firefighting operations at mines; investigate mines for compliance with all relevant safety and health laws and regulations, and issue citations when violations are detected; and survey miners for complaints about work conditions, following up on such complaints through investigation.

Mine inspection is a potentially rewarding line of work for someone who enjoys working in remote locations. The job requires frequent travel—some inspectors spend up to two weeks per month on the road, although most travel less than that—which could be either a drawback or a benefit, depending on your point of view. Mines, it goes without saying, are not the nicest work environments even under optimal conditions, and this work certainly would not suit someone who desperately craves sunshine or who is susceptible to claustrophobia. Because mines are relatively dangerous places (compared to, say, an office building), the job also entails some inherent risks.

Positive Aspects of Federal Civil Service Jobs

There are many good reasons to work for the U.S. government: Government work offers plenty of opportunities, a good salary and benefits, job security, and more. Federal employment provides:

- **Challenging work.** Civil service positions are important, varied, and necessary to the smooth operation of our government.
- **Pay comparability.** Salaries are based on private sector comparisons. In 2009, the average full-time federal employee earned nearly $80,000 per year.
- **Extra pay.** Salaries may be augmented by locality pay and special pay provisions (such as extra pay for law enforcement jobs).
- **Job security.** Federal workers are always in demand, and federal layoffs are rare.
- **Step increases within grade.** Time on the job can lead to step increases that bring higher salaries.
- **Merit promotions.** It is possible to compete for merit increases in salary. Internal promotion allows employees to climb the federal ladder, assuming more responsibility and earning better pay.
- **Health and life insurance.** Insurance costs are shared with the government, which offers a wide range of plans.
- **Retirement.** Workers receive benefits from the Federal Employees Retirement System and Social Security.
- **Holidays and vacation/sick days.** Federal employees receive ten paid holidays every year and accrue between 13 and 26 paid vacation days and 13 paid sick days per year. Family and medical leaves may also be available.
- **Alternative work schedules.** Flexible hours, compressed workweek, telecommuting, part-time work, and job transfers may be options, depending on the job.
- **Appeals and grievances process.** There are outlets for complaint—among them are unions, the Merit Systems Protection Board, the Federal Labor Relations Authority, and the Office of Personnel Management (OPM).
- **Training opportunities.** Government-paid training and tuition reimbursement are available.

If you get a federal job, you'll be in good company: The federal government is the largest single employer in the United States, with just under 2.7 million civilian employees as of January 2009. That figure includes nearly three-quarters of one million postal workers and more than 1.9 million employees of the executive branch (which includes the president's office, the Department of State, the Department of Defense, the Department of Justice, the Department of Education, etc.) as of 2008. You'll find just about every type of job in the federal government that you'd find in the private sector. These jobs range from entry-level custodial and clerical positions all the way up to high-power white-collar jobs.

Every year, hundreds of thousands of positions open up because of employee promotions and retirements. The government frequently grows and creates new positions (as it did when it created a new agency, the Department of Homeland Security, in 2002), but even in times of tight budgets and downsizing, there are always lots of jobs available. The government always needs postal workers to deliver the nation's mail; police officers and firefighters to protect us; and clerks, secretaries, and maintenance personnel to keep the government running. During the last decade, the federal government has typically hired between 200,000 and 300,000 new employees during each non-census year (the number spikes to about one million in census years; the extra hires consist of temporary workers employed to conduct the census).

General Vessel Assistant, National Oceanographic and Atmospheric Administration, Department of Commerce

If you're looking for an opportunity to work on the open sea but aren't quite ready to join the Navy, Coast Guard, or Merchant Marine, the National Oceanographic and Atmospheric Administration (NOAA) may be the place for you. The NOAA operates research ships that conduct survey, sampling, and fishing operations to support its mission of leading in environmental research and preservation.

One of the NOAA's entry-level positions is general vessel assistant (GVA). GVA jobs include ordinary seaman, ordinary fisherman, wiper, and messman. Seamen and fishermen load and unload supplies; they also clean, paint, and maintain fishing gear. Wipers work in the engine room, maintaining the engine by wiping down machines, cleaning oil spills, and assisting in all engine repairs. A messman works under the steward; he or she washes dishes and prepares and cleans the dining area and mess deck. Many GVAs gain valuable experience in scientific research by participating in the operation, handling, and maintenance of scientific equipment on the open seas. All GVAs are employed year-round and work a 40-hour workweek. When docked at their homeport, GVAs help prepare for upcoming voyages or complete the work of recently finished voyages.

A GVA must be a U.S. citizen and must receive clearance via medical and dental exams. A drug test is also mandatory. No written exam is required. GVAs do not need to produce U.S. Coast Guard or Merchant Mariner's documents, as do applicants to more advanced positions on NOAA ships.

At a 2009 starting salary of about $32,000, GVAs won't get rich. However, because they typically spend about 240 days a year at sea, they can often forego rent, a considerable expense. Meals are also covered, and because they are typically at sea, GVAs have relatively few opportunities to spend their pay. Thus, a savvy GVA could actually squirrel away a decent amount of savings. Among other benefits of the job, duty locations include some pretty nice locations, such as Charleston, South Carolina; Honolulu, Hawaii; Norfolk, Virginia; San Diego, California; Seattle, Washington; Woods Hole, Massachusetts; Pascagoula, Mississippi; and various port towns in Alaska. Finally, GVAs accrue experience, through which they may earn promotion to positions with greater responsibility and greater pay. For example, five years' experience qualifies a seaman, angler, or wiper for a job as chief boatswain, a position that paid about $58,000 in 2009.

Opportunities to Work Anywhere

The federal government offers jobs all over the country; you don't have to live in or even near Washington, D.C. to hold a federal civil service job. In fact, fewer than 200,000 of the federal government's workforce work in Washington, D.C. There are actually more civilian federal jobs in California than there are in D.C. There are federal workforces of well more than 100,000 in Florida, Maryland, New York, Pennsylvania, Texas, and Virginia as well. Cities with large federal workforces include Atlanta, Baltimore, Chicago, Denver, Los Angeles/Long Beach, New York City, Philadelphia, San Antonio, and San Diego. But you don't have to live in a big city to find work with the federal government. In many small towns, a large percentage of civilians are federal employees. Look at the blue pages of your local telephone book to see just how many federal employees there are in your area. The federal government also employs nearly 20,000 workers in U.S. territories and another 75,000 in foreign countries.

Minimum Qualifications

All you need for a career with the government is a high school diploma (or GED) and, for most positions, U.S. citizenship. (There are also some part-time positions for high school students; we'll discuss them later.) If you are a male born after December 31, 1959, you must also have registered with (or be exempt from) the Selective Service. Many kinds of positions are available for people with no education beyond high school and for those with little or no job experience. Beyond the minimum requirements, your education, skills, experience, and location will determine what specific jobs you are eligible for within the federal government.

Types of Employees

Federal employees are classified as **full time**, **part time**, **interns**, and **work-study** employees. Full-time employees fall into four subcategories:

- **Temporary** employees hold positions that last for less than one year. They enjoy no special privileges or benefits, but as temporary employees, they get their foot in the door to government employment. This is a great advantage; temporary workers not only get insider knowledge of job openings, but also, if they do their jobs well, have a terrific advantage over other candidates when it comes time to hire for better jobs.

- **Term** employees work for a specified time, usually in the service of a particular project or study. Term employment can last from one to three years and can, on occasion, extend beyond the three-year limit. Term employees often receive health benefits; they are usually not eligible for pension benefits. Like temporary employees, term hires can find out about job openings early and, if they do their jobs well, have an edge in competing for permanent positions.

- **Career-conditional** employees are typically new federal hires on track to a career position. During their first three years of employment, career-conditional employees serve a probation, during which they are evaluated and after which they become eligible for instatement as full-time permanent employees. This three-year period is critical for those who seek career status. It includes most career benefits, although with various restrictions upon them (disability insurance, for example, is often excluded or limited for career-conditional employees).

- **Career** employees are those with full-time, full-benefit-level jobs. These jobs are not only the best paying in the federal system, but also among the safest; career employees are rarely affected by downsizing and layoffs.

Part-time employees, **interns**, and **work-study employees** work in a variety of agencies, and the parameters of their positions vary widely. In general, if you are at least 16 years old, you can begin working part time for the government, so long as you are a student in good standing and remain so until you graduate. Many agencies, including the U.S. Postal Service (USPS), also have regular part-time and seasonal positions.

The Series and Grade System of Classification

In the federal government, civilian employees are organized—and paid—according to the kind of work they do (called the *series*) and the level of difficulty (called the *grade*) of their position. Salaries and wages, called *schedules*, are determined by these classifications. Each grade consists of several *steps*, or raises. For example, a Grade 5 Park Ranger earns a base salary of $30,772 at Step 1, $34,875 at Step 5, and $40,005 at Step 10. If he or she is promoted to Grade 7, he or she earns $38,117 at Step 1, $43,200 at Step 5, and $49,553 at Step 10 (all figures as of 2009). Note that these salaries are based upon the location in which the ranger works (see **Federal Pay Schedule** and **Percentage Pay Adjustments by Geographic Locality** tables on page 17).

Because the federal government consists of numerous departments and independent agencies, there are many different job series and pay schedules that apply to federal employees. Still, excluding postal workers, most entry-level employees fall into one of two main series and schedules:

- The **General Schedule (GS)** applies to most professional, technical, administrative, and clerical positions.
- The **Wage Grade (WG)** series and schedule apply to most blue-collar workers employed by the federal government.

GS employees account for approximately two-thirds of the government civilian workforce (this figure excludes employees of the USPS); the remaining one-third are WG employees.

General Schedule Jobs

There are 23 different *occupational groups* (general job categories) in the General Schedule, and each group can have up to 50 *job series* (jobs that fall within the general job category). For example, the medical, hospital, dental, and public health occupational group includes such job series as autopsy assistant series, nurse series, podiatrist series, etc. Each of these jobs series can, in turn, include numerous *job titles*. The nurse series, for example, includes nurses in hospitals, nurses in clinics, nurses who specialize in a particular field of medicine, etc.

Here's how the hierarchy of GS categories works:

Occupational Group
↓
Job Series
↓
Job Titles

Employees in different GS series—even those in jobs as diverse as computer scientist and food inspector—will receive the same salary if they are at the

Information Management Officer, Office of the Director of National Intelligence (ODNI)

There can be little doubt that intelligence and homeland security will be among the major growth areas in government in the coming years. They are also areas that should offer some of the most gratifying jobs in government; given the state of the world today, it's hard to imagine that workers in these fields will ever wonder whether their work is important.

The director of national intelligence (DNI) is a heavy hitter in D.C. He or she advises the president, the National Security Council, and the Homeland Security Council on intelligence matters. The DNI also supervises the implementation of the National Intelligence Program. The office of the DNI (ODNI) is one of the government's major hubs of crucial intelligence activity.

Information management officers hold entry-level full-time permanent positions in the ODNI. They assist in the implementation of records- and knowledge-management systems. They also assist in the documentation of the ODNI's operations, policies, decisions, procedures, and functions; creation, storage, and cataloging of records; and the promotion the ODNI through marketing, training, and awareness.

To qualify for this position, a candidate must be a U.S. citizen capable of obtaining top secret security clearance. He or she must have a basic understanding of and interest in the intelligence and defense communities, their missions, and their business practices. A solid understanding of current world events is also required. Communication skills (oral and written) in a variety of formats (one on one, small group, presentation, e-mail, report) and the ability to work well in a team environment are also considered essential, as are project management skills. Desirable additional skills include familiarity with the Federal Records Act and federal record-keeping requirements as they apply to the federal government, intelligence agencies, and the defense community; and familiarity with the Freedom of Information and Protection of Privacy Act and all relevant regulations and procedures.

Applicants who meet the aforementioned minimum required qualifications are further evaluated on the basis of supplemental application materials, including a biographic profile or resume, a narrative statement describing the applicant's knowledge, skills, and abilities as they pertain to the job requirements (specific examples should be included), and performance reviews for the prior two years. In 2009, this position offered a starting salary in the $37,000 to $58,000 range, depending on previous experience and qualifications.

same grade and work in the same location; that's because the grading system says that their jobs are equally difficult and equally important. This is also true for the wage schedule. Note, however, that salaries are adjusted for location, meaning that a clerk in New York City will earn more than a clerk at the same grade level who works in Dayton, Ohio.

General Schedule Occupational Groups

There are 23 different occupational groups in the GS.

0000	Miscellaneous Occupations Group
0100	Social Science, Psychology, and Welfare Group
0200	Human Resources Management Group
0300	General Administrative, Clerical, and Office Services Group
0400	Biological Sciences Group
0500	Accounting and Budget Group
0600	Medical, Hospital, Dental, and Public Health Group
0700	Veterinary Medical Science Group
0800	Engineering and Architecture Group
0900	Legal and Kindred Group
1000	Information and Arts Group
1100	Business and Industry Group
1200	Copyright, Patent, and Trademark Group
1300	Physical Sciences Group
1400	Library and Archives Group
1500	Mathematics and Statistics Group
1600	Equipment, Facilities, and Services Group
1700	Education Group
1800	Investigation Group
1900	Quality Assurance, Inspection, and Grading Group
2000	Supply Group
2100	Transportation Group
2200	Information Technology Group

Many personnel-intensive jobs fall into the GS-300 category; the government employs more than 70,000 clerks and assistants (GS-0303), more than 60,000 administrators (GS-0310), more than 50,000 secretaries (GS-0318), and more than 50,000 computer specialists (GS-0334).

The General Schedule includes 15 grades for its positions. They are designated GS-1 through GS-15, with GS-1 the lowest level and GS-15 the highest. Entry-level jobs typically fall into the GS-1 to GS-7 range. Jobs at the GS-5 level typically require a four-year undergraduate degree or comparable work experience; jobs at the GS-7 level and above typically require either graduate-level education or comparable work experience.

All competitive GS jobs are listed at the USAJOBS website (www.usajobs.gov). Many excepted GS positions are listed there as well, although you should check the websites of individual agencies to make sure you find all listings for such positions.

Wage Grade Employees

Federal wage employees are paid at an hourly rate set through the Federal Wage System (FWS), which was established in 1972 to create a uniform wage system that ensured fair compensation. Under FWS, the Federal Prevailing Rate Advisory Committee, which is comprised of both federal agency and labor union representatives, advises the Director of the Office of Personnel Management on the setting of federal wages.

The fundamental principle of FWS pay is that federal wage earners should earn comparable pay to their peers in the private sector. Wage levels are set by locality to reflect differences in cost of living. Each wage-grade position has five steps. At Step 2, wage earners earn the full prevailing rate paid in the private sector; at Step 5, wage earners typically earn 12% above the prevailing rate.

2500	Wire Communications Equipment Installation and Maintenance Family
2600	Electronic Equipment Installation and Maintenance Family
2800	Electrical Installation and Maintenance Family
3100	Fabric and Leather Work Family
3300	Instrument Work Family
3400	Machine Tool Work Family
3500	General Services and Support Work Family
3600	Structural and Finishing Work Family
3700	Metal Processing Family
3800	Metal Work Family
3900	Motion Picture, Radio, Television, and Sound Equipment Operating Family
4000	Lens and Crystal Work Family
4100	Painting and Paperhanging Family

4200	Plumbing and Pipefitting Family
4300	Pliable Materials Work Family
4400	Printing Family
4600	Woodwork Family
4700	General Maintenance and Operations Work Family
4800	General Equipment Maintenance Family
5000	Plant and Animal Work Family
5200	Miscellaneous Occupations Family
5300	Industrial Equipment Maintenance Family
5400	Industrial Equipment Operation Family
5700	Transportation/Mobile Equipment Operation Family
5800	Heavy Mobile Equipment Mechanic Family
6500	Ammunition, Explosives, and Toxic Materials Work Family
6600	Armament Work Family
6900	Warehousing and Stock Handling Family
7000	Packing and Processing Family
7300	Laundry, Dry Cleaning, and Pressing Family
7400	Food Preparation and Serving Family
7600	Personal Services Family
8200	Fluid Systems Maintenance Family
8600	Engine Overhaul Family
8800	Aircraft Overhaul Family
9000	Film Processing Family

Salaries and Benefits

As a government employee, you'll earn a respectable income, even at the entry level. Positions that require little or no education or work experience often offer higher pay than comparable jobs in the private sector. In addition, federal employees with relevant education or experience are far more likely than their private-sector counterparts to be promoted to better, higher-paying positions.

Federal Pay Schedule and Locality Adjustments

The following table shows the pay schedule for full-time salaried employees by grade and step. A second table shows the amount by which pay is increased for those working in various cities; these increases are provided to offset the expense of living in cities in which rents and mortgages, groceries, automobile insurance, etc. are relatively expensive.

SALARY TABLE 2009-GS INCORPORATING THE 2.90% GENERAL SCHEDULE INCREASE ANNUAL RATES BY GRADE AND STEP-EFFECTIVE JANUARY 2009 (In dollars)										
GRADE	STEP 1	STEP 2	STEP 3	STEP 4	STEP 5	STEP 6	STEP 7	STEP 8	STEP 9	STEP 10	WITHIN GRADE AMOUNTS
1	$ 17,540	$ 18,126	18,709	19,290	19,873	20,216	20,792	21,373	21,396	21,944	VARIES
2	19,721	20,190	20,842	21,396	21,635	22,271	22,907	23,543	24,179	24,815	VARIES
3	21,517	22,234	22,951	23,668	24,385	25,102	25,819	26,536	27,253	27,970	717
4	24,156	24,961	25,766	26,571	27,376	28,181	28,986	29,791	30,596	31,401	805
5	27,026	27,927	28,828	29,729	30,630	31,531	32,432	33,333	34,234	35,135	901
6	30,125	31,129	32,133	33,137	34,141	35,145	36,149	37,153	38,157	39,161	1,004
7	33,477	34,593	35,709	36,825	37,941	39,057	40,173	41,289	42,405	43,521	1,116
8	37,075	38,311	39,547	40,783	42,019	43,255	44,491	45,727	46,963	48,199	1,236
9	40,949	42,314	43,679	45,044	46,409	47,774	49,139	50,504	51,869	53,234	1,365
10	45,095	46,598	48,101	49,604	51,107	52,610	54,113	55,616	57,119	58,622	1,503
11	49,544	51,195	52,846	54,497	56,148	57,799	59,450	61,101	62,752	64,403	1,651
12	59,383	61,362	63,341	65,320	67,299	69,278	71,257	73,236	75,215	77,194	1,979
13	70,615	72,969	75,323	77,677	80,031	82,385	84,739	87,093	89,447	91,801	2,354
14	83,445	86,227	89,009	91,791	94,573	97,355	100,137	102,919	105,701	108,483	2,782
15	98,156	101,428	104,700	107,972	111,244	114,516	117,788	121,060	124,332	127,604	3,272

PERCENT PAY INCREASE-BY CITY			
Atlanta	18.55%	Miami/Fort Lauderdale	20.21%
Boston/Worcester	23.98%	Milwaukee	17.65%
Buffalo	16.39%	Minneapolis–St. Paul	20.36%
Chicago	24.47%	New York metro region	27.96%
Cincinnati	18.28%	Philadelphia	21.25%
Cleveland	18.16%	Phoenix	16.08%
Columbus	16.62%	Pittsburgh	15.86%
Dallas–Fort Worth	19.95%	Portland	19.71%
Dayton	15.90%	Raleigh-Durham	17.38%
Denver/Boulder	22.03%	Richmond	16.10%
Detroit	23.56%	Sacramento	21.53%
Hartford	25.08%	San Diego	23.44%
Houston	28.28%	San Francisco/San Jose	34.35%
Huntsville/Decatur	15.46%	Seattle/Tacoma	21.06%
Indianapolis	14.23%	Washington, D.C./Baltimore/No. Virginia	23.10%
Los Angeles	26.51%	Rest of continental U.S.	13.86%

Benefits

Federal benefits are hard to beat. Benefit packages vary from department to department and from position to position, but most career employees receive the following:

- Ten paid holidays per year
- 13 to 26 days of paid vacation per year
- 13 days of sick leave per year
- Regular cost of living adjustments
- Death and disability insurance
- Group life insurance
- Healthcare (medical and dental benefits)
- Government pension

Special Programs

The federal government offers a number of special programs that can make your job even more lucrative. All employees are eligible for the government's Incentive Rewards Program, which provides prizes and bonuses of up to $500,000 to workers who find innovative ways to reduce government costs and improve efficiency. Other programs include the Federal Employee Education and Assistance Fund (FEEAF), which provides grants and scholarships to federal employees and their dependents. Because this program is funded by employee contributions, it doesn't cost the taxpayers a single penny!

Information Technology (IT) Specialist, Bureau of the Census

The Constitution of the United States mandates a census every ten years, making the Bureau of the Census one of the oldest agencies of the federal government. Originally little more than a head count, the census has evolved over the centuries into a collection of compledemographic, social, and economic data.

The management of such varied and important data requires sophisticated computer systems; as a result, IT specialists will find a broad range of opportunities at the Census Bureau. Depending on their level of academic advancement and previous work experience, IT specialists can start anywhere between the GS-5 level to the GS-11 level. They can sign on as systems administration specialists, network services specialists, or security specialists. Each track offers room for advancement to GS-12 level. IT specialists at the Census Bureau plan and coordinate hardware and software installations; manage the bureau's network systems; develop and implement privacy tools; support and improve existing software applications; and plan, develop, and troubleshoot data storage and retrieval systems.

All applicants must be U.S. citizens. GS-5 hires must have a bachelor's degree with a major in a computer-related field, or three years of work experience as a computer assistant, program analyst, or some other position that required the development or adaptation of computer programs, or an acceptable combination of schooling (without achieving a degree) and work experience. GS-7s must have a computer-related bachelor's degree with superior academic achievement or a bachelor's plus one year of computer-related graduate work and/or one year of professional experience as an IT Specialist. GS-9s must have a master's degree in computer science or extensive experience in a VMS, Unix, Novell, or Windows NT environment. GS-11s must have a PhD in computer science or extensive professional experience and expertise in the field. Veterans who received honorable or general discharge receive preferential treatment in hiring.

Like all permanent full-time federal jobs, Census Bureau IT positions provide job security, a solid living wage, and a number of plum benefits, including health insurance with more than 100 optional plans to choose from; basic life insurance plus three types of optional supplemental insurance; long-term care insurance for employees, their parents, spouses, children, parents-in-law, and stepparents; annual and sick leave; health and dependent-care flexible spending accounts; and a three-tiered retirement program.

Some agencies have their own programs as well. The USPS, for example, has the Postal Employee's Relief Fund, which provides monetary relief to employees who have been victims of natural disasters.

Federal Hiring System

Competitive Service and Excepted Service

The federal government offers two classes of jobs: **competitive service** and **excepted service.**

Competitive service jobs are supervised by the Office of Personnel Management, which sets qualification requirements and pay rates. Competitive service jobs are subject to acts of Congress that ensure fair and equal treatment in hiring. Hiring is based upon the applicants' knowledge, skills, and abilities (often abbreviated as *KSAs*) with no regard to such external factors as race, religion, gender, etc. Applicants for competitive service positions receive a score based upon their qualifications (which may include level of education, years of experience, test scores, and results of personal interview); this score is used to compare candidates and select those most qualified for the job. Hiring authorities have the power to review as many applicants as they like but must evaluate them solely on the basis of job-related criteria.

Excepted service jobs are not subject to the appointment, pay, and classification rules outlined under Title 5 of the United States Code (they are, however, subject to veterans' preferences). Excepted service agencies (which include the U.S. Postal Service, the Federal Bureau of Investigation, the Central Intelligence Agency, the Federal Reserve System, the Foreign Service, and the General Accounting Office) are free to set their own qualification requirements.

Some agencies offer a miof competitive and excepted service jobs; certain divisions of the agency (or merely specific jobs within each division) may be designated "excepted" with the rest classified as "competitive."

Types of Candidates

Hiring agencies typically choose candidates from among three groups of candidates:

1. a **competitive list of eligible candidates**, ranked by their qualification score for a specific position
2. a **list of eligible candidates with previous civil service status** who are therefore eligible for non-competitive hiring within a competitive service; these candidates are selected under agency merit-promotion guidelines and can receive appointment by promotion, reassignment, transfer, or reinstatement
3. a **list of eligible candidates who qualify for special noncompetitive appointment under law or executive order** such as the Veterans Readjustment Appointment (VRA), which allows agencies to hire eligible veterans without competition

Ranking Candidates

All competitive service and many excepted service agencies rate applicants on a scale of 1 to 100 according to specific job-related criteria; these criteria are clearly delineated on the job vacancy announcement. Veterans receive a five- or ten-point bonus (ten points are awarded to those with service-related disabilities, to certain unmarried spouses of deceased veterans, or to mothers of deceased or disabled veterans—more on veterans' preference later in this chapter). In the past, the Office of Personnel Management handled grading. Today, many agencies are empowered to grade their own applicant pools; a number of these agencies subcontract the grading back to OPM.

As you are probably aware, in the private sector, a good interview can make or break your application. In government, it doesn't work quite that way; because the interview comes so much later in the hiring process, it does not hold the potential for catapulting a questionable candidate to "must hire" status. While the interview is still very important, much more important are your application or resume and your performance on exams. If these fail to impress, you'll never get the chance to win your employer over during the interview.

Until recently, the OPM maintained registers and eligibility lists of qualified applicants who had not been placed. This allowed the agency to dip into a reserve of potential employees whenever there was a new job opening; often that meant that the job could be filled by a previous applicant without the government's having to post the job and screen a new wave of candidates. As various federal agencies have been given more freedom to evaluate and grade their own candidates, however, this system has become impractical.

As a result, the register and eligibility list systems have been eliminated. Fortunately, anyone interested in a federal job can go to the USAJOBS website (www.usajobs.com) and complete an online resume that can be submitted to any federal employer. The resume is stored in the USAJOBS system, so there is no need to recomplete it every time you apply for a new job (you may want to tweak your resume, however, to highlight skills required for the open position).

Veterans' Preference

If you've served on active duty in the military, you may be eligible for veterans' preference: an additional five points—or ten points to those with service-related disabilities, to certain unmarried spouses of deceased veterans, or to mothers of deceased or disabled veterans—to your rating in the job selection process. To be eligible, you must have been discharged under honorable conditions or, if you began serving after October 15, 1976, you must have a campaign badge, an expeditionary medal, or a service-related disability.

To claim the five-point preference, you need to attach proof of your eligibility in the form of a copy of your DD-214, Certificate of Release or Discharge from Active Duty, or other eligible form. For the ten-point preference, you must attach SF-15, the Application for Ten-Point Veterans' Preference, and the eligibility proofs it requires. For more information regarding Veterans' Preference, visit the USAJOBS website or visit the Department of Labor's Veterans' Preference Advisor page at www.dol.gov/elaws/vetspref.htm.

Unassembled Exams

If there is no exam, then the application itself is considered the entrance test (and is sometimes referred to as an "unassembled exam"). Rating is based solely upon the application and accompanying materials. Applicants achieving the highest scores are placed on the "best qualified" list and are typically invited to interview.

Assembled Exams and Band Testing

The assembled exam—the legendary *civil service test*—is less and less commonly used as time passes. Today, written tests are not required for most federal civil service jobs. Such tests are most often used for clerical jobs at the GS-2, GS-3, and GS-4 level and for technical aid jobs at the GS-2 and GS-3 levels. Tests are used only rarely for jobs at the GS-5 level and above.

When an exam is administered, the hiring agency either:

- holds an *assembled exam* (so named because all applicants are assembled at the same time and place) for all candidates, OR
- calls only the top-ranked candidates for the exam (this is often referred to as *band testing*).

In the case of an assembled exam, your test results can significantly improve your qualification score, which, in turn, can land you the job. In the case of band testing, you will already need to be relatively highly qualified *before* sitting for the exam, as only the best candidates reach the exam stage.

Job Vacancy Announcements

All jobs filled through competitive application are posted at the USAJOBS website (www.usajobs.gov). Positions classified as "excepted"—meaning that they fall outside the legal requirements imposed on competitive hiring—do not have to be posted at the USAJOBS website, but most are anyway. The FBI, for example, hires through the excepted process only, yet still posts all its opening at USAJOBS. To be safe, you should check for job postings at the websites of individual agencies at which you wish to work if you are interested in one of the agency's excepted positions.

Every job vacancy notice provides an overview of the available position, a detailed description of the duties associated with the position, a list of job requirements, an outline of the hiring process, and a list of benefits. Specific information includes:

- Open and close dates (*filing period* or *application window*)
- Job title
- Job number
- Geographic location
- Number of vacancies
- Hiring office/agency
- Salary range
- Terms (part/full time)
- Benefits
- Job duties
- Job qualifications
- Criteria for evaluation or rating (education, experience, etc.)
- Any supplemental information required of candidate
- Who may apply (*area of consideration* or *limits of consideration*)
- Description of application process
- Whom to call for forms
- To whom to address further questions
- Where to mail/e-mail completed forms
- Application deadline

If an agency wants to offer the position to a limited group of current or former employees, the job announcement will list the specific types of applicants to which the job is open; this is often described as the *area of consideration*. When the job is offered to external candidates, the positions may still be restricted to persons within a certain geographical area. It is important to read job announcements carefully to make sure that you are eligible for consideration.

Finding a Job and Getting It

Applying for a federal position is a three-step process. Those steps are:

1. Creating a USAJOBS Account and Creating a Resume
2. Searching and Applying for Jobs
3. Managing Your Career

Step 1: Creating a USAJOBS Account and Creating a Resume

The easiest way to create a USAJOBS account is via the Internet. Point your browser to the USAJOBS website (www.usajobs.gov) and click the "MY USAJOBS" tab. This will take you to a page from which you can either (1) create an account, or (2) access an already existing account. Click the "Account" button.

The next screen asks you to input:

- your name
- your address
- your telephone number
- your email address

- your username and password (You get to choose both; your username must be unique in the USAJOBS system. Don't forget to write them down somewhere where you will not lose them, because you will need them every time you access your account.)
- a password question that provides a hint about your password (e.g., "What is your favorite hobby?" Answer the question correctly and the USAJOBS website will give you your password.)
- your citizenship status
- your Veterans' Preference status

Click "I agree. Log me in." and presto! Your USAJOBS account has been created. Now you are ready to create a resume. USAJOBS allows you to create and save multiple resumes, so you will be able to tailor your resume to specific job opportunities.

When building your USAJOBS resume(s), follow these tips:

- **Use key words.** Remember that employers will scan your resume for key words that reflect your knowledge, skills, and abilities (KSAs). Think carefully about your word choice. Your goal is to communicate that you have the skills and experiences that the employer is seeking. Read job postings for positions in which you are interested and incorporate key words from the description into your resume. When rewriting your resume for a particular position, add words from that specific job description.
- **Keep your resume brief.** Recruiters receive many applications for every position, and during their first review of resumes, they will scan them briefly, looking for qualities that make a candidate stand out. Highlight those qualities and keep all other information to a minimum; this will increase the chances that the recruiter will see the most important information on that first go-round. USAJOBS

says that the hiring manager should be able to find your key credentials within ten to 15 seconds of looking at your resume. If he or she can't, your resume is too long and contains too much information.

- **Highlight numbers that emphasize your achievements.** Specific details are much more powerful than nonspecific statements. Don't just say, "I saved my company money by developing new software." Say, "I created software that saved my company $60,000 during the first year of implementation." Because the latter offers a concrete number, it is much more impressive than the former example.

The USAJOBS website provides step-by-step instructions to guide you through the resume-building process. Resume building consists of entering all types of information, such as work experience, educational background, training, references, and skills, into a web-based form. Click "Save" when you're done and your resume will remain on file at the website until you decide to edit or delete it.

You may also submit a hard copy of your resume if you prefer. If you do, make sure that you include all the information included in an online resume and all the information requested in the job vacancy announcement; if you don't, you will not be considered for the position. Remember that your hard-copy resume, like your online resume, should be brief, focusing only on relevant points.

Following is a list of the information you should include in a hard-copy resume.

- **Job information**
  Job announcement number
  Job title
  Grade(s) for which you are applying
- **Personal information**
  Full name and mailing address, with zip code

Daytime and evening telephone numbers, with area code

Country of citizenship

Veterans' preference, if applicable

- **Education**

The name, city, state, and zip code, if possible, of your high school, along with the date on which you earned your diploma or GED

The name, city, state, and zip code, if possible, of any colleges and universities you attended, as well as your major(s) and the type of degree(s) you received. If you did not receive a degree, indicate the total number of credits earned and indicate whether they were quarter or semester credits. Do not send a college transcript unless required to do so by the job vacancy announcement.

- **Work experience**

Include the following information for all paid and unpaid work experience relating to the job vacancy you would like to fill:

Job title

Duties and accomplishments

Name and address of employer

Name and phone number of supervisor (indicate whether your current supervisor may be contacted)

Dates employment began and ended (month and year)

Number of hours worked per week

Salary/wages

- **Other qualifications**

The OPM requests that you provide dates for these accomplishments, but do not send documentation unless specifically requested to do so:

Any job-related training courses you've taken (include course title and year)

Job-related skills, such as foreign languages, computer software/hardware proficiency, machine operability, and typing speed

Current job-related certificates and licenses

Job-related honors, awards, and special accomplishments, such as membership in a professional or honor society, leadership activities, publications, and performance awards

Step 2: Searching and Applying for Jobs

Searching for job openings with the federal government has never been easier, thanks to USAJOBS, the government's "one-stop source for federal jobs and employment information." The site includes many helpful tutorials (at www.usajobs.gov/firsttimers.asp) that will help you get started. Once you've learned how to navigate the site, you'll be ready to search for jobs by region, state, zip code, country, department, and salary range. You may also contact USAJOBS by telephone at 703-724-1850 or, for TDD service, at 978-461-8404.

One of the great features of the USAJOBS website is its search agent function, which allows you to create and save up to ten different collections of job-search parameters. Suppose you were looking for an administrative job. You might be willing to accept a job at one pay level if it were in the area where you currently live, but you might be willing to relocate only for a better-paying job. You could create two search agents, one that searched only for administrative jobs in your area and one that searched for administrative jobs nationally. You can fine-tune your search by job category, occupational series, hiring agency or department, salary range, and pay grade. The USAJOBS website will automatically run all your search agents for you as often as you like (monthly, biweekly, weekly, or daily) and will e-mail you the results.

You can also search for job openings at an individual agency's website, a good strategy if you're interested in working at a particular agency. You should also take a look at the Call to Serve website (www.ourpublicservice.org/workforusa/workforusa.htm); it's run by The Partnership for Public Service, a private organization dedicated to "helping revitalize the federal civil service." The Best Places to Work in the Federal Government website (www.bestplacestowork.org) ranks federal jobs by employee satisfaction levels; that's certainly useful information. No matter where you find your job listing, you will likely have to apply through the USAJOBS website.

The Internet is the best resource for your job search, but it isn't the only one. If you live near an OPM service center or a Federal Executive Board (FEB) office, give them a call; they may have printed versions of job listings. You might also consider subscribing to the *Federal Jobs Digest*, an excellent biweekly newsletter. (You can also visit the Federal Jobs Digest website at www.jobsfed.com; it features a very user-friendly search engine for locating open positions in the federal government). Other books worth considering (besides this one) include Dennis V. Damp's *The Book of U.S. Government Jobs*. It, too, has a website (federaljobs.net) that provides an overview of government work and links to many government agency employment sites.

Once you have found a position that interests you, you will have to decipher the job announcement and complete an application. Take special note of the *filing period* or *application window*, which is the specific time period during which applications will be accepted. Be sure you are aware of the filing period; otherwise, you may miss the deadline. Once the filing period ends, you will not be able to apply for the position.

After you submit your resume, what happens next depends on the type of position for which you are applying. Some civil service jobs require that you take a written exam (most federal jobs do not have this requirement, by the way). Others require different qualifying procedures before you can be employed.

Written Exams

When you apply for a competitive position that requires an assembled exam, you will receive a test scheduling card. This is particularly important for positions with the USPS as well as for law enforcement, firefighting, and clerical and secretarial positions. These entry-level jobs require a written test, and because there is often an oversupply of applicants, you'll need to make a reservation to take the exam. Fill out and return the test scheduling card and you'll be notified of exactly when and where you need to be to take the exam. Be aware that sometimes certain areas have such high demand for certain jobs, including clerical workers, that these exams can be taken on a walk-in basis without reservation. Contact your area Federal Job Information Center in the Office of Personnel Management for more details.

For most entry-level positions that require exams, the tests start out by measuring your basic reading, writing, and (sometimes) math skills. The hiring agency is generally more interested in your ability to be trained than in the knowledge you already have about the job. Sample exams testing these basic skills, as well as chapters that teach you how to improve your performance in reading, grammar, vocabulary, spelling, math, and civil service skills, such as coding and memory, are included in this book.

Depending on the position you seek, the exams may also assess your common sense and logic or your memory. There are also different kinds of questions that test specific work-related skills. For instance, postal workers are required to memorize and check addresses; clerical workers are tested on aspects of filing, such as alphabetization. The exams usually present scenarios that would arise in a typical job situation and are almost always multiple choice.

In general, you can retake tests if you fail, and you can always retake a test during a subsequent testing period or for a subsequent job posting in order to improve your score. Improving your score will, of course, improve your job ranking.

Physical Performance Tests

The majority of civilian government jobs don't require any special physical ability, but there are several important exceptions. At the USPS, for example, many jobs require physical strength and stamina, so the USPS requires all applicants to be able to lift 70 pounds in order to be considered.

Firefighters and law enforcement employees, among others, *do* need special physical capacities and skills, and they must pass a series of physical tests before they can be hired. These physical ability tests may include timed runs, obstacle courses, ladder climbs, weight lifting, weight pulling, sit-ups, and push-ups.

Interviews

Interviews for government positions almost always come *after* your agency has determined that you are otherwise qualified for the job. These interviews often serve more as a final checkpoint in the hiring process than as a first step, as in the private sector. Most interviewers will go into detail about the type of work the job entails, the benefits of the position, and the procedures of the agency. They will also probably ask questions that will help them ascertain how motivated, cooperative, intelligent, and logical you are, as well as what kind of work habits, goals, and personal values you have.

The first question almost any interview will ask is "tell me a little bit about yourself." Prepare for this question; it is your chance to create a positive tone for the rest of the interview. Describe where you are from, tell about your education and experience, and state how your skills will help the hiring agency. Maintain a positive attitude throughout the interview; you are acting as a salesperson, and the product you are selling is

yourself. Believe in your product or your customer never will. Dress appropriately, and remember that too formal is better than too casual. After the interview, don't forget to send a thank-you letter. This will communicate that you are a thoughtful person and will indicate to the agency that you are very interested in the job.

You can also give yourself an edge in the interview by showing some knowledge of the agency and its business. During the application process, seek out others in the position you desire. Find out what their work is like and what qualities are valued. If you know something about the position and the agency, you'll demonstrate your interest and motivation, two characteristics employers value highly.

You'll also be more likely to succeed if you're able to explain, comfortably, any gaps in your education or experience. Tell the truth; you'll be respected if you can admit to past failures and faults, especially if you can explain how you overcame, or plan to overcome, them.

Finally, you should be able to discuss your short- and long-term career goals. Clearly, if your goals are in line with the goals of the department, you're in a better position to be hired. Here again, your research—talking to people already working with the department—and your overall awareness of the business of the agency will help.

Other Requirements

Before you're hired, Uncle Sam wants to make sure you're government material. That's why you will be asked to fill out a Declaration for Federal Employment (OF-306). This form is used to determine your suitability for working for the federal government and to authorize a background investigation. You must answer personal questions on subjects like loan defaults, felonies, and misdemeanors. Please note: Answering yes to questions does not disqualify you, but your answers will certainly be taken into consideration during the selection process.

You must also certify that all of the information you've provided is accurate and correct to the best of your knowledge. Know that your application will be checked. If investigators find out that you have falsified information on your application or resume, you may suffer any or all of three possible consequences: You won't be hired; you'll be fired (if you are applying for promotion within the federal government); or you may be fined or jailed.

Many positions—especially those that deal directly with public safety, such as those in the police and firefighter series, as well as those that require security clearance—require an employee who not only meets all qualifications criteria and excels in all stages of the hiring process, but also meets certain citizenship standards. That's why before employees are hired for these jobs, they may be subject to one or more of the following:

- a background investigation
- a drug screening test
- a medical examination
- a psychological evaluation or a personality test

These checks may significantly lengthen the hiring process, but they're important to ensure the well-being of all the citizens who interact with these employees. Security concerns are, of course, heightened in this post–9/11 world, so expect such checks to increase in number and duration for the foreseeable future, rather than decrease.

Step 3: Managing Your Career

Once you've created a USAJOBS account and created a resume, you'll be able to use the website's Manage Your Career options to, well, manage your career. Your options include:

- **The Career Interest Guide:** This guide includes a questionnaire designed to gauge your interest level in various types of federal work. When you have completed the questionnaire, your results—suggesting career areas in which you would be most happy—are displayed immediately. It also contains a function that allows you to search available jobs by the following career-interest areas: business detail, humanitarian, leading/influencing, mechanical, plants and animals, protective, scientific, and other. These categories correspond to the results of the career-interest questionnaire.

- **Job Interest Matching:** This function allows you to explore three broad career areas: clerical and technical; professional and administrative; and supervisory, managerial, and executive. In each area, you are asked to read a list of possible tasks and identify those that appeal to you. Your results will produce a list of jobs that match your interests.

- **Specific Job Exploration:** This function allows you to explore jobs by their specific general series number. Input a number to see the job description and a list of minimum qualifications for the job.

- **Match Federal Jobs to Private Sector Jobs:** This function allows you to see what jobs in the private sector correspond to various federal job categories.

The U.S. Postal Office Uses an Entirely Different Hiring Process

The U.S. Postal Service (USPS)—which, with nearly 660,000 employees, is the nation's second largest employer (Wal-Mart is the first with about 1.9 million)—has its own unique hiring process. New appointments at the USPS enter as either casual (temporary) or part-time flexible (career); either track can lead to full-time career employment, but be aware that competition for such positions can be fierce. Nearly all entry-level positions require applicants to pass an examination that tests address checking, forms completion, coding, and memory; it also includes a personal inventory. To learn more about the USPS and its hiring practices, check out LearningExpress's *Postal Worker Exam*.

Contact Information

The Office of Personnel Management (OPM) maintains nine regional service centers. Although their primary mission is to serve federal agencies, these offices can also provide information about available jobs and assistance with specific application queries.

OPM Service Centers

Atlanta Services Branch
75 Spring Street SW, Suite 1000
Atlanta, GA 30303
Fax: 404-730-9738
E-mail: atlanta@opm.gov

Chicago Services Branch
230 South Dearborn Street, DPN 30-3
Chicago, IL 60604
Fax: 312-353-6211
E-mail: chicago@opm.gov

Denver Services Section
12345 Alameda Parkway
P.O. Bo25167
Denver, CO 80225
Fax: 303-236-8580
E-mail: denver@opm.gov

Kansas City Services Section
601 East 12th Street, Room 131
Kansas City, MO 64106
Fax: 816-426-5104
E-mail: kansascity@opm.gov

Norfolk Services Section
200 Granby Street, Room 500
Norfolk, VA 23510-1886
Fax: 757-441-6280
E-mail: norfolk@opm.gov

Philadelphia Services Branch
600 Arch Street, Room 3400
Philadelphia, PA 19106
Fax: 215-861-3030
E-mail: philadelphia@opm.gov

Raleigh Services Branch
4407 Bland Road, Suite 200
Raleigh, NC 27609-6296
Fax: 919-790-2824
E-mail: raleigh@opm.gov

San Antonio Services Section
8610 Broadway, Room 305
San Antonio, T78217
Fax: 210-805-2429
E-mail: sanantonio@opm.gov

San Francisco Services Branch

120 Howard Street, Room 735
San Francisco, CA 94105
Fax: 415-281-7095
E-mail: sanfrancisco@opm.gov

Washington, D.C. Services Branch

1900 E Street NW, Room 2469
Washington, D.C. 20415
Fax: 202-606-1768
E-mail: washington@opm.gov

Federal Executive Boards (FEBs) coordinate federal activities outside of Washington, D.C.; because these activities comprise 88% of the federal workforce, that's a pretty big job! Your local FEB can provide you with an exhaustive list of federal agencies within its area, along with contact information. If you're hoping not to relocate, a visit to your local FEB will provide you with a thorough list of your potential job options. The following is a list of all 26 FEBs.

Atlanta, GA

Jimmy Bridgeman, Chairperson
Gwendolyn Campbell, Executive Director
Federal Executive Board
Richard B. Russell Federal Building
75 Spring Street SW, Room 1140
Atlanta, GA 30303
Phone: 404-331-4400
Fax: 404-331-4270
Web: www.atlanta.feb.gov
E-mail: gwenne.campbell@gsa.gov

Baltimore, MD

George King, Chairperson
Richard Howell, Executive Director
Federal Executive Board
Fallon Federal Building
31 Hopkins Plaza, Room 820A
Baltimore, MD 21201
Phone: 410-962-4047
Fax: 410-962-6198
E-mail: baltimore.feb@verizon.net

Boston, MA

Manuel J. Vaz, Chairperson
Kim Ainsworth, Executive Director
Federal Executive Board
10 Causeway Street, Suite 350
Boston, MA 02222
Phone: 617-565-6769
Fax: 617-565-8178
Web: www.boston.feb.gov
E-mail: kim.ainsworth@gsa.gov

Buffalo, NY

Philip C. Dissek, Chairperson
Paul Kendzierski, Executive Director
Federal Executive Board
130 South Elmwood Avenue, Suite 416
Buffalo, NY 14202
Phone: 716-551-5655
Fax: 716-551-3007
Web: www.buffalo.feb.gov
E-mail: director@buffalofeb.org

Chicago, IL

David A. Schnell, Chairperson
Jean Brown, Executive Director
Federal Executive Board
230 South Dearborn Street, Room 3770
Chicago, IL 60604
Phone: 312-353-6790
Fax: 312-353-3058
Web: www.chicagoinfo.gov/chicagofeb
E-mail: jan.stinson@gsa.gov

Cincinnati, OH

Jack Craig, Chairperson
Tina Toca, Program Specialist
Greater Cincinnati Federal Executive Board
1116 JWP Federal Office Building
550 Main Street, Suite 1-116
Cincinnati, OH 45202-3215
Phone: 513-684-2102
Fax: 513-684-2103
Web: www.cincinnati.feb.gov
E-mail: tina@gcfeb.com; tina.tora@va.gov

Cleveland, OH

Martha Smith, Chairperson
Michael Goin, Executive Director
Federal Executive Board
A. J. Celebrezze Federal Building
1240 East Ninth Street, Room 355
Cleveland, OH 44199
Phone: 216-433-6633
Fax: 216-433-9463
Web: www.cleveland.feb.gov
E-mail: michael.w.goin@nasa.gov

Dallas–Ft. Worth, TX

Teresa Bruner, Chairperson
Gladean Butler, Executive Director
Federal Executive Board
525 South Griffin Street, Suite 870-LB102
Dallas, TX 75202
Phone: 214-767-5370
Fax: 214-767-5380
E-mail: gladean.butler@gsa.gov

Denver, CO

Paul Sherbo, Chairperson
Gay Page, Executive Director
Denver Federal Executive Board
Denver Federal Center
6760 East Irvington Place
Building 810, Room 5014
Denver, CO 80279
Phone: 303-202-4588
Fax: 303-202-4583
Web: www.denver.feb.gov
E-mail: gpage@denver.feb.gov

Detroit, MI

Michael Jansen, Chairperson
Michelle Rhodes, Executive Director
Federal Executive Board
477 Michigan Avenue, Room M10
Detroit, MI 48226
Phone: 313-226-3534
Fax: 313-226-2155
Web: www.detriot.feb.gov
E-mail: Michelle.rhodes@gsa.gov

Honolulu Pacific, HI

Kirk E. Bruno, Chairperson

Gloria Uyehara, Executive Director

Federal Executive Board

300 Ala Moana Boulevard, Room 1-120

Box 50268

Honolulu, HI 96850

Phone: 808-541-2638

Fax: 808-541-3429

Web: www.honolulu-pacific.feb.gov

E-mail: guyehara@hpfeb.org

Houston, TX

Edward Pringle, Chairperson

Mike Mason, Executive Director

Federal Executive Board

2350 N. San Parkway E., Suite 1,000

Houston, TX 77032

Phone: 713-724-9210

Fax: 936-597-7436

Web: www.houston.feb.gov

E-mail: houstonfeb@gmail.com

Kansas City, MO

Romell Looks, Chairperson

Cindy Hillman, Executive Director

Federal Executive Board

1500 East Bannister Road, Suite 1176

Kansas City, MO 64131-3009

Phone: 816-823-5100

Fax: 816-823-5104

Web: http://kcfeb.gsa.gov

E-mail: feb.mail@gsa.gov

Los Angeles, CA

Glen Banks, Chairperson

Kathrene Hansen, Executive Director

Federal Executive Board

501 West Ocean, Suite 3200

Long Beach, CA 90802

Phone: 562-951-6970

Fax: 562-951–6902

Web: www.losangeles.feb.gov

E-mail: kathrene.hansen@dhs.gov

St. Paul, Minnesota

W. Charles Becoat, Chairperson

Ray Morris, Executive Director

Federal Executive Board

1 Federal Drive, Room 510

St. Paul, MN 55111-4008

Phone: 612-713-7201

Fax: 612-713-7203

Web: www.doi.gov/febtc

E-mail: ray_morris@ios.doi.gov

Newark, NJ

Scott McShaffrey, Chairperson

Angela A. Zaccardi, Executive Director

Federal Executive Board

970 Broad Street, Room 1434-B

Newark, NJ 07102

Phone: 973-645-6217

Fax: 973-645-6218

Web: www.newark.feb.gov

E-mail: angela.zaccardi@gsa.gov

Albuquerque, NM
John Woolsey, Co-Chairperson
Georgia Marchbanks, Co-Chairperson
John Kwait, Executive Director
Federal Executive Board
P.O. Box 156
Albuquerque, NM 87103-1056
Phone: 505-248-6415
Fax: 505-248-6414
Web: www.newmexico.feb.gov
E-mail: John_Kwait@fws.gov

New Orleans, LA
Keith T. Hill, Chairperson
Kathy Barré, Executive Director
Federal Executive Board
P.O. Box 53206
New Orleans, LA 70153-3206
Phone: 504-426-0106
Fax: 303-205-3005
Web: http://sig.nfc.usda.gov/feb
E-mail: kathy.barre@usda.gov

New York, NY
Carmine Gallo, Chairperson
Cynthia Gable, Executive Director
Federal Executive Board
26 Federal Plaza, Room 3016
New York, NY 10278
Phone: 212-264-1890
Fax: 212-264-1172
Web: www.newyorkcity.feb.gov
E-mail: cynthia.gable@gsa.gov

Oklahoma City, Oklahoma
David Nikodym, Chairperson
LeAnn Jenkins, Executive Director
Federal Executive Board
215 Dean A. McGee Avenue, Suite 153
Oklahoma City, OK 73102
Phone: 405-231-4167
Fax: 405-231-4165
Web: www.oklahoma.feb.gov
E-mail: leann.jenkins@gsa.gov

Portland, Oregon
David Ferguson, Chairperson
Ron Johnson, Executive Director
Federal Executive Board
1220 SW Third Avenue, Suite 1776
Portland, OR 97204-2823
Phone: 503-326-2060
Fax: 503-326-2070
E-mail: rjohnson@pcez.com

Philadelphia, PA
Brenda M. Laroche, Chairperson
Jack Ratcliffe, Executive Director
Federal Executive Board
William J. Green, Jr., Federal Building
600 Arch Street, Room 4320
Philadelphia, PA 19106
Phone: 215-861-3665
Fax: 215-861-3667
Website: www.philadelphia.feb.gov
E-mail: jack.ratcliffe@gsa.gov

Pittsburgh, PA

Terry Wolf, Chairperson
George Buck, Executive Director
Federal Executive Board
1000 Liberty Avenue, Room 1303
Pittsburgh, PA 15222
Phone: 412-395-6223
Fax: 412-395-6221
Web: www.pittsburgh.feb.gov
E-mail: george.buck@opm.gov

St. Louis, MO

John Gilles, Chairperson
Rose Garland, Executive Director
Federal Executive Board
1222 Spruce, Room 2.202c
St. Louis, MO 63103
Phone: 314-539-6312
Fax: 314-539-6314
Web: www.stlouis.feb.gov
E-mail: rose.garland@gsa.gov

San Antonio, TX

Leopold Vasquez, Chairperson
Rebecca Froboese, Executive Director
Federal Executive Board
17319 San Pedro, Suite 2-200
San Antonio, TX 78232
Phone: 210-403-5938
Fax: 210-403-5948
Web: www.sanantonio.feb.gov
E-mail: rebecca.froboese@gmail.com

San Francisco, CA

Rosemary Melville, Chairperson
Dianna Louie, Executive Director
Federal Executive Board
1301 Clay Street, Room 1400
Oakland, CA 94612-5209
Phone: 510-637-1571
Fax: 510-637-1579
E-mail: dianna.louie@gsa.gov

Seattle, WA

Rory Westberg, Chairperson
Anne Tiernan, Executive Director
Federal Executive Board
Jackson Federal Building, Room 2942
915 Second Avenue
Seattle, WA 98174-1010
Phone: 206-220-6171
Fax: 206-220-6132
E-mail: anne.tiernan@gsa.gov

South Florida

Ron Demes, Chairperson
Jaqueline Arroyo, Executive Director
Federal Executive Board
4780 SW 64th Avenue, Suite 103
Davie, FL 33314
Phone: (954) 792-1109
FAX: (954) 792-5969
Website: www.southflorida.feb.gov
Email: jarroyo@doc.gov

3 ▶ CIVIL SERVICE AT THE STATE AND LOCAL LEVELS

You don't have to work for Uncle Sam to work for the government. Hundreds of thousands of people work for state and local governments in jobs that parallel just about every occupation in the private sector, from the receptionist at the public library to the maintenance crews who fill in potholes to the police officers who direct traffic and chase criminals across interstates. There's a lot of work that needs to be done to maintain a state, county, city, or town, and many of these opportunities are available to people with little special training or expertise.

Bus Driver

If you prefer working without a supervisor looking over your shoulder and you don't mind the stresses involved in dealing with traffic and sometimes demanding customers, driving a bus may be the right job for you. It's also a great opportunity for someone looking for part-time civil service work, because most entry-level bus drivers begin as part-timers, picking up shifts nobody else wants and gradually working their way up the ladder to more and better shifts.

There are two basic groups of bus drivers on the public payroll: school bus drivers and transit bus drivers. School bus drivers begin and typically remain part-time workers, because their jobs generally can be completed in two two-hour shifts, one in the morning and one in the afternoon. Many school bus drivers perform other jobs within the school system, handling maintenance or janitorial duties at one of the schools they serve. Others pick up occasional jobs driving to and from field trips, sporting events, and other school-related activities. A good school bus driver must have the patience to deal with children and possess good policing skills in order to ensure that students travel safely.

Transit bus drivers generally work more hours and are better paid than their school bus driving peers. They typically have more responsibilities as well; besides transporting passengers safely to their destinations, transit bus drivers must also sell tickets, collect money, prepare trip reports, answer passengers' questions about routes and schedules, and, in some locations, maintain their buses. All bus drivers must drive carefully under challenging weather and traffic conditions, mindful that they neither fall behind nor get ahead of schedule.

State and local law establishes the qualifications for bus driving jobs. In some areas, bus drivers must be at least 24 years of age; other areas set a lower minimum. Bus drivers must have good vision and hearing (with or without correction), must be in good physical condition, and must have normal use of their arms and legs. Many localities require bus drivers to pass a background and/or drug test; such tests are more common for school bus drivers. Bus drivers must hold a special driver's license, the acquisition of which requires passing written and skills tests.

Bus drivers typically earn between $10 and $20 per hour, although wages outside both extremes are not uncommon. Nearly one-third of all bus drivers in the United States work part time. More than two-thirds drive school buses.

Positive Aspects of State and Municipal Civil Service Jobs

The following sections review the many advantages to civil service employment at the state and local level.

Good Prospects

According to the Bureau of Labor Statistics' publication *Occupational Outlook Handbook*, new jobs should be continually created at the state and local level into the foreseeable future. There are two primary reasons for this: First, state populations are increasing, requiring an increase in the size of the government that serves the people. Second, the federal government has shifted some responsibilities from the national to the state and local level. It should be noted, on the other hand, that state and local budgets are typically pretty tight, a factor that dampens job growth somewhat. Some governments have sought to outsource certain functions, a

Types of State and Local Government Jobs

While specific job titles may vary considerably, state and local government jobs generally fall into one of the following categories:

- Accounting/financial management
- Agriculture/conservation
- Clerical/administrative
- Education/information services
- Engineering/architecture
- Legal/licensing
- Medical/health services
- Public safety/law enforcement
- Skilled trades/maintenance
- Social services

process that also reduces the number of state and local jobs.

The biggest employment sectors at the state and local level appear in the professional and service occupations; these account for more than half of all such government jobs. Information technology remains an area of strong growth. Look also for the dramatic growth in the areas of social services, health services, and protective services, with a focus on service to the elderly, children, and the mentally impaired.

One way to learn about what type of positions are available in a specific state is to visit the state's website. You can find links to the official websites of all 50 states, as well as U.S. territories and outlying areas, at www.usa.gov/Agencies/State_and_Territories.shtml.

Diverse Opportunities and Job Security

State and local governments provide many of the services that we take for granted in our communities. Public education (not only elementary schools and secondary schools, but also community colleges and universities), parks, hospitals, libraries, prisons, trans-portation, sanitation, public utilities, fire and police departments, and courts all fall under the jurisdiction of state and local government. Government agencies and departments provide us with all these essential services, ensuring that even during tough economic times, state and local government jobs will still be available. And in most cases, state and local government career employees, like their counterparts in the federal civil service, are well protected from layoffs.

And remember, you don't have to be a teacher to work in a school, a doctor to work in a hospital, or a lawyer to work in a courthouse. All these agencies need a wide variety of personnel to fulfill their mission: clerical support staff, maintenance workers, skilled workers such as carpenters and plumbers, security guards, and so on.

To give you a better idea of exactly what kind of jobs are out there, here is a list of available entry-level jobs found on a random day at the websites of one state and one municipal government:

- Auditor
- Bus operator
- Computer network administrator

- Corrections officer
- Dental assistant
- Financial analyst
- Food services employee
- Housekeeper
- Instructor, Technical college
- Laboratory technician
- Mechanic
- Nurse
- Occupational therapist
- Pharmacy technician
- Police officer
- Program assistant, Division of Family Services
- Recycling collector
- Sanitation worker

- Secretary
- Security personnel
- Social services provider
- Tree trimmer
- Vehicle operator
- Watershed inspector

Good Starting Salaries

Starting salaries range greatly from job to job, state to state, and locality to locality. The following table shows the median average salary for a range of state and municipal positions in 2006, the last year for which the government collected such figures. As you can see, the pay is pretty good.

MEDIAN ANNUAL SALARY FOR SELECTED EXECUTIVE AND MANAGERIAL OCCUPATIONS IN LOCAL GOVERNMENT 2006	
OCCUPATION	SALARY
City manager	$92,799
Assistant chief administrative officer	$83,155
Information services director	$75,118
Engineer	$79,648
Chief financial officer	$76,101
Economic development director	$73,140
Public works director	$71,360
Fire chief	$75,645
Human resources director	$72,527
Chief law enforcement official	$69,600
Human services director	$70,958

Parks and recreation director	$68,284
Health officer	$67,275
Purchasing director	$63,043
Chief librarian	$58,750
Treasurer	$54,803
Clerk	$45,497

Source: *U.S. Bureau of Labor Statistics*

Generous Benefits

Like salaries, exact benefits vary widely among governments, but most state and local government employees can expect a reasonable benefits package that includes:

- health insurance
- life insurance
- disability insurance
- paid vacation and holidays
- sick leave
- educational incentives
- pension plan

you will not be considered. Your interview for a state or local job typically won't come until several steps into the selections process, so you cannot get around not having minimum qualifications by winning an employer over in an interview.

If you are a veteran, you may be entitled to special treatment in the hiring process at both the state and local level. This is especially true when the selection process entails a clearly defined ranking system. Veterans applying for firefighter or police officer positions, for example, often have five or ten points added to their scores. For more details, you should contact your state or local personnel department.

Minimum Qualifications for State and Local Civil Service

Qualifications for state and local jobs vary widely depending on the kind of job. Some jobs require nothing more than a high school diploma or GED, and a few don't even require that much. Whatever type of job you're looking for, be sure to check the specific job qualifications on the job announcement before you apply.

State and local governments, like the federal government, rank applicants according to specific, clear criteria. If you don't meet the minimum qualifications,

The Hiring Process at the State and Local Level

There is no uniform process for finding and securing a civil service job at the state or local level, but the following steps provide a pretty good rundown of what you can expect in most places.

Finding a Job Opening

All state governments and nearly all local governments have decided to take advantage of the Internet by making it their primary portal for job searches and job applications. These days, all you need do is find the

Tax Collector

Taxes are collected at the federal, state, and local levels, and everywhere that taxes are collected there will be those who try to avoid paying their fair share. That's when tax examiners and tax collectors spring to action.

Examiners, as their name suggests, examine tax forms for irregularities. When they find them, they notify the taxpayer (individual or business) about the discrepancy. If the response is unsatisfactory, a collector is assigned to the case. Collectors are the muscle in the tax-collecting business; they go after folks who either cannot or will not pay their tax bills. Tax collection is a year-round business; state and local collectors are responsible for collecting not only delinquent income taxes but also taxes that are paid continually, such as sales tax, cigarette tax, and gasoline tax. Work conditions are generally pleasant, with much of the work completed from a comfortable office during a 40-hour workweek, with occasional trips to courthouses, halls of records, and the businesses and homes of delinquent taxpayers.

State tax collectors have a number of options in performing their duties. In many cases, a simple phone call is all that is necessary to get a violator to comply. In other instances, the collector may have to institute legal proceedings that may include the garnishment of wages or the seizure of property. As you might imagine, this is not work for the faint of heart. Confronting delinquent taxpayers, whether at home, in their offices, or at the courthouse, is stressful work that occasionally results in hostile encounters.

Entry-level tax collectors often serve an apprenticeship of up to two years, during which a mentor provides on-the-job training. Ambitious collectors never stop training; they stay abreast of the latest developments in tax laws and collection methods through workshops, conferences, and academic courses. Those who succeed in the field can rise to management level, which affords them greater decision-making authority. Tax collection will never go away, because there will always be taxes and there will always be citizens who cannot or do not pay them. Even so, jobs in this field are quite competitive. This situation is exacerbated by the fact that some state and local governments are starting to outsource their tax collection business. Increased automation within tax departments has facilitated personnel reductions, further stiffening competition for new job openings.

appropriate website that lists the jobs you desire in the area you prefer, point and click, and just like that, you are ready to apply for work.

All states now allow you to complete an application and submit it online; some states, in fact, *only* process applications submitted in this manner. If you do not have online access, your local library should be able to provide it for you. Your regional state government office should also have Internet portals available to the public to facilitate job applications.

Local governments are, of course, more varied in their practices. Some allow for online applications.

Others list jobs online but require you to submit a hard-copy application (by mail, fax, or in person). A few don't even list jobs online; instead, you must visit a government office to study job postings and submit your application.

At both the state and local levels, don't forget to visit the websites of specific agencies for which you wish to work as well as the main website that lists all job opportunities. In theory, all job postings should appear at the central site, but websites are operated by human beings and human beings make mistakes or fall behind in their work and don't post a job notice in a

Social Worker, Department of Corrections

Not everyone who works in a prison is a guard or warden (that's just the way it is in the movies!). Prisons need maintenance workers, kitchen staff, and a full support staff that includes medical personnel and social workers.

Social workers fulfill a number of important roles in helping prisons operate. They assess prisoners on the basis of their potential for rehabilitation and for the potential risks they pose to the prison community. They provide direct counseling to prisoners and to their families, and they place prisoners in counseling, educational, religious, and self-help programs, including substance abuse treatment programs, where appropriate. They help design practical, meaningful release programs for inmates whose sentences will soon expire, and they work with parole officers before, during, and after release to manage each parolee's readjustment to society. The job involves a lot of record keeping and a substantial amount of interaction with prison officials and the courts, but it primarily focuses on efforts to redirect inmates to productive, lawful lives outside of prison.

Social workers must hold a license, a process that typically requires the applicant to hold at least a bachelor's degree in a social work-related field. Some jobs require an advanced degree. Required skills include familiarity with social work methodology, strong interviewing techniques, strong interpersonal skills, an understanding of the dynamics of human relations, problem identification and resolution skills, familiarity with the criminal justice system and victims' issues, strong investigative skills, case planning skills, and effective communication skills (oral and written). Like all prison employees, a prison social worker must pass a criminal background check prior to employment.

Social work is not a lucrative field, but the pay is not bad either. Starting salaries range from around $30,000 to more than $40,000 and typically include state benefits packages, which are usually quite good. This job should be especially attractive to individuals interested in working in the field of substance abuse. Many prison systems, recognizing that substance abuse contributes heavily to in-prison problems as well as to failures in the rehabilitation process, are increasingly requiring inmates to undergo substance abuse therapy upon arrival and/or as a condition of release. As a result, the number of opportunities in this particular field are growing rapidly.

timely manner, or . . . well, you get the point. Better safe than sorry; that's why you should visit specific agencies' websites to double-check for job opportunities.

Each job description will provide specific details about the nature of the job, the required qualifications for the job, and the procedure for applying. Follow the directions carefully! A mistake may result in your being disqualified from consideration. Also, make sure to submit all materials by the stated deadline. Deadlines are typically written in stone; miss one and you are out of the running for the job.

What happens after you submit your application depends on the nature of the job. For many jobs, you will be required to take a written exam. Other jobs include a number of other screening processes, which are described in the following sections.

Written Exams

Many state and local government jobs have a written exam as part of the selection process. The type of test will vary greatly from job to job and from location to location, but most exams will include at least some basic reading, writing, and (sometimes) math skills. You can hone your skills in these areas by taking the practice exams in this book and by studying the review material provided here.

Beyond these basic skills, here are some of the areas most often tested for specific occupations:

- **Clerical/office support:** sorting items alphabetically and numerically, proofreading to catch discrepancies in a series of numbers and letters, coding, typing or word processing speed and accuracy, and/or stenography
- **Corrections officer:** memory and observation, logic (placing events in a logical order), using judgment and common sense in a given situation, coding, understanding and applying written rules and procedures
- **Firefighter:** following directions, judgment and reasoning (for example, what you think is the most important thing to do in a certain situation), reading and understanding maps and floor plans, memory and observation. Some municipalities and counties will provide you with a study guide that they'll expect you to study before the exam, so both your understanding and your ability to remember the materials will be tested.
- **Police officer:** memory and observation, map reading, using common sense and good judgment in a given situation

Many other jobs may not include a written test but will require various levels of certification, degrees, or job experience. Whether you have to go through other steps in the selection process depends on what kind of job you seek. Entry-level applicants for almost any public safety job—law enforcement, including corrections, or firefighting, for example—will have to pass through most if not all of these steps: one or more interviews, a physical ability test, a background investigation, a psychological investigation, and a medical evaluation. Clerical workers, on the other hand, may have only an interview—or perhaps not even that;

their written exam scores and applications may be enough to land them their jobs.

Physical Ability Test

People who are applying for almost any physically demanding job, including police officer, firefighter, or sanitation worker, can count on having to pass a physical ability test. These tests vary widely from job to job and from location to location. In some cases, you will be tested on the number of push-ups and sit-ups you can do in a specified period of time, how quickly you can run a mile, and/or how much weight you can bench-press. Other tests of physical fitness may also be administered.

Other tests may be more closely job-related. You may be asked to complete some sort of obstacle course in order to be considered for a police or firefighting job. Sanitation workers may be required to drag a heavy object and then lift and toss it as though they were throwing it onto a collection truck, and then carry several other objects a specified distance. Firefighters might have to crawl through a tunnel, climb stairs, drag a hose, drag a dummy, raise and climb a ladder, and/or jump over a wall—all while wearing full protective gear.

Whatever the parameters of the test, physical tests are usually timed, requiring you to complete a given exercise or program in a given length of time. In some cases, the test is pass/fail; if you come in under the time, you pass, and if you don't, you fail. In other cases, you are ranked based on your time; the better your time, the better your ranking and the better your chances of being hired.

If your job requires a physical ability test, you'll need to be in tip-top shape before you attempt the test. It's important that you do well on your first try, especially if the score weighs into your ranking. A few cities will allow you to retake the physical test if you fail, but most will not allow you to retake an exam until the

Few jobs are as exciting, as dangerous, or as essential as firefighting. Each year firefighters save thousands of lives and prevent many billions of dollars worth of property damage, often while working under extremely perilous conditions. Because nearly two-thirds of the nation's fire departments provide medical services, many firefighters are also trained and engaged in emergency medical service. Firefighters are frequently the first responders to all types of civil disruption, from automobile accidents to forest fires to chemical spills to medical emergencies.

Firefighters must be prepared to work long, irregular hours; some departments require 24-hour shifts, and anything less than a ten-hour shift is rare. Forty-eight-hour workweeks are more the norm than is the traditional 40-hour workweek. The pay isn't commensurate with the value of the work. Firefighters may start earning in the $30,000 range. Higher-ups are more fairly compensated; a captain can earn a base salary between $49,000 and $59,000 annually, while a fire chief can earn a base salary of up to $90,000. For all firefighters, opportunities for overtime are often available. Most firefighters also enjoy generous benefits packages that provide plenty of vacation and sick leave, medical and life insurance, pension plans, and tuition reimbursement.

Despite the challenges and the risks involved, firefighting jobs are tough to land. The field is highly competitive, with many applicants for each open position. Candidates for the job must pass a written test; tests of strength, coordination, agility, and stamina; a background investigation that may include a polygraph test; a medical examination that includes a drug screening test; and a board-conducted interview. The completion of a firefighting-related curriculum at a community college may improve one's chances of employment but is rarely mandatory. Some departments require entering firefighters to arrive with EMT-basic training. Others provide this training as part of their entry-level training programs. Apprenticeship programs of up to four years' duration are available in some locations.

An effective firefighter must be able to function as part of a team under stressful conditions. Alertness, courage, endurance, self-discipline, and a commitment to public service are all essential. The best firefighters continually study to improve their skills and knowledge, learning about new techniques, new medical technology, the latest programs in public education, and the latest research on the detection and prevention of arson. Promotion, like hiring, is often contingent at least in part on performance on written examinations.

current application period ends and the following application period begins.

Interviews

In the private sector, an initial interview is often one of the first steps in the process of getting hired. You submit your application or resume, and then the company calls you in for an interview to see whether you're the type of person they want. In the public sector, an interview—when there is one—is likely to come later in the process. On the basis of your application and any supporting materials (including your exam score when an exam is required), the agency has already decided that you're the type of person that they want. The interview is to make sure. You'll probably face most of the standard interview questions: who you are, what your experience is and how it has prepared you for this job, where you want to be in simonths or five years. Although the interview doesn't give you a chance to make up for a spotty application or bad test scores—

you won't be called if you have those—it does give you a chance to convince the interviewer that you have good verbal communication skills and poise.

People applying for public safety jobs, including police officer, corrections officer, or firefighter, are likely to face a different type of interview than are people applying for office-based jobs. They may also be required to submit to several interviews, perhaps one with a chief or deputy chief, another with a board that includes officers, officials from outside the hiring department, and civilians. In most cases, the primary goal in this type of interview is to assess your communication skills, your interpersonal skills, and your judgment. You'll probably be asked why you want a job in public safety and what qualities you have that will make you good at the job. You will probably also be asked to speak about your background: your upbringing, your education, and any relevant life experiences. You may be presented with hypothetical situations that are job related; these will be designed to measure your ethical and moral standards, not your knowledge of the job. For example, you may be asked what you would do if you caught a fellow officer stealing during an investigation.

Background Information

Many government employers conduct at least a cursory background check of most or all potential employees. For most jobs, the investigation does little more than confirm the facts on your application, checking to make sure that you did indeed attend that fancy university and work for that prestigious company you listed on your resume.

Law enforcement agents and firefighters are subjected to much more rigorous background checks. You might not even be aware that you're being investigated, but if the background investigator—often a federal agent or a detective in the police department—uncovers any discrepancies in your application or

other information you've submitted, you can be sure that you will be questioned about them. Therefore, it is critical that you be open and honest throughout all stages of the application and selection process.

Psychological Evaluation

People applying for public safety jobs are also subject to a psychological evaluation. These are stressful jobs, so hiring departments want to make sure that candidates have the emotional stability to handle the pressure. After all, the lives of the employee, his or her fellow officers, and citizens could be at stake. The psychological examination for police officers is generally more extensive than for firefighters and correctional officers. You'll be tested to determine that you won't be hampered by serious emotional disturbances, nervous disorders, or drug and/or alcohol dependence. Sometimes the psychological evaluation consists of one or more written tests. Sometimes an interview with a psychiatrist is also included.

Medical Evaluation

To work for the state, city, or county, you may be asked to submit a letter from your physician certifying that you are in generally good physical health, particularly if your job involves physical stress. You may also have to submit to a drug test.

Candidates for public safety positions usually have to be examined by a doctor of the department's choosing. The medical exam is like a regular physical. Your blood pressure, height, weight, and other vital data will be recorded. Your eyes and ears will probably be checked, and you may have a blood and/or urine test, which may or may not also serve as a drug test. But that's about all. If you've made it this far in the hiring process, you'll probably have a job offer waiting for you once you receive the doctor's okay.

Preparing for the Hiring Process

The best way to prepare for the ordeal that getting hired entails is to talk to people already in the position you desire. They are best able to tell you about the demands of the job and what you can expect both during the hiring process and on the job. You can learn what qualities are most valued by those departments and what techniques successful candidates have used to prepare for exams and interviews.

You can use the practice exams in this book to help you get ready for the parts of your test that include reading, writing, math, and civil service skills. LearningExpress also publishes more specific guides on the tests and selection process for many civil service jobs. Check out the titles we publish at our website, www.learnatest.com.

Contacts for Government Jobs at the State Level

ALABAMA

Jackie B. Graham, Director
Paul Thomas, Deputy Director
State of Alabama Personnel Department
300 Folsom Administrative Building
64 North Union Street
Montgomery, AL 36130-4100
Phone: 334-242-3389
Web: www.personnel.state.al.us

ALASKA

Mailing Address:
Department of Administration
Division of Personnel
P.O. Bo110201
Juneau, AK 99811-0201

Street Address:
State Office Building
333 Willoughby Avenue, Tenth Floor
Juneau, AK 99801-1770

Phone: 800-587-0430 (statewide toll-free number); 907-465-4095 (Juneau and out-of-state callers)
Fax: 907-465-2576
Web: dop.state.ak.us (Click "Workplace Alaska" link.)

ARIZONA

Web: http://azstatejobs.gov (Apply via the Internet and follow up by contacting the Human Resources Department of the agency to which you are applying.)

ARKANSAS

Mailing Address:
P.O. Box 3278
Little Rock, AR 72203

Street Address:
Office of Personnel Management
DFA Building
1509 West Seventh Street, Suite 201
Little Rock, AR 72201

Phone: 501-682-1823
Fax: 501-682-5104
Web: www.ark.org/arstatejobs/index.php
E-mail: opmhelp@dfa.state.ar.us

CALIFORNIA

California State Personnel Board
801 Capitol Mall
Sacramento, CA 95814
Phone: 916-653-1705
Web: http://spb.ca.gov/jobs

COLORADO

Department of Personnel and Administration
633 17th Street, Suite 1600
Denver, CO 80202
Phone: 303-866-6566
Fax: 303-866-3034
Web: www.gssa.state.co.us (Click "Colorado
    State Government Classified Jobs System"
    link.)
E-mail: comments@state.co.us

CONNECTICUT

Department of Administrative Services
Web: www.das.state.ct.us/exam/default.asp

Brenda Sisco, Commissioner
165 Capitol Avenue, Room 491
Hartford, CT 06106
Phone: 860-713-5100
Fax: 860-713-7481
E-mail: brendasisco@ct.gov

Dr. Martin Anderson, Deputy Commissioner
165 Capitol Avenue, Room 491
Hartford, CT 06106
Phone: 860-713-5100
Fax: 860-713-7481
E-mail: martinanderson@ct.gov

Pamela L. Libby, Ph.D., Director, Human
    Resource Management
165 Capitol Avenue, Room 411
Hartford, CT 06106
Phone: 860-713-5204
Fax: 860-622-2965
E-mail: pamela.libby@po.state.ct.us

DELAWARE

24-Hour Job Line: 302-739-7750 (in Delaware);
   800-345-1789 (out of state)
Web: www.delawarestatejobs.com

Carvel State Office Building
New Castle County
820 North French Street
Wilmington, DE 19801
Phone: 302-577-8277

Haslet Armory
Kent County
122 William Penn Street
Dover, DE 19901
Phone: 302-739-5458

Del Tech Owens Campus
Sussex County
Route 18
Georgetown, DE 19947
Phone: 302-856-5966

FLORIDA

Phone: 866-663-4735; 866-221-0268 (TTY)
Web: http://peoplefirst.myflorida.com

GEORGIA

2 Martin Luther King Jr. Drive SE
Room 418, West Tower
Atlanta, GA 30334-5100
Phone: 404-656-2725
Web: www.careers.ga.gov (Contact individual
   agency's human resources department to
   inquire about posted positions. Contact
   information is available online at
   www.careers.ga.gov/careerscontact.asp

HAWAII

Department of Human Resources Development
Leiopapa a Kamehameha Building
235 South Beretania Street, 11th Floor
Honolulu, HI 96813-2437
Phone: 808-587-1111
Web: www.hawaii.gov/hrd

IDAHO

Mailing Address:

Division of Human Resources

P.O. Box 83720

Boise, ID 83720-0066

Phone: 208-334-2263 (local);
    800-554-5627 (toll-free)

Fax: 208-334-3182

Web: http://dhr.idaho.gov

ILLINOIS

Illinois Department of Central Management
    Services

Web: www.work.illinois.gov

CMS Assessment Centers:

(Examining/employment applications are avail-
    able at any other Illinois Employment and
    Training Center (IETC) operated by the Illi-
    nois Department of Employment Security.)

James R. Thompson Center

100 West Randolph Street, Suite 3-300

Chicago, IL 60601

Phone: 312-793-3565; 312-814-4458 (TTY)

Capital City Center

130 West Mason Street, Second Floor

Springfield, IL 62702

Phone: 217-557-6885; 217-785-3979 (TTY)

State Regional Office Building

2125 South First Street, Main Level

Champaign, IL 61820

Phone: 217-278-3435

Illinois Relay Center: 800-526-0844

State Regional Office Building

2309 West Main Street, Suite 112

Marion, IL 62959

Phone: 618-993-7005

Illinois Relay Center: 800-526-0844

E. J. "Zeke" Giorgi Center

200 South Wyman Street, Lower Level

Rockford, IL 61101

Phone: 815-987-7004

Illinois Relay Center: 800-526-0844

Department of Central Management Services
    Examining and Counseling Division Office

401 S. Spring Street, Room 500

Springfield, IL 62706

Phone: 217-782-7100; 217-785-3979 (TTY)

INDIANA

Indiana State Personnel Department
402 West Washington Street, Room W161
Indianapolis, IN 46204
Phone: 317-232-0200
Web: www.in.gov/spd
(All applications must be submitted online; the
state does not accept applications submitted
by mail or fax.)

IOWA

Department of Administrative Services,
Human Resources Enterprise
Hoover State Office Building
1305 East Walnut Street
Des Moines, IA 50319
Phone: 515-281-5889
Office Hours: 8:00 A.M.–4:30 P.M.,
Monday–Friday
Web: http://das.hre.iowa.gov/state_jobs.html
E-mail: dashre.info@iowa.gov

KANSAS

Division of Personnel Services
Phone: 785-296-4278
Web: http://da.state.ks.us/ps/aaa/recruitment
E-mail: psweb@da.state.ks.gov
(Apply online or by mail and then follow up with
a call to the human resources department of
the agency to which you are applying.)

KENTUCKY

Kentucky Personnel Cabinet
State Office Building
501 High Street
Frankfort, KY 40601
Phone: 866-PAL-LINE (866-725-5463) (toll-
free); 502-564-8339 (in Frankfort)
Web: http://personnel.ky.gov/employment

LOUISIANA

Mailing Address:
Staffing Division, Department of Civil Service
P.O. Box 94111, Capitol Station
Baton Rouge, LA 70821
Fax: 225-342-2386

Phone: 225-342-8536
Web: www.dscs.state.la.us/asp/csjobsearch/
search/jobs.htm

MAINE

Department of Administrative and Financial
Services
Bureau of Human Resources
Burton M. Cross Building, Fourth Floor
#4 State House Station
Augusta, ME 04333-0004
Office Hours: 8:00 A.M.–5:00 P.M.,
Monday–Friday
Phone: 207-624-7761; 888-577-6690 (TTY)
Fax: 207-287-4414
Web: www.maine.gov/bhr/state_jobs/index.htm

MARYLAND

Maryland Department of Budget and Management
45 Calvert Street
Annapolis, MD 21401
Phone: 800-705-3493
Web: www.dbm.maryland.gov (Click "Job Seekers" link. Find job listings online and then submit application to hiring agency.)
E-mail: marylandgov@dbm.state.md.us

MASSACHUSETTS

Commonwealth of Massachusetts Human Resources Division
Executive Office for Administration and Finance
One Ashburton Place, Room 301
Boston, MA 02108
Hours: 8:45 A.M.–5:00 P.M., Monday–Friday, except holidays
Phone: 617-727-3555; 800-392-6178 (toll-free)
Web: www.mass.gov

MICHIGAN

Web: www.michigan.gov

Lansing Office:
Capitol Commons Center
400 South Pine Street
Lansing, MI 48909
Phone: 517-241-6674; 800-788-1766 (toll-free); 517-335-0191 (TDD)
Fax: 517-373-7690

Detroit Office:
Cadillac Place
3042 West Grand Boulevard, Suite 4-400, Fourth Floor
Detroit, MI 48202
Phone: 313-456-4400; 313-456-4409 (TDD)
Fax: 313-456-4411

MINNESOTA

Department of Employee Relations
658 Cedar Street
200 Centennial Building
St. Paul, MN 55155
Phone: 651-259-5888
Web: www.dnr.state.mn.us/jobs/index.html

MISSISSIPPI

State Personnel Board
Robert G. Clark, Jr. Building
301 North Lamar, Suite 203
Jackson, MS 39201
Phone: 601-359-1406
Fax: 601-359-2729
Web: www.spbrez.ms.gov/appltest/starteapp.html

MISSOURI

Mailing Address:
Division of Personnel
Office of Administration
P.O. Box 388
Jefferson City, MO 65102

Street Address:
Division of Personnel
Office of Administration
Harry S. Truman Building
301 West High Street, Room 430
Jefferson City, MO 65102

Phone: 573-751-4162
Fax: 573-751-8641
Web: www.oacentral.oa.mo.gov/dopweb/
joa.aspx
E-mail: persmail@oa.mo.gov

MONTANA

Mailing Address:
Human Resource Office
P.O. Box 200108
Helena, MT 59620-0113

Phone: 406-444-2511
Fax: 406-444-2701
Web: mt.gov/statejobs/statejobs.asp

NEBRASKA

DAS State Personnel
301 Centennial Mall South, Mall Level
Lincoln, NE 68509
Phone: 402-471-2075
Fax: 402-471-3754
Web: www.das.state.ne.us/personnel/
nejobs/per.htm

NEVADA

Department of Personnel
209 East Musser Street
Carson City, NV 89701-4267

Carson City Training Center
2527 North Carson Street, Suite 275
Carson City, NV 89701

Las Vegas Training Center
555 East Washington Avenue
Las Vegas, NV 89101-1083

Phone: 775-684-0160 (Carson City); 702-486-
2920 (Las Vegas); 800-992-0900 ext. 0160 (in
Nevada)
Web: dop.nv.gov/fshome.html

NEW HAMPSHIRE

Human Resources Director
State of New Hampshire Division of Personnel
25 Capitol Street
Concord, NH 03301-6313
Phone: 603-271-3262; 800-735-2964 (TDD)
Fax: 603-271-1422
Web: www.nh.gov/hr/employmentlisting.html

NEW JERSEY

Street Address:
Department of Personnel
44 South Clinton Avenue
Trenton, NJ 08625

Mailing Address:
Department of Personnel
P.O. Box 310
Trenton, NJ 08625

Phone: 609-292-4144
Web: www.state.nj.us/nj/employ/

NEW MEXICO

New Mexico State Personnel Office
2600 Cerrillos Road
Santa Fe, NM 87505
Web: www.spo.state.nm.us/ (Click on the "Job
    seekers" link.)

NEW YORK

New York State Department of Civil Service
Alfred E. Smith State Office Building
Albany, NY 12239
Office Hours: 8:30 A.M.–5 P.M., Monday–Friday
Phone: 518-457-2487 (in Albany);
    877-NYS-JOBS (877-697-5627) (toll-free)
Web: www.cs.state.ny.us/jobseeker/public
E-mail: pio@cs.state.ny.us

NORTH CAROLINA

Office of State Personnel
Web: www.osp.state.nc.us/jobs

Mailing Address:
1331 Mail Service Center
Raleigh, NC 27699-1331

Street Address:
Administration Building, Third Floor
116 West Jones Street
Raleigh, NC 27603-1300
Phone: 919-807-4800
Fax: 919-733-0653

Personnel Development Center
101 West Peace Street
Raleigh, NC 27603-1127
Phone: 919-733-2474

Temporary Solutions
620 North West Street, Suite 102
Raleigh, NC 27603-5938
Phone: 919-733-7927

NORTH DAKOTA

Human Resources Management Services
600 East Boulevard Avenue, Department 113
Bismarck, ND 58505-0120
Phone: 701-328-3293
Fax: 701-328-1475
Web: www.nd.gov/hrms
E-mail: hrms@nd.gov

OHIO

Civil Service Testing and State Job Information
   Office
30 East Broad Street, 28th Floor
Columbus, OH 43215-3414
Phone: 614-466-4666
Fax: 614-466-3419
E-mail: careers@ohio.gov
Web: http://careers.ohio.gov

OKLAHOMA

Office of Personnel Management
Jim Thorpe Building
2101 North Lincoln Boulevard
Oklahoma City, OK 73105
Office Hours: 8 A.M.–5 P.M., Monday–Friday
Phone: 405-521-2177
Fax: 405-524-6942
Web: www.ok.gov/opm/state-jobs/index.html

OREGON

Department of Administrative Services
155 Cottage Street NE, U-30
Salem, OR 97301-3967
Office Hours: 8 A.M.–5 P.M., Monday–Friday
Phone: 503-378-8344
Web: www.oregonjobs.org
E-mail: statejobs.info@state.or.us

PENNSYLVANIA

State Civil Service Commission
Web: www.scsc.state.pa.us/scsc/site/default.asp

Harrisburg Office:
320 Market Street
Strawberry Square Complex, Second Floor
P.O. Box 569
Harrisburg, PA 17108-0569
Phone: 717-783-3058; 717-772-2685 (TDD)

Philadelphia Office:
10 South 11th Street, Second Floor
Philadelphia, PA 19107-3618
Phone: 215-560-2253; 215-560-4367 (TDD)

Pittsburgh Office:
300 Liberty Avenue
State Office Building, Room 1503
Pittsburgh, PA 15222-1210
Phone: 412-565-7666; 412-565-2484 (TDD)

RHODE ISLAND

Cheryl A. Burrell, Human Resources Program
   Administrator
Department of Administration, Human
   Resources Outreach and Diversity Office
One Capitol Hill
Providence, RI 02908-5860
Phone: 401-222-6397
Fax: 401-222-6391
Web: www.dlt.ri.gov/webdev/jobsri/
   statejobs.htm
E-mail: cburrell@hr.ri.gov

SOUTH CAROLINA

Office of Human Resources
State Career Center
1401 Senate Street
Columbia, SC 29201
Phone: 803-734-9080
Web: www.ohr.sc.gov/ohr/ohr-index.phtm
E-mail: webinfo@ohr.sc.gov

SOUTH DAKOTA

Bureau of Personnel
Web: bop.sd.gov/
E-mail: bopinfo@state.sd.us

Central Office
Capitol Building
500 East Capitol Avenue
Pierre, SD 57501-5070
Phone: 605-773-3148
Fax: 605-773-4344

Training
Foss Building
523 East Capitol Avenue
Pierre, SD 57501-3182
Phone: 605-773-3461
Fax: 605-773-5389

TENNESSEE

Tennessee Department of Personnel
Applicant Services
James K. Polk Building
505 Deaderick Street, First Floor
Nashville, TN 37219
Phone: 615-251-5200
Web: www.tennesseeanytime.org/
government/employment.html

TEXAS

Texas Workforce Commission
101 East 15th Street
Austin, TX 78778-0001
Phone: 800-832-2829
Web: https://wit.twc.state.tx.us
E-mail: laborinfo@twc.state.tx.us

UTAH

Utah Department of Human Resource
Management
State Office Building, Suite 2120
Salt Lake City, UT 84114-1531
Phone: 801-538-3025; 801-538-3696 (TDD)
Fax: 801-538-3081
Web: www.dhrm.utah.gov
E-mail: dhrmweb@utah.gov

Utah Department of Workforce Services
P.O. Box 45249
Salt Lake City, UT 84145-0249
Phone: 801-526-WORK (801-526-9675)
Fax: 801-526-9211
Web: https://statejobs.utah.gov
E-mail: dwscontactus@utah.gov

VERMONT

Commissioner, Department of Human
Resources
110 State Street
Montpelier, VT 05620-3001
Phone: 802-828-3491
Fax: 802-828-3409

Recruitment and Classification
144 State Street
Montpelier, VT 05620-1701
Phone: 802-828-1509
Fax: 802-828-1515

Workforce Development and Wellness
The Summit: Center for State Employee
Development
Osgood Building
103 South Main Street
Waterbury, VT 05671-2801
Phone: 802-241-1115
Fax: 802-241-1119

Help Desk: 7:45 A.M.–4:30 P.M., Monday–Friday
Phone: 802-828-0407; 800-253-0191 (TTY)
Web: www.vermontpersonnel.org/
jobapplicant/index.php
E-mail: recruit@per.state.vt.us

VIRGINIA

Department of Human Resource Management
101 North 14th Street, 12th Floor
Richmond, VA 23219
Phone: 804-225-2131
Fax: 804-371-7401
Web: http://jobs.virginia.gov

WASHINGTON

Department of Personnel
600 South Franklin Street SE
Olympia, WA 98501-1314
Phone: 360-664-1960; 360-664-6211 (TTY)
Web: http://careers.wa.gov
E-mail: information@dop.wa.gov

WEST VIRGINIA

West Virginia Division of Personnel
Charleston Capitol Complex
1900 Kanawha Boulevard East
Building 6, Room 420
Charleston, WV 25305-0139
Phone: 304-558-3950 (job opportunity
announcements: ext. 503);
304-558-1237 (TDD)
Fax: 304-558-1399
Web: www.state.wv.us/admin/personnel/jobs

WISCONSIN

Mailing Address:
Office of State Employment Relations
P.O. Bo7855
Madison, WI 53707-7855

Street Address:
Office of State Employment Relations
101 East Wilson Street, Fourth Floor
Madison, WI 53702

Phone: 608-267-1012
Web: wisc.jobs/public/index.asp
E-mail: wiscjobs@wisconsin.gov

WYOMING

State of Wyoming Human Resources Division
Emerson Building
2001 Capitol Avenue
Cheyenne, WY 82002-0060
Phone: 307-777-7188
Fax: 307-777-6562
Web: personnel.state.wy.us/stjobs/index.htm
E-mail: stjobs@state.wy.us

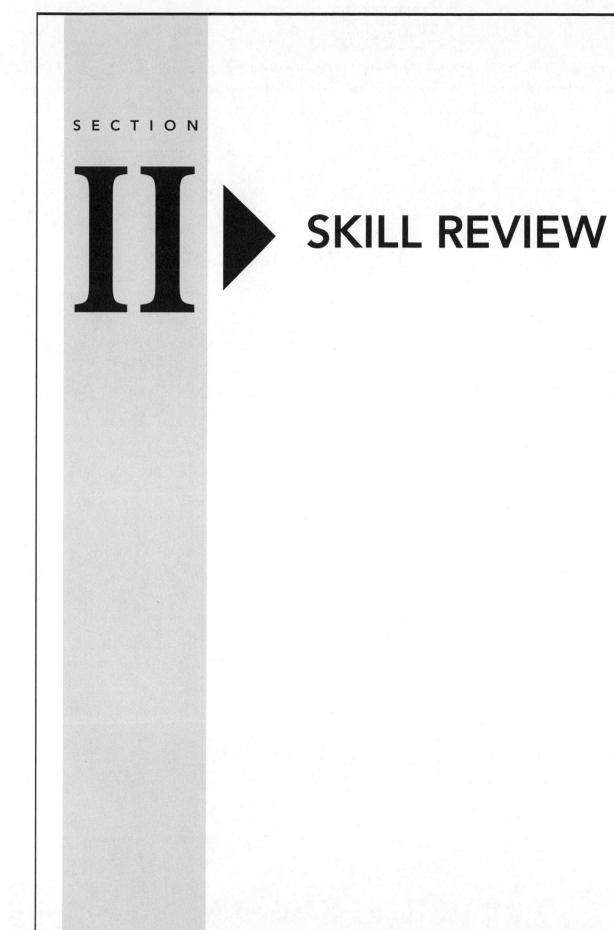

II ▶ SKILL REVIEW

CHAPTER

4 ▶ THE LEARNINGEXPRESS TEST PREPARATION SYSTEM

CHAPTER OVERVIEW

Taking any written exam can be tough. It demands a lot of preparation if you want to achieve a top score, and your rank on the eligibility list is often determined largely by this score. The LearningExpress Test Preparation System, developed exclusively for LearningExpress by leading test experts, gives you the discipline and attitude you need to be a winner.

Taking this written exam is no picnic, and neither is getting ready for it. Your future career in civil service depends on you getting a high score on the various parts of the test, but there are all sorts of pitfalls that can keep you from doing your best on this all-important exam. Here are some of the obstacles that can stand in the way of your success:

- being unfamiliar with the format of the exam
- being paralyzed by test anxiety
- leaving your preparation to the last minute or not preparing at all
- not knowing vital test-taking skills: how to pace yourself through the exam, how to use the process of elimination, and when to guess
- not being in tip-top mental and physical shape
- messing up on exam day by having to work on an empty stomach or shivering through the exam because the room is cold

What's the common denominator in all these test-taking pitfalls? One word: *control*. Who's in control, you or the exam?

The LearningExpress Test Preparation System puts you in control. In just nine easy-to-follow steps, you will learn everything you need to know to make sure that you are in charge of your preparation and your performance on the exam. Other test takers may let the exam get the better of them; other test takers may be unprepared or out of shape, but not you. After completing this chapter, you will have taken all the steps you need to get a high score on any civil service exam.

Here's how the LearningExpress Test Preparation System works: nine easy steps lead you through everything you need to know and do to get ready for your exam. Each of the steps listed below and on the following pages includes both reading about the step and one or more activities. It's important that you do the activities along with the reading, or you won't be getting the full benefit of the system. Each step tells you approximately how much time that step will take you to complete.

Step 1. Get Information (30 minutes)

Step 2. Conquer Test Anxiety (20 minutes)

Step 3. Make a Plan (50 minutes)

Step 4. Learn to Manage Your Time (10 minutes)

Step 5. Learn to Use the Process of Elimination (20 minutes)

Step 6. Know When to Guess (20 minutes)

Step 7. Reach Your Peak Performance Zone (10 minutes)

Step 8. Get Your Act Together (10 minutes)

Step 9. Do It! (10 minutes)

Total time for complete system (180 minutes-3 hours)

We estimate that working through the entire system will take you approximately three hours. It's perfectly okay if you work at a faster or slower pace. If you can take a whole afternoon or evening, you can work through the whole LearningExpress Test Preparation System in one sitting. Otherwise, you can break it up, and do just one or two steps a day for the next several days. It's up to you—remember, you are in control.

Step 1: Get Information

Time to complete: 30 minutes

Activities: Read Chapter 2

Knowledge is power. The first step in the Learning-Express Test Preparation System is finding out everything you can about the types of civil service exams offered. For example, the Civil Service page of Federal Jobs Net (federaljobs.net/exams.htm) outlines the details about taking a civil service exam. *The Book of U.S. Government Jobs* (Tenth Edition) will have additional information for you on civil service exam requirements.

What You Should Find Out

The more details you can find out about the exam, the more efficiently you will be able to study. Here's a list of some things you might want to find out about your exam:

- What skills are tested?
- How many sections are on the exam?
- How many questions are in each section?
- Are the questions ordered from easy to hard, or is the sequence random?
- How much time is allotted for each section?
- Are there breaks between sections?
- What is the passing score, and how many questions do you have to answer right in order to get that score?
- Does a higher score give you any advantages, like a better rank on the eligibility list?

- How is the exam scored, and is there a penalty for wrong answers?
- Are you permitted to go back to a prior section or move on to the next section if you finish early?
- Can you write in the exam booklet, or will you be given scratch paper?
- What should you bring with you on exam day?

What's on Most Civil Service Exams

The skills that are tested on civil service exams vary from occupation to occupation. That's why it's important to contact your local state association to find out what skills are covered. Then, move on to the next step to get rid of that test anxiety.

Step 2: Conquer Test Anxiety

Time to complete: 20 minutes
Activity: Practice Overcoming Test Anxiety
Having complete information about the exam is the first step in getting control of it. Next, you have to overcome one of the biggest obstacles to test success: test anxiety. Test anxiety can not only impair your performance on the exam itself, but it can even keep you from preparing properly. In Step 2, you will learn stress management techniques that will help you succeed on your exam. Learn these strategies now, and practice them as you work through the questions in this book, so they'll be second nature to you by exam day.

Combating Test Anxiety

The first thing you need to know is that a little test anxiety is a good thing. Everyone gets nervous before a big exam—and if that nervousness motivates you to prepare thoroughly, so much the better. It's said that Sir Olivier, one of the foremost British actors of the twentieth century, threw up before every performance. His stage fright didn't impair his performance; in fact, it

probably gave him a little extra edge—just the kind of edge you need to do well, whether on a stage or in an examination room.

Stress Management before the Exam

If you feel your level of anxiety is getting the best of you in the weeks before the exam, here is what you need to do to bring the level down again:

- **Get prepared.** There's nothing like knowing what to expect, and being prepared for it, to put you in control of test anxiety. That's why you're reading this book. Use it faithfully, and remind yourself that you're better prepared than most of the people taking the exam.
- **Practice self-confidence.** A positive attitude is a great way to combat test anxiety. This is no time to be humble or shy. Stand in front of the mirror and say to your reflection, "I'm prepared. I'm full of self-confidence. I'm going to ace this exam. I know I can do it." Say it into a recorder, and play it back once a day. If you hear it often enough, you will believe it.
- **Fight negative messages.** Every time someone starts telling you how hard the exam is or how it's almost impossible to get a high score, start using your self-confidence messages. If the someone with the negative messages is you—telling yourself you don't do well on exams, that you just can't do this—don't listen. Turn on your recorder and listen to your self-confidence messages.
- **Visualize.** Imagine yourself reporting for duty on your first day of your civil service job. Think of yourself performing your job with pride and learning skills you will use for the rest of your life. Visualizing success can help make it happen—and it reminds you of why you're doing all this work in preparing for the exam.

- **Exercise.** Physical activity helps calm down your body and focus your mind. Besides, being in good physical shape can actually help you do well on the exam. Go for a run, lift weights, go swimming—and do it regularly.

Stress Management on Exam Day

There are several ways you can bring down your level of test stress and anxiety on exam day. They'll work best if you practice them in the weeks before the exam, so you know which ones work best for you.

- **Deep breathing.** Take a deep breath while you count to five. Hold it for a count of one, and then let it out on a count of five. Repeat several times.
- **Move your body.** Try rolling your head in a circle. Rotate your shoulders. Shake your hands from the wrist. Many people find these movements very relaxing.
- **Visualize again.** Think of the place where you are most relaxed: lying on the beach in the sun, walking through the park, or whatever relaxes you. Now, close your eyes and imagine you're actually there. If you practice in advance, you will find that you need only a few seconds of this exercise to experience a significant increase in your sense of well-being.

When anxiety threatens to overwhelm you during the exam, there are still things you can do to manage your stress level:

- **Repeat your self-confidence messages.** You should have them memorized by now. Say them quietly to yourself, and believe them!
- **Visualize one more time.** This time, visualize yourself moving smoothly and quickly through the exam, answering every question correctly and finishing just before time is up. Like most visualization techniques, this one works best if you've practiced it ahead of time.
- **Find an easy question.** Skim over the test until you find an easy question, and answer it. Getting even one circle filled in gets you into the test-taking groove.
- **Take a mental break.** Everyone loses concentration once in a while during a long exam. It's normal, so you shouldn't worry about it. Instead, accept what has happened. Say to yourself, "Hey, I lost it there for a minute. My brain is taking a break." Put down your pencil, close your eyes, and do some deep breathing for a few seconds. Then, you're ready to go back to work.

Try these techniques ahead of time, and see if they work for you!

Take the Test Anxiety Quiz on the following page to find out whether or not your level of test anxiety is something you should worry about.

You need to worry about test anxiety only if it is extreme enough to impair your performance. The following questionnaire will provide a diagnosis of your level of test anxiety. In the blank before each statement, write the number that most accurately describes your experience.

0 = Never

1 = Once or twice

2 = Sometimes

3 = Often

_____ I have gotten so nervous before an exam that I simply put down the books and didn't study for it.

_____ I have experienced disabling physical symptoms such as vomiting and severe headaches because I was nervous about an exam.

_____ I have simply not showed up for an exam because I was scared to take it.

_____ I have experienced dizziness and disorientation while taking an exam.

_____ I have had trouble filling in the little circles because my hands were shaking too hard.

_____ I have failed an exam because I was too nervous to complete it.

_____ **Total: Add up the numbers in the blanks above.**

Understanding Your Test Stress Scores

Here are the steps you should take, depending on your score. If you scored:

- **Below 3:** Your level of test anxiety is nothing to worry about. It's probably just enough to give you that little extra edge.
- **Between 3 and 6:** Your test anxiety may be enough to impair your performance, and you should practice the stress-management techniques listed in this section to try to bring your test anxiety down to manageable levels.
- **Above 6:** Your level of test anxiety is a serious concern. In addition to practicing the stress-management techniques listed in this section, you may want to seek additional, personal help. Call your local high school or community college and ask for the academic counselor. Tell the counselor that you have a level of test anxiety that sometimes keeps you from being able to take the exam. The counselor may be willing to help you or may suggest someone else you should talk to.

Step 3: Make a Plan

Time to complete: 50 minutes
Activity: Construct a study plan, using Schedules A-D (pages 64-66)

Many people do poorly on exams because they forget to make a study schedule. The most important thing you can do to better prepare yourself for your exam is to create a study plan or schedule. Spending hours the day before the exam poring over sample test questions not only raises your level of anxiety, but it is also not a substitute for careful preparation and practice over time.

Don't cram. Take control of your time by mapping out a study schedule. There are four examples of study schedules on the following pages, based on the amount of time you have before the exam. If you're the kind of person who needs deadlines and assignments to motivate you for a project, here they are. If you're the kind of person who doesn't like to follow other people's plans, you can use the suggested schedules to construct your own.

In constructing your plan, you should take into account how much work you need to do. If your score on the sample test wasn't what you had hoped, consider taking some of the steps from Schedule A and fitting them into Schedule D, even if you do have only three weeks before the exam. (See Schedules A-D on the next few pages.)

Even more important than making a plan is making a commitment. You have to set aside some time every day for studying and practice. Try to set aside at least 20 minutes a day. Twenty minutes daily will do you more good than two hours crammed into a Saturday.

If you have months before the exam, you're lucky. Don't put off your study until the week before the exam. Start now. Even ten minutes a day, with half an hour or more on weekends, can make a big difference in your score—and in your chances of working in civil service.

Schedule A: The Leisure Plan

This schedule gives you at least six months to sharpen your skills and prepare for your exam. The more prep time you give yourself, the more relaxed you'll feel.

TIME	PREPARATION
Exam minus 6 months:	Read Chapters 1, 2, and 3. Start going to the library once every two weeks to read books, magazines, or websites in your desired field. Start gathering information about working. Find other people who are preparing for the exam, and form a study group.
Exam minus 5 months:	Read Chapter 5 and work through the exercises.
Exam minus 4 months:	Read Chapter 6 and work through the excercises. You're still continuing with your reading, aren't you?

TIME	PREPARATION
Exam minus 3 months:	Read Chapter 7 and work through the exercises.
Exam minus 2 months:	Use your scores from the chapter exercises to help you decide where to concentrate your efforts this month. Go back to the relevant chapters and use the additional resources listed there. Continue working with your study group.
Exam minus 1 month:	Take and review the sample exams in Chapters 8, 9, and 10. See how much you've learned in the past months. Concentrate on what you've done well, and decide not to let any areas where you still feel uncertain bother you.
Exam minus 1 week:	Review any areas that are still giving you trouble.
Exam minus 1 day:	Relax. Do something unrelated to the civil service exam. Eat a good meal and go to bed at your usual time.

Schedule B: The Just—Enough—Time Plan

If you have three to six months before the exam, that should be enough time to prepare. This schedule assumes four months; stretch it out or compress it if you have more or less time.

TIME	PREPARATION
Exam minus 4 months:	Read Chapters 1, 2, and 3. Start going to the library once every two weeks to read books, magazines, or websites about civil service jobs. Start gathering information about civil service jobs.
Exam minus 3 months:	Read Chapters 5–6 and work through the exercises.
Exam minus 2 months:	Read Chapter 7 and work through the exercises.
Exam minus 1 month:	Take one of the sample exams in Chapters 8, 9, or 10. Use your score to help you decide where to concentrate your efforts this month. Go back to the relevant chapters and use the extra resources listed there, or get the help of a friend or teacher.
Exam minus 1 week:	Review the sample exams in Chapters 8, 9, or 10. See how much you've learned in the past months. Concentrate on what you've done well, and decide not to let any areas where you still feel uncertain bother you.
Exam minus 1 day:	Relax. Do something unrelated to your civil service exam. Eat a good meal and go to bed at your usual time.

Schedule C: More Study in Less Time

If you have one to three months before the exam, you still have enough time for some concentrated study that will help you improve your score. This schedule is built around a two-month time frame. If you have only one month, spend an extra couple of hours a week to get all these steps in. If you have three months, take some of the steps from Schedule B and fit them in.

TIME	PREPARATION
Exam minus 8 weeks:	Read Chapters 1, 2, and 3.
Exam minus 6 weeks:	Read Chapters 5 and 6 and work through the exercises.
Exam minus 4 weeks:	Read Chapter 7 and work through the exercises.
Exam minus 2 weeks:	Take one of the sample exams in Chapters 8, 9, or 10. Then, score it and read the answer explanations until you're sure you understand them. Review the areas where your score is lowest.
Exam minus 1 week:	Review the sample exams, concentrating on the areas where a little work can help the most.
Exam minus 1 day:	Relax. Do something unrelated to the civil service exam. Eat a good meal and go to bed at your usual time.

Schedule D: The Cram Plan

If you have three weeks or less before the exam, you may have your work cut out for you. Carve half an hour out of your day, every day, for studying. This schedule assumes you have the whole three weeks to prepare; if you have less time, you will have to compress your schedule accordingly.

TIME	PREPARATION
Exam minus 3 weeks:	Read Chapters 1–3.
Exam minus 2 weeks:	Work through the exercises in Chapters 5–7. Review areas you're weakest in.
Exam minus 1 week:	Evaluate your performance on the chapter exercises. Review the parts of Chapters 5–7 that you had the most trouble with. Get a friend or teacher to help you with the section you had the most difficutlty with.
Exam minus 2 days:	Take the sample exams in Chapters 8, 9, and 10. Review your results. Make sure you understand the answer explanations.
Exam minus 1 day:	Relax. Do something unrelated to the civil service exam. Eat a good meal and go to bed at your usual time.

Step 4: Learn to Manage Your Time

Time to complete: 10 minutes to read, many hours of practice
Activities: Practice these strategies as you take the sample exams.

Steps 4, 5, and 6 of the LearningExpress Test Preparation System put you in charge of your exam by showing you test taking strategies that work. Practice these strategies as you take the sample exams in Chapters 8, 9 and 10. Then, you will be ready to use them on exam day.

First, you will take control of your time on the exam. The first step in achieving this control is to find out the format of the exam you're going to take. Civil service exams may have different sections that are each timed separately. If this is true of the exam you will be taking, you will want to practice using your time wisely on the practice exams and trying to avoid mistakes while working quickly. Other types of exams don't have separately timed sections. If this is the case, just practice pacing yourself on the practice exams so you don't spend too much time on difficult questions.

- **Listen carefully to directions.** By the time you get to the exam, you should know how the test works, but listen just in case something has changed.
- **Pace yourself.** Glance at your watch every few minutes, and compare the time to how far you've gotten in the section. Leave some extra time for review, so that when one-quarter of the time has elapsed, you should be more than a quarter of the way through the section, and so on. If you're falling behind, pick up the pace.
- **Keep moving.** Don't spend too much time on one question. If you don't know the answer, skip the question and move on. Circle the number of

the question in your test booklet in case you have time to come back to it later.
- **Keep track of your place on the answer sheet.** If you skip a question, make sure you skip on the answer sheet, too. Check yourself every five to ten questions to make sure the question number and the answer sheet number match.
- **Don't rush.** You should keep moving, rushing won't help. Try to keep calm and work methodically and quickly.

Step 5: Learn to Use the Process of Elimination

Time to complete: 20 minutes
Activity: Practice using the process of elimination on practice tests.

After time management, the next most important tool for taking control of your exam is using the process of elimination wisely. It's standard test-taking wisdom that you should always read all the answer choices before choosing your answer. This helps you find the right answer by eliminating wrong answer choices. And, sure enough, that standard wisdom applies to this exam, too.

Let's say you're facing a question that goes like this:

13. "Biology uses a binomial system of classification." In this sentence, the word *binomial* most nearly means
   a. understanding the law.
   b. having two names.
   c. scientifically sound.
   d. having a double meaning.

If you happen to know what *binomial* means, you don't need to use the process of elimination, but let's assume that, like most people, you don't. So, you look at the answer choices. "Understanding the law" sure doesn't sound very likely for something having to do with biology. So, you eliminate choice **a**—and now you only have three answer choices to deal with. Mark an **X** next to choice **a** so you never have to read it again.

Move on to the other answer choices. If you know that the prefix *bi-* means *two*, as in *bicycle*, you will flag choice **b** as a possible answer. Make a check mark beside it, meaning "good answer, I might use this one."

Choice **c**, "scientifically sound," is a possibility. At least it's about science, not law. It could work here, though, when you think about it, having a "scientifically sound" classification system in a scientific field is kind of redundant. You remember the *bi-* in *binomial*, and probably continue to like choice **b** better. But you're not sure, so you put a question mark next to choice **c**, meaning "well, maybe."

Now, look at choice **d**, "having a double meaning." You're still keeping in mind that *bi-* means *two*, so this one looks possible at first. But then you look again at the sentence the word belongs in, and you think, "Why would biology want a system of classification that has two meanings? That wouldn't work very well!" If you're really taken with the idea that *bi-* means *two*, you might put a question mark here. But if you're feeling a little more confident, you will put an **X**. You've already got a better answer picked out.

Now, your question looks like this:

13. "Biology uses a *binomial* system of classification."
In this sentence, the word *binomial* most nearly means
   X **a.** understanding the law.
   ✓ **b.** having two names.
   ? **c.** scientifically sound.
   ? **d.** having a double meaning.

You've got just one check mark, for a good answer. If you're pressed for time, you should simply mark choice **b** on your answer sheet. If you've got the time to be extra careful, you could compare your check mark answer to your question mark answers to make sure that it's better. (It is: The *binomial* system in biology is the one that gives a two-part genus and species name like homo sapiens.)

It's good to have a system for marking good, bad, and maybe answers. We recommend using this one:

X = bad
✓ = good
? = maybe

If you don't like these marks, devise your own system. Just make sure you do it long before <u>exam</u> day—while you're working through the practice exams in this book—so you won't have to worry about it during the exam.

Even when you think you're absolutely clueless about a question, you can often use the process of elimination to get rid of one answer choice. If so, you're better prepared to make an educated guess, as you will see in Step 6.

More often, the process of elimination allows you to get down to only two possibly right answers. Then you're in a strong position to guess. And sometimes, even though you don't know the right answer, you find it simply by getting rid of the wrong ones, as you did in the previous example.

Try using your powers of elimination on the questions in the Using the Process of Elimination worksheet, beginning on the next page. The answer explanations there show one possible way you might use the process to arrive at the right answer.

The process of elimination is your tool for the next step, which is knowing when to guess.

1. Ilsa is as old as Meghan will be in five years. The difference between Ed's age and Meghan's age is twice the difference between Ilsa's age and Meghan's age. Ed is 29. How old is Ilsa?
   a. 4
   b. 10
   c. 19
   d. 24

2. "All drivers of commercial vehicles must carry a valid commercial driver's license whenever operating a commercial vehicle." According to this sentence, which of the following people need **NOT** carry a commercial driver's license?
   a. a truck driver idling his engine while waiting to be directed to a loading dock
   b. a bus operator backing her bus out of the way of another bus in the bus lot
   c. a taxi driver driving his personal car to the grocery store
   d. a limousine driver taking the limousine to her home after dropping off her last passenger of the evening

3. Smoking tobacco has been linked to
   a. increased risk of stroke and heart attack.
   b. all forms of respiratory disease.
   c. increasing mortality rates over the past ten years.
   d. juvenile delinquency.

4. Which of the following words is spelled correctly?
   a. incorrigible
   b. outragous
   c. domestickated
   d. understandible

Answers

Here are the answers, as well as some suggestions as to how you might have used the process of elimination to find them.

1. d. You should have eliminated choice **a** off the bat. Ilsa can't be four years old if Meghan is going to be Ilsa's age in five years. The best way to eliminate other answer choices is to try plugging them in to the information given in the problem. For instance, for choice **b**, if Ilsa is 10, then Meghan must be 5. The difference in their ages is 5. The difference between Ed's age, 29, and Meghan's age, 5, is 24. Is 24 two times 5? No. Then choice **b** is wrong. You could eliminate choice **c** in the same way and be left with choice **d**.

2. c. Note the word *not* in the question, and go through the choices one by one. Is the truck driver in choice **a** "operating a commercial vehicle"? Yes, idling counts as "operating," so he needs to have a commercial driver's license. Likewise, the bus operator in choice **b** is operating a commercial vehicle; the question doesn't say the operator has to be on the street. The limo driver in choice **d** is operating a commercial vehicle, even if it doesn't have passenger in it. However, the cabbie in choice **c** is not operating a commercial vehicle, but his own private car.

3. a. You could eliminate choice **b** simply because of the presence of the word *all*. Such absolutes hardly ever appear in correct answer choices. Choice **c** looks attractive until you think a little about what you know—aren't fewer people smoking these days, rather than more? So how could smoking be responsible for a higher mortality rate? (If you didn't know that *mortality rate* means the rate at which people die, you might keep this choice as a possibility, but you'd still be able to eliminate two answers and have only two to choose from.) Choice **d** is plain silly, so you could eliminate that one, too. You're left with the correct choice, **a**.

4. a. How you used the process of elimination here depends on which words you recognized as being spelled incorrectly. If you knew that the correct spellings were *outrageous*, *domesticated*, and *understandable*, then you were home free. You probably knew that at least one of those words was wrong.

Step 6: Know When to Guess

Time to complete: 20 minutes
Activity: Practice guessing on practice test questions.
Armed with the process of elimination, you're ready to take control of one of the big questions in test-taking: Should I guess? The first and main answer is yes. Unless the exam has a so-called "guessing penalty," you have nothing to lose and everything to gain from guessing. The more complicated answer depends both on the exam and on you-your personality and your "guessing intuition."

Most civil service exams don't use a guessing penalty. The number of questions you answer correctly yields your score, and there's no penalty for wrong answers. So most of the time, you don't have to worry—simply go ahead and guess. But if you find that your exam does have a guessing penalty, you should read the section below to find out what that means to you.

How the Guessing Penalty Works

A guessing penalty really only works against random guessing—filling in the little circles to make a nice pattern on your answer sheet. If you can eliminate one or more answer choices, you're better off taking a guess than leaving the answer blank, even on the sections that have a penalty.

Here's how a guessing penalty works: Depending on the number of answer choices in a given exam, some proportion of the number of questions you get wrong is subtracted from the total number of questions you got right. For instance, if there are four answer choices, typically the guessing penalty is $\frac{1}{3}$ of your wrong answers. Suppose you took an exam of 100 questions. You answered 88 of them right and 12 wrong.

If there's no guessing penalty, your score is simply 88. But if there's a $\frac{1}{3}$ point guessing penalty, the scorers take your 12 wrong answers and divide by three to come up with 4. Then they subtract that four from your correct answer score of 88 to leave you with a score of 84. Thus, you would have been better off if you had simply not answered those 12 questions. Then your total score would still be 88 because there wouldn't be anything to subtract.

What You Should Do About the Guessing Penalty

You now know how a guessing penalty works. The first thing this means for you is that marking your answer sheet at random doesn't pay. If you're running out of time on an exam that has a guessing penalty, you should not use your remaining seconds to mark a pretty pattern on your answer sheet. Take those few seconds to try to answer one more question right.

But as soon as you get out of the realm of random guessing, the guessing penalty no longer works against you. If you can use the process of elimination to get rid of even one wrong answer choice, the odds stop being against you and start working in your favor.

Sticking with our example of an exam that has four answer choices, eliminating just one wrong answer makes your odds of choosing the correct answer one in three. That's the same as the one-out-of-three guessing penalty—even odds. If you eliminate two answer choices, your odds are one in two—better than the guessing penalty. In either case, you should go ahead and choose one of the remaining answer choices.

When There Is No Guessing Penalty

As noted, most civil service exams don't have a guessing penalty. That means that, all other things being equal, you should always go ahead and guess, even if you have no idea what the question means. Nothing can happen to you if you're wrong. But all other things aren't necessarily equal. The other factor in deciding whether or not to guess, besides the guessing penalty, is you. There are two things you need to know about yourself before you go into the exam:

- Are you a risk-taker?
- Are you a good guesser?

Your risk-taking temperament matters most on exams with a guessing penalty. Without a guessing penalty, even if you're a play-it-safe person, guessing is perfectly safe. Overcome your anxieties, and go ahead and mark an answer.

But what if you're not much of a risk-taker, and you think of yourself as the world's worst guesser? Complete the Your Guessing Ability worksheet on the next two pages to get an idea of how good your intuition is.

The following are ten really hard questions. You are not supposed to know the answers. Rather, this is an assessment of your ability to guess when you don't have a clue. Read each question carefully, just as if you did expect to answer it. If you have any knowledge at all about the subject of the question, use that knowledge to help you eliminate wrong answer choices. Use this answer grid to fill in your answers to the questions.

ANSWER GRID

1. (a) (b) (c) (d)   5. (a) (b) (c) (d)   9. (a) (b) (c) (d)
2. (a) (b) (c) (d)   6. (a) (b) (c) (d)   10. (a) (b) (c) (d)
3. (a) (b) (c) (d)   7. (a) (b) (c) (d)
4. (a) (b) (c) (d)   8. (a) (b) (c) (d)

1. September 7 is Independence Day in
   a. India.
   b. Costa Rica.
   c. Brazil.
   d. Australia.

2. Which of the following is the formula for determining the momentum of an object?
   a. $p = mv$
   b. $F = ma$
   c. $P = IV$
   d. $E = mc^2$

3. Because of the expansion of the universe, the stars and other celestial bodies are all moving away from each other. This phenomenon is known as
   a. Newton's first law.
   b. the big bang.
   c. gravitational collapse.
   d. Hubble flow.

4. American author Gertrude Stein was born in
   a. 1713.
   b. 1830.
   c. 1874.
   d. 1901.

5. Which of the following is NOT one of the Five Classics attributed to Confucius?
   a. *I Ching*
   b. *Book of Holiness*
   c. *Spring and Autumn Annals*
   d. *Book of History*

6. The religious and philosophical doctrine that holds that the universe is constantly in a struggle between good and evil is known as
   a. Pelagianism.
   b. Manichaeanism.
   c. neo-Hegelianism.
   d. Epicureanism.

7. The third Chief Justice of the U.S. Supreme Court was
   a. John Blair.
   b. William Cushing.
   c. James Wilson.
   d. John Jay.

8. Which of the following is the poisonous portion of a daffodil?
   a. the bulb
   b. the leaves
   c. the stem
   d. the flowers

9. The winner of the Masters golf tournament in 1953 was
   a. Sam Snead.
   b. Cary Middlecoff.
   c. Arnold Palmer.
   d. Ben Hogan.

10. The state with the highest per capita personal income in 1980 was
   a. Alaska.
   b. Connecticut.
   c. New York.
   d. Texas.

Answers

Check your answers against the correct answers below.

1. c.
2. a.
3. d.
4. c.
5. b.
6. b.
7. b.
8. a.
9. d.
10. a.

How Did You Do?

You may have simply gotten lucky and actually known the answer to one or two questions. In addition, your guessing was more successful if you were able to use the process of elimination on any of the questions. Maybe you didn't know who the third Chief Justice was (question 7), but you knew that John Jay was the first. In that case, you would have eliminated choice **d** and therefore improved your odds of guessing correctly from one in four to one in three.

According to probability, you should get $2\frac{1}{2}$ answers correct, so getting either two or three right would be average. If you got four or more right, you may be a really terrific guesser. If you got one or none right, you may be a really bad guesser.

Keep in mind, though, that this is only a small sample. You should continue to keep track of your guessing ability as you work through the sample questions in this book. Circle the numbers of questions you guess on as you make your guess; or, if you don't have time while you take the practice exams, go back afterward and try to remember which questions you guessed at. Remember, on an exam with four answer choices, your chances of getting a right answer is one in four. So keep a separate "guessing" score for each exam. How many questions did you guess on? How many did you get right? If the number you got right is at least one-fourth of the number of questions you guessed on, you are at least an average guesser, maybe better—and you should always go ahead and guess on a real exam. If the number you got right is significantly lower than one-fourth of the number you guessed on, you would, frankly, be safe in guessing anyway, but maybe you would feel more comfortable if you guessed only selectively, when you can eliminate a wrong answer or at least have a good feeling about one of the answer choices.

Step 7: Reach Your Peak Performance Zone

Time to complete: 10 minutes to read; weeks to complete!

Activity: Complete the Physical Preparation Checklist (page 75)

To get ready for a challenge like a big exam, you also have to take control of your physical, as well as your mental, state. Exercise, proper diet, and rest will ensure that your body works with, rather than against, your mind on test day, as well as during your preparation.

Exercise

If you don't already have a regular exercise program going, the time during which you're preparing for an exam is actually an excellent time to start one. And if you're already keeping fit—or trying to get that way—don't let the pressure of preparing for an exam fool you into quitting now. Exercise helps reduce stress by pumping wonderful good-feeling hormones called endorphins into your system. It also increases the oxygen supply throughout your body, including your brain, so you will be at peak performance on exam day.

A half hour of vigorous activity—enough to raise a sweat—every day should be your aim. If you're really pressed for time, every other day is OK. Choose an activity you like and get out there and do it. Jogging with a friend always makes the time go faster, as does running with a radio.

But don't overdo it. You don't want to exhaust yourself. Moderation is the key.

Diet

First of all, cut out the junk. Go easy on caffeine, and try to eliminate alcohol and nicotine from your system at least two weeks before the exam.

What your body needs for peak performance is simply a balanced diet. Eat plenty of fruits and vegetables, along with protein and carbohydrates. Foods that are high in lecithin (an amino acid), such as fish and beans, are especially good "brain foods."

The night before the exam, you might "carbo-load" the way athletes do before a contest. Eat a big plate of spaghetti, rice and beans, or whatever your favorite carbohydrate is.

Rest

You probably know how much sleep you need every night to be at your best, even if you don't always get it. Make sure you do get that much sleep, though, for at least a week before the exam. Moderation is important here, too. Too much sleep will just make you groggy.

If you're not a morning person and your exam will be given in the morning, you should reset your internal clock so that your body doesn't think you're taking an exam at 3 A.M. You have to start this process well before the exam. The way it works is to get up half an hour earlier each morning, and then go to bed half an hour earlier that night. Don't try it the other way around; you will just toss and turn if you go to bed early without having gotten up early. The next morning, get up another half an hour earlier, and so on. How long you will have to do this depends on how late you're used to getting up. Use the Physical Preparation Checklist on the next page to make sure you're in tip-top form.

Physical Preparation Checklist

For the week before the test, write down 1) what physical exercise you engaged in and for how long and 2) what you ate for each meal. Remember, you're trying for at least half an hour of exercise every other day (preferably every day) and a balanced diet that's light on junk food.

Exam minus 7 days

Exercise: _____ for _____ minutes

Breakfast: _____

Lunch: _____

Dinner: _____

Snacks: _____

Exam minus 6 days

Exercise: _____ for _____ minutes

Breakfast: _____

Lunch: _____

Dinner: _____

Snacks: _____

Exam minus 5 days

Exercise: _____ for _____ minutes

Breakfast: _____

Lunch: _____

Dinner: _____

Snacks: _____

Exam minus 4 days

Exercise: _____ for _____ minutes

Breakfast: _____

Lunch: _____

Dinner: _____

Snacks: _____

Exam minus 3 days

Exercise: _____ for _____ minutes

Breakfast: _____

Lunch: _____

Dinner: _____

Snacks: _____

Exam minus 2 days

Exercise: _____ for _____ minutes

Breakfast: _____

Lunch: _____

Dinner: _____

Snacks: _____

Exam minus 1 day

Exercise: _____ for _____ minutes

Breakfast: _____

Lunch: _____

Dinner: _____

Snacks: _____

Step 8: Get Your Act Together

Time to complete: 10 minutes to read; time to complete will vary
Activity: Take control of your test preparation.
You're in control of your mind and body; you're in charge of test anxiety, your preparation, and your test-taking strategies. Now, it's time to take charge of external factors, like the exam site and the materials you need to take the exam.

Find Out Where the Exam Is and Make a Trial Run

The test administer will notify you when and where your exam is being held. Do you know how to get to the exam site? Do you know how long it will take to get there? If not, make a trial run, preferably on the same day of the week at the same time of day. Make note, on the Final Preparations worksheet on the next page, of the amount of time it will take you to get to the exam site. Plan on arriving 10–15 minutes early so you can get the lay of the land, use the bathroom, and calm down. Then, figure out how early you will have to get up that morning, and make sure you get up that early every day for a week before the exam.

Gather Your Materials

The night before the exam, lay out the clothes you will wear and the materials you have to bring with you to the exam. Plan on dressing in layers; you won't have any control over the temperature of the examination room. Have a sweater or jacket you can take off if it's warm.

Don't Skip Breakfast

Even if you don't usually eat breakfast, do so on exam morning. A cup of coffee doesn't count. Don't do doughnuts or other sweet foods, either. A sugar high will leave you with a sugar low in the middle of the exam. A mix of protein and carbohydrates is best. Cereal with milk and just a little sugar or eggs with toast will do your body a world of good.

Step 9: Do It!

Time to complete: 10 minutes, plus test-taking time
Activity: Ace your civil service exam!
Fast forward to exam day. You're ready. You made a study plan and followed through. You practiced your test-taking strategies while working through this book. You're in control of your physical, mental, and emotional state. You know when and where to show up and what to bring with you. In other words, you're better prepared than most of the other people taking the exam with you. You're psyched.

Just one more thing. When you're done with the exam, you will have earned a reward. Plan a celebration. Call up your friends and plan a party, have a nice dinner for two, or pick out a movie to see—whatever your heart desires. Give yourself something to look forward to.

And then do it. Go into the exam, full of confidence, armed with test-taking strategies you've practiced until they're second nature. You're in control of yourself, your environment, and your performance on the exam. You're ready to succeed. So do it. Go in there and ace the exam. And look forward to your future career as a civil servant.

Getting to the testing site

Location of testing site: _____

Date: _____

Departure time: _____

Do I know how to get to the testing site?   Yes ___   No ___

If no, make a trial run.

Time it will take to get to the testing site: _____

Things to lay out the night before

Clothes I will wear   ___

Sweater/jacket   ___

Watch   ___

Photo ID   ___

4 No. 2 pencils   ___

Other Things to Bring/Remember

_____   _____

_____   _____

_____   _____

CHAPTER

5 ▶ MATH SKILLS FOR CIVIL SERVICE EXAMS

Not all civil service exams test your math knowledge, but many do. Knowledge of basic arithmetic, as well as the complereasoning necessary for algebra, are important qualifications for almost any profession. You have to be able to add up dollar figures, evaluate budgets, compute percentages, and perform similar mathematical tasks in many civil service jobs. Many jobs require someone able to read and interpret data presented in the form of tables and graphs. So even if your exam doesn't include math, you'll probably find that the material in this chapter will help you on the job.

The math portion of the test covers subjects you probably studied in grade school and high school. While every test is different, most emphasize arithmetic skills and word-problem solving.

Strategies for Multiple-Choice Tests

Have you ever wondered why some people are naturally good test takers, while others never seem to reach their potential under test conditions? Good test takers are those who intuitively understand what strategies work best on a multiple-choice test. If you're not one of those people, don't worry: You can learn these strategies. They are not complicated or elaborate, and they will help you greatly improve your test scores. Here they are:

- **Perform all work on paper.** Don't try to solve problems in your head. It is too easy to make a careless mistake that way. And, if you do make a mistake, you will be much less likely to find and correct it because you won't be able to review your work. That's why you should write everything out. Solve equations on paper and draw diagrams whenever necessary. You will not only make fewer careless mistakes, but also be able to recheck your work at the end of the test, time permitting.

- **Skip questions that you find difficult or time consuming.** Remember that you need only to pass this test; you do not need a perfect score. Therefore, you do not have to answer every question. If you can't answer a question, just skip it and move on. There will be other questions ahead that you will be able to answer, and you want to make sure to get to them. Also, because your final score will be based on the number of questions you answer correctly, you do not want to work on time-consuming questions until you have answered every question that you can answer quickly. Circle questions that you skip to make them easier to locate if and when you return to them.

- **Break questions down into component parts.** Don't try to ingest the problem whole. Look at each piece of information to determine its significance in solving the problem. Later in this chapter, we'll discuss techniques you can use to translate word problems into equations. Breaking down questions into component parts helps with this translation technique.

- **Reread the question before you record your final answer.** Some of the incorrect answer choices on multiple-choice tests represent partial answers; these are answers that represent only *some* of the calculations necessary to answer the question. For example, if the question asks you to add two numbers and multiply the sum by a third number, the sum of the two numbers may be one of the incorrect answers. Choosing a partial answer is one of the most common careless errors people make on mathematics multiple-choice exams.

- **Use approximate values whenever you can.** Take a look at the answer choices: Are the values bunched close together, or are they greatly different? If the answer choices are far apart, you can probably approximate to find the correct answer. This is a great time-saver. Suppose a problem asks you to multiply $5.97 and $9.04. It's much easier to multiply $6 and $9, so if the question allows you to approximate, do it! You're also much less likely to make a careless error when you calculate with approximate values. If a question asks you to multiply $5.97 and $9.04, look at the answer choices. If only one answer is near $54 (the product of $6 and $9), you know that you can use approximate values to solve.

- **Before recording your answer, ask yourself if the answer is reasonable.** The most common miscalculation on civil service mathematics exams involves misplacement of a decimal point. Other common errors yield results that are clearly impossible. Use common sense to make sure that your answer is reasonable and that you didn't make a careless error of some type. For example, suppose a question asked you to multiply 10.3 and 1.8. Suppose you calculated the answer 185.4. Check your answer using common sense and approximate values. 10.3 is almost 10 and 1.8 is almost 2, so the correct answer should be somewhere around 20. In this way, you would know that you made a careless error and could correct it.

- **Take advantage of the multiple-choice format of the test.** Multiple-choice tests give you the correct answer. Of course, they bury the answer among three incorrect answers. Even so, the fact that the correct answer already appears in the test means that you do not have to solve every problem from scratch. You can answer some problems by testing the answers. We call this technique "working backwards."

Working Backwards

You can answer some questions simply by testing the answer choices against the problem. When you test the correct answer choice against the question, the question will read as a true statement. Each of the incorrect answers will turn the question into a false statement.

Choose an answer choice that will be easy to work with, preferably one that is neither the greatest nor the least value among the answer choices. That way, if the answer you get is too low, you know to try one of the higher numbers. Then, plug your selection into the text of the problem to see whether it is the correct solution.

Example: Juan ate $\frac{1}{3}$ of the jelly beans in a bag. Maria then ate $\frac{3}{4}$ of the remaining jelly beans in the bag, after which there were 10 remaining jelly beans. How many jelly beans were originally in the bag?

    a. 60   **b.** 90   **c.** 120   **d.** 140

Start by testing 90 or 120 (instead of 60 or 140, which are the smallest and largest choices). $\frac{1}{3}$ of 90 is 30, meaning that Juan ate 30 jelly beans, leaving 60 jelly beans in the bag. If there were 90 jelly beans in the bag originally, then there will be 10 jelly beans remaining in the bag after Juan eats $\frac{1}{3}$ of them, and then Maria eats $\frac{3}{4}$ of the remaining jelly beans. Maria then ate $\frac{3}{4}$ of the remaining jelly beans; $\frac{3}{4}$ of 60 is 45, leaving 15 jelly beans in the bag. Therefore, 90 is not the correct answer. The correct answer is probably the smaller answer 60. (Do you see how starting with an answer that is neither the least nor the greatest value allows you to eliminate more than one incorrect answer at a time?) Let's test 60 just to be sure.

Juan eats $\frac{1}{3}$ of the 60 jelly beans in the bag. $\frac{1}{3}$ of 60 is 20, meaning that 40 jelly beans remain in the bag. Maria eats $\frac{3}{4}$ of the 40 remaining jelly beans. $\frac{3}{4}$ of 40 is 30, which means that 10 jelly beans remain in the bag. That's true; the problem tells us that 10 jelly beans remain in the bag. 60 is the correct answer; when you plug it into the question, the result is a true statement.

Word Problems

Many of the math problems on civil service tests are word problems. A word problem can include any kind of math, including simple arithmetic, fractions, decimals, percentages, and even algebra.

The hardest part of any word problem is translating the problem into an equation. Fortunately, there are a few reliable tricks that help you translate English statements into mathematical statements. At other times, a key word in the problem hints at the mathematical operation to be performed. Study the following information to see how to translate word problems into mathematical statements and equations.

Equals   key words: is, are, has, was, were, had

English	Math
Bob is 18 years old.	$B = 18$
There are 7 hats.	$H = 7$
Judi has 5 books.	$J = 5$

Addition   key words: sum, together, more, total, greater, or older than

English	Math
The sum of two numbers is 10.	$x + y = 10$
Karen has $5 more than Sam.	$K = 5 + S$
Judi is 2 years older than Tony.	$J = T + 2$
The total of the three numbers is 25.	$a + b + c = 25$
Joan and Tom together have $16.	$J + T = 16$

Subtraction   key words: difference; less than, fewer, or younger than; remain; left over

*For *less than* and *fewer*, it is important to remember to switch the order of the things being subtracted. For example, "Jacob has 5 fewer coins than Leslie" would be "Leslie – 5 = Jacob."

English	Math
The difference between the two numbers is 17.	$x - y = 17$
Mike has 5 fewer cats than twice the number Jan has.	$M = 2J - 5$
Jay is 2 years younger than Brett.	$J = B - 2$
After Carol ate 3 apples, R apples remained.	$R = C - 3$

Multiplication   key words: product, times, of

English	Math
20% of the students	$\frac{20}{100} \times S$
Half of the boys	$\frac{1}{2} \times b$
The product of two numbers is 12.	$a \times b = 12$ or $ab = 12$

Division   key words: per, evenly

English	Math
15 drops per teaspoon	$\frac{15 \text{ drops}}{\text{tsp}}$
22 miles per gallon	$\frac{22 \text{ miles}}{\text{gal}}$
100 gifts divided evenly among 10 people	$100 \div 10$

Distance Formula:
Rate × Time = Distance

Distance formula problems include key words such as *speed, plane, train, boat, car, walk, run, climb,* and *swim.* They provide two of the three elements—rate, time, and distance—in the distance formula. Plug those two elements into the formula and solve for the third. Don't forget that rate and time have to be measured in common units. If the rate is measured in miles per hour, the time has to be measured in hours, not minutes or days.

Example: How far did the plane travel in 4 hours if it traveled at an average speed of 300 miles per hour?

$rt = d$

$r = 300$

$t = 4$

$300 \times 4 = d$

$1{,}200 = d$

The plane traveled 1,200 miles.

Example: Ben walked 20 miles in 4 hours. What was his average speed?

$rt = d$

$t = 4$

$d = 20$

$r \times 4 = 20$

$(r \times 4) \div 4 = 20 \div 4$

$r = 5$

Ben walked at a rate of 5 miles per hour.

Example: Jill drives 12 miles in 15 minutes. How far does she drive in 1 hour?

$rt = d$

Convert all measurements to a common unit. Because the question asks for an answer in terms of hours, convert all time measurements to hours. 15 minutes equals $\frac{15}{60}$ hours. $\frac{15}{60}$ reduces to $\frac{1}{4}$.

$t = \frac{1}{4}$

$d = 12$

$r \times \frac{1}{4} = 12$

$(r \times \frac{1}{4}) \times 4 = 12 \times 4$

$r = 48$

Jill drives 48 miles in 1 hour.

Two Ways to Solve Word Problems

There are two methods to approaching word problems. The first way is to translate the problem into an algebraic equation and then solve for the missing information. The second way is to work backwards by plugging in one of the answer choices. Let's solve the following problem using both methods.

David has a box of doughnuts. He gives $\frac{1}{3}$ of the doughnuts in the box to Wanda, and then gives 2 doughnuts to Andrew, after which 8 doughnuts remain in the box. How many doughnuts were originally in the box?

  a. 9　　　　**b.** 12　　　　**c.** 15　　　　**d.** 18

Remember, there are two ways to solve this problem. The first is to translate the problem into an equation and solve.

- David has a box of doughnuts.

  Call the box of doughnuts D.

- He gives $\frac{1}{3}$ of the doughnuts in the box to Wanda . . .

  Subtract one-third of the number of doughnuts from the box.
  $D - \frac{1}{3}D$, which equals $\frac{2}{3}D$

- then gives 2 doughnuts to Andrew . . .

  $\frac{2}{3}D - 2$

- after which 8 doughnuts remain in the box.

  $\frac{2}{3}D - 2 = 8$

Now you have an equation you can solve.

  $\frac{2}{3}D - 2 = 8$

Add 2 to both sides.

  $\frac{2}{3}D - 2 + 2 = 8 + 2$
  $\frac{2}{3}D = 10$

Multiply both sides by 3.

  $3 \times \frac{2}{3}D = 3 \times 10$
  $\frac{3}{1} \times \frac{2}{3}D = 3 \times 10$
  $\frac{3 \times 2}{1 \times 3}D = 3 \times 10$
  $\frac{6}{3}D = 30$
  $2D = 30$

Finally, divide both sides by 2.

$$2D \div 2 = 30 \div 2$$
$$D = 15$$

Therefore, there were originally 15 doughnuts in the box.

Method 2:

Work backwards from the answer choices to see which one is correct. Let's work backwards from choice **b**, 12.

- David has a box of doughnuts.

    David has 12 doughnuts.

- He gives $\frac{1}{3}$ of the doughnuts in the box to Wanda . . .

    David gives Wanda $\frac{1}{3}$ of his 12 doughnuts. Thus, he gives her 4 doughnuts and has 8 doughnuts left.

- then gives 2 doughnuts to Andrew . . .

    $8 - 2 = 6$

- so when starting with 12 doughnuts, 6 will remain in the box.

Since 8 doughnuts were supposed to remain in the box, 12 is not the correct answer to the question. There are too few doughnuts left in the box; therefore, the correct choice is greater than 12. Test choices **c**, 15, or **d**, 18, next to determine which is correct. Let's test choice **c**, 15. David gives $\frac{1}{3}$ of his 15 doughnuts to Wanda; he gives her 5, keeping 10. He gives 2 to Andrew, after which 8 doughnuts remain in the box. That's right! The correct answer is **c**, 15.

Fractions and Decimals

Fractions are used to describe the relationship between a part and a whole. The number representing the *part* appears in the top half of the fraction, called the *numerator*. The number representing the *whole* appears in the bottom half of the fraction, called the *denominator*.

Consider the following example:

Example: A pizza is cut into 8 equal slices. You eat 3 of the slices.

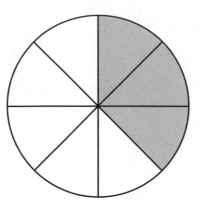

The whole pizza consists of 8 slices, of which you ate a part consisting of 3 slices. In fractional terms, that means you ate $\frac{3}{8}$ of the pizza.

Fractions appear in three different forms:

In a *proper fraction*, the numerator is smaller than the denominator.

$\frac{1}{2}, \frac{6}{11}, \frac{3}{7}, \frac{5}{9}$

In an *improper fraction*, the numerator is larger than the denominator.

$\frac{7}{3}, \frac{10}{2}, \frac{38}{7}, \frac{125}{2}$

A *mixed number* consists of a whole number and a proper fraction. Improper fractions can be rewritten as mixed numbers.

$3\frac{1}{2}, 7\frac{5}{9}, 21\frac{1}{13}, 4\frac{11}{25}$

To **convert an improper fraction to a mixed number**, use the following procedure:

1. Divide the numerator by the denominator. The result will be a whole number, with or without a remainder.
2. Write the whole number.
3. If there is a remainder, write a fraction with the remainder in the numerator and the original denominator as the denominator.

Example: Convert $\frac{17}{5}$ to a mixed number.
$17 \div 5 = 3$ with a remainder of 2
$\frac{17}{5} = 3\frac{2}{5}$

To **convert a mixed number to an improper fraction**, use the following procedure:

1. Multiply the whole number in the mixed number by the denominator of the fraction.
2. Add the result to the numerator of the fraction.

Example: Convert $5\frac{1}{6}$ to an improper fraction.

$5 \times 6 = 30$

$30 + 1 = 31$

$5\frac{1}{6} = \frac{31}{6}$

You should convert mixed numbers to improper fractions whenever you are asked to multiply or divide mixed numbers. Improper fractions are easier to multiply and divide than are mixed numbers.

Reducing Fractions

When the numerator and the denominator of a fraction are divisible by the same number, we say that the fraction can be *reduced*. When you reduce a fraction, you rewrite it with smaller numbers in the numerator and the denominator without changing the value of the fraction. When a fraction cannot be reduced further, we say that it has been written in *lowest terms* or in its *simplest form*.

Reduce a fraction by dividing both the numerator and denominator by a single value that divides evenly into both of them.

Example: Reduce $\frac{5}{10}$.

Both 5 and 10 are divisible by 5.

$\frac{5 \div 5}{10 \div 5} = \frac{1}{2}$

A fraction is reduced to simplest terms when you divide it by the largest value that will divide evenly into the numerator and denominator. Sometimes you won't be able to think of the largest number that divides evenly into the numerator and denominator. That's okay; just divide both by whatever number you can think of that divides evenly into both, and then study your result to see whether you can think of another number that divides evenly.

Example: Reduce $\frac{33}{132}$.

Both 33 and 132 are divisible by 33, but that's not so easy to see. It's much easier to see that both are divisible by 3. (**Here's a neat trick:** To determine whether a number is divisible by 3, add all its digits. If the sum of the digits is divisible by 3, the number itself is divisible by 3. We know that 132 is divisible by 3 because $1 + 3 + 2 = 6$, and 6 is divisible by 3. This trick works for 9, too!) So, divide by 3 first.

$\frac{33 \div 3}{132 \div 3} = \frac{11}{44}$

Now it's much easier to see that 11 and 44 are both divisible by 11. Reduce again.

$\frac{11 \div 11}{44 \div 11} = \frac{1}{4}$

$\frac{33}{132}$ reduces to $\frac{1}{4}$.

Raising Fractions to Higher Terms

When you reduce a fraction, you rewrite it so that the numerator and denominator are smaller. Raising a fraction to a higher term reverses the process; it allows you to rewrite a fraction with a larger numerator and denominator. You often need to raise one or more fractions to higher terms in order to add or subtract them.

Example: Raise $\frac{2}{3}$ to higher terms with 24 in the denominator.

1. Divide 24 by the denominator, 3. The quotient is 8.
2. Then multiply the denominator by the quotient, 8.
3. $\frac{2 \times 8}{3 \times 8} = \frac{16}{24}$

Adding Fractions

It is easy to add fractions that have a common denominator. Simply perform the appropriate calculation on the numerators and write the result over the denominator. **Do NOT add the denominators!**

Example: $\frac{3}{5} + \frac{1}{5} = \frac{3+1}{5} = \frac{4}{5}$

When adding mixed numbers, add the whole numbers together and then add the fractions together.

Example: $3\frac{1}{9} + 12\frac{4}{9} = 3 + 12 + \frac{1}{9} + \frac{4}{9} = 15 + \frac{1+4}{9} = 15\frac{5}{9}$

If the sum of the fractions is an improper fraction, convert the improper fraction to a mixed number.

Examples: $\frac{4}{7} + \frac{6}{7} = \frac{4+6}{7} = \frac{10}{7}$
$10 \div 7 = 1$ remainder 3, so $\frac{10}{7} = 1\frac{3}{7}$

$2\frac{2}{3} + 4\frac{2}{3} = 2 + 4 + \frac{2}{3} + \frac{2}{3} = 6 + \frac{2+2}{3} = 6\frac{4}{3}$
$4 \div 3 = 1$ remainder 1, so $\frac{4}{3} = 1\frac{1}{3}$
$6 + 1\frac{1}{3} = 7\frac{1}{3}$

Don't forget to reduce your answer to lowest terms.

Example: $\frac{4}{9} + \frac{2}{9} = \frac{4+2}{9} = \frac{6}{9}$
$\frac{6 \div 3}{9 \div 3} = \frac{2}{3}$

You cannot add fractions unless they share a common denominator. If the denominators are not equal, you must first rewrite one or all of the fractions until the denominators are equal.

To find a common denominator, look at the denominators of all the fractions in the problem. Do they all divide evenly into the largest denominator? If they do, great! That number is your common denominator. If they don't, run through the multiplication table of the largest denominator until you find a number that all the other denominators divide into evenly.

Example: $\frac{2}{3} + \frac{1}{5} =$

Does 3 divide evenly into 5? No.

So, run through the multiplication table for 5 in your mind: 10, 15, 20, 25, etc. Does 3 divide evenly into 10? No. Does it divide evenly into 15? Yes! So, 15 is your common denominator.

Now, use the technique you learned to raise fractions to higher terms to rewrite $\frac{2}{3}$ and $\frac{1}{5}$ so that each has a denominator of 15.

$$\frac{2 \times 5}{3 \times 5} = \frac{10}{15}$$

$$\frac{1 \times 3}{5 \times 3} = \frac{3}{15}$$

$$\frac{10}{15} + \frac{3}{15} = \frac{10 + 3}{15} = \frac{13}{15}$$

Adding three fractions is only a little more complicated.

Example: $\frac{1}{4} + \frac{1}{3} + \frac{1}{6} =$

Do 4 and 3 divide evenly into 6? 3 does, but 4 does not. All three fractions must be written over a common denominator, so 6 cannot be the common denominator.

Run through the multiples of 6: 12, 18, 24, etc. Do 4 and 3 divide evenly into 12? Yes, so 12 is your common denominator.

Use the technique for raising fractions to higher terms to rewrite all three fractions with a denominator of 12.

$$\frac{1 \times 3}{4 \times 3} = \frac{3}{12}$$

$$\frac{1 \times 4}{3 \times 4} = \frac{4}{12}$$

$$\frac{1 \times 2}{6 \times 2} = \frac{2}{12}$$

$$\frac{3}{12} + \frac{4}{12} + \frac{2}{12} = \frac{3 + 4 + 2}{12} = \frac{9}{12}$$

Don't forget to reduce to lowest terms.

$$\frac{9 \div 3}{12 \div 3} = \frac{3}{4}$$

Subtracting Fractions

Subtracting fractions is like adding fractions. When the fractions share a common denominator, the job is easy. Simply subtract the numerators. Do NOT subtract the denominators.

Example: $\frac{7}{8} - \frac{4}{8} = \frac{7-4}{8} = \frac{3}{8}$

To subtract mixed numbers, subtract the whole number from the whole number and the fraction from the fraction.

Example: $5\frac{3}{4} - 1\frac{2}{4} = (5-1) + (\frac{3}{4} - \frac{2}{4}) = 4\frac{1}{4}$

Sometimes you will have to perform an extra step. If the fraction in the second mixed number is larger than the fraction in the first mixed number, you will have to borrow in order to rewrite the first number.

Example: $12\frac{1}{5} - 7\frac{3}{5} =$

Can you subtract $\frac{3}{5}$ from $\frac{1}{5}$? No, because $\frac{3}{5}$ is greater than $\frac{1}{5}$. You must rewrite $12\frac{1}{5}$ by borrowing. Because $\frac{5}{5}$ equals 1, you can borrow 1 from the 12 and add $\frac{5}{5}$ to $\frac{1}{5}$. In this way, you can rewrite $12\frac{1}{5}$ as $11\frac{1+5}{5}$, or $11\frac{6}{5}$. Now you can complete the calculation.

$$12\frac{1}{5} - 7\frac{3}{5} =$$
$$11\frac{6}{5} - 7\frac{3}{5} =$$
$$(11-7) + (\frac{6}{5} - \frac{3}{5}) = 4\frac{6-3}{5} = 4\frac{3}{5}$$

To subtract numbers that do not share common denominators, you must first rewrite one or all of the fractions until the denominators are equal. To find a common denominator, look at the denominators of all the fractions in the problem. Do they all divide evenly into the largest denominator? If they do, great! That number is your common denominator. If they don't, run through the multiplication table of the largest denominator until you find a number that all the other denominators divide into evenly.

Example: $\frac{3}{4} - \frac{1}{6} =$

Do the fractions share a common denominator? No. Does 4 divide evenly into 6? No.

So, run through the multiplication table for 6 in your mind: 12, 18, 24, 30, etc. Does 4 divide evenly into 12? Yes! So, 12 is your common denominator.

Now, use the technique you learned to raise fractions to higher terms to rewrite $\frac{3}{4}$ and $\frac{1}{6}$ so that each has a denominator of 12.

$$\frac{3 \times 3}{4 \times 3} = \frac{9}{12}$$
$$\frac{1 \times 2}{6 \times 2} = \frac{2}{12}$$
$$\frac{9}{12} - \frac{2}{12} = \frac{9-2}{12} = \frac{7}{12}$$

The same holds true for mixed numbers that do not share a common denominator. You must first rewrite the fractions so that their denominators are equal.

Example: $7\frac{1}{6} - 2\frac{4}{5} =$

Do the fractions share a common denominator? No. Does 5 divide evenly into 6? No.

So, run through the multiplication table for 6 in your mind: 12, 18, 24, 30, etc. Does 5 divide evenly into 12? No, nor does it divide evenly into 18 or 24. Your common denominator is 30.

$$\frac{1 \times 5}{6 \times 5} = \frac{5}{30}$$

$$\frac{4 \times 6}{5 \times 6} = \frac{24}{30}$$

$$7\frac{5}{30} - 2\frac{24}{30} =$$

Because you cannot subtract $\frac{24}{30}$ from $\frac{5}{30}$, you must rewrite $7\frac{5}{30}$ by borrowing 1, or $\frac{30}{30}$, from the 7.

$$7\frac{5}{30} =$$

$$6 + 1 + \frac{5}{30} =$$

$$6 + \frac{30}{30} + \frac{5}{30} =$$

$$6 + \frac{30 + 5}{30} = 6\frac{35}{30}$$

$$6\frac{35}{30} - 2\frac{24}{30} =$$

$$(6 - 2) + \frac{35}{30} - \frac{24}{30} =$$

$$4 + \frac{35 - 24}{30} =$$

$$4\frac{11}{30}$$

Multiplying Fractions

Multiplying fractions is actually easier than adding them. All you have to do is multiply the numerators and multiply the denominators.

Example: $\frac{2}{3} \times \frac{5}{7} = \frac{2 \times 5}{3 \times 7} = \frac{10}{21}$

Example: $\frac{1}{2} \times \frac{3}{5} \times \frac{7}{4} = \frac{1 \times 3 \times 7}{2 \times 5 \times 4} = \frac{21}{40}$

Sometimes you can cancel diagonally *before* multiplying. Canceling diagonally is a shortcut that lets you multiply smaller numbers. It's just like reducing: You find a number that divides evenly into a top number and bottom number and do the division before you multiply. If you don't cancel, it's no big deal; you'll still be able to reduce after you multiply. Canceling just makes your calculations a little bit easier.

Example: $\frac{5}{6} \times \frac{9}{20}$

1. Both 6 and 9 are divisible by 3, so you can cancel. Divide each by 3. $\frac{5}{\,_2 6} \times \frac{9^3}{20}$

2. Both 5 and 20 are divisible by 5, so you can cancel. Divide each by 5. $\frac{^1 5}{\,_2 6} \times \frac{9^3}{20_4}$

3. Now you can multiply. $\frac{1 \times 3}{2 \times 4} = \frac{3}{8}$

To multiply a fraction by a whole number, first rewrite the whole number as a fraction with a denominator of 1.

Example: $5 \times \frac{2}{3} = \frac{5}{1} \times \frac{2}{3} = \frac{10}{3}$

If the question asks for the answer in the form of a mixed number, use the technique discussed earlier to rewrite $\frac{10}{3}$ as $3\frac{1}{3}$.

To multiply mixed numbers, rewrite the mixed numbers as improper fractions before multiplying.

Example: $4\frac{2}{3} \times 5\frac{1}{2}$

1. Convert $4\frac{2}{3}$ to an improper fraction. $\qquad\qquad$ $(4 \times 3) + 2 = 14.\ 4\frac{2}{3} = \frac{14}{3}$
2. Convert $5\frac{1}{2}$ to an improper fraction. $\qquad\qquad$ $(5 \times 2) + 1 = 11.\ 5\frac{1}{2} = \frac{11}{2}$
3. Cancel and multiply. $\qquad\qquad\qquad\qquad\quad$ $\frac{\overset{7}{\cancel{14}}}{3} \times \frac{11}{\underset{1}{\cancel{2}}} = \frac{77}{3}$

If the question asks for the answer in the form of a mixed number, use the technique discussed earlier to rewrite $\frac{77}{3}$ as $25\frac{2}{3}$.

Example: 8,400 fans attended a college football game. $\frac{3}{4}$ of the fans rooted for the home team. The rest rooted for the visiting team. How many fans rooted for the home team?

To solve, multiply 8,400 by $\frac{3}{4}$:

$\frac{8,400}{1} \times \frac{3}{4} =$

$\frac{8,400 \times 3}{1 \times 4} =$

$\frac{25,200}{4}$

A fraction is one way of writing a division problem. When you see a fraction with a numerator larger than a denominator, you can divide (that's also how we convert improper fractions to mixed fractions).

$25,200 \div 4 = 6,100$

There were 6,100 fans rooting for the home team.

Dividing Fractions

Dividing fractions is like multiplying fractions, but with one extra step. In order to divide two fractions, use the reciprocal of the second fraction and turn the division sign into a multiplication sign.

Example: $\frac{1}{2} \div \frac{3}{5}$

1. Take the reciprocal of $\frac{3}{5}$. $\qquad\qquad\qquad\qquad\qquad$ $\frac{3}{5} \rightarrow \frac{5}{3}$
2. Change the division sign to a multiplication sign.
3. Calculate to solve. $\qquad\qquad\qquad\qquad\qquad$ $\frac{1}{2} \times \frac{5}{3} = \frac{1 \times 5}{2 \times 3} = \frac{5}{6}$

To divide a fraction by a whole number, first change the whole number to a fraction by putting the whole number in the numerator of a fraction with a denominator of 1. Then follow the aforementioned steps.

Example: $\frac{3}{5} \div 2 = \frac{3}{5} \div \frac{2}{1} = \frac{3}{5} \times \frac{1}{2} = \frac{3 \times 1}{5 \times 2} = \frac{3}{10}$

To divide mixed numbers, rewrite them as improper fractions.

Example: $3\frac{1}{5} \div 1\frac{1}{2}$

1. Convert $3\frac{1}{5}$ to an improper fraction. $(3 \times 5) + 1 = 16$, so $3\frac{1}{5} = \frac{16}{5}$
2. Convert $1\frac{1}{2}$ to an improper fraction. $(1 \times 2) + 1 = 3$, so $1\frac{1}{2} = \frac{3}{2}$
3. Calculate.

$$\frac{16}{5} \div \frac{3}{2} =$$

$$\frac{16}{5} \times \frac{2}{3} =$$

$$\frac{16 \times 2}{5 \times 3} = \frac{32}{15}$$

If the problem asks for an answer in the form of a mixed number, use the conversion technique to convert $\frac{32}{15}$ to $2\frac{2}{15}$.

Decimals

A decimal is a way to write a fraction without a numerator or denominator. You use decimals every day when you deal with money—$10.35 is a decimal that represents 10 dollars and 35 cents. The period separating the dollars from the cents is called a decimal point. In $10.35, 35 represents a fraction; because 1 cent equals $\frac{1}{100}$ of a dollar, 35 in $10.35 represents $\frac{35}{100}$ of a dollar.

Every decimal digit to the right of the decimal point has a name.

$0.1 = 1$ tenth $= \frac{1}{10}$
$0.02 = 2$ hundredths $= \frac{2}{100}$
$0.003 = 3$ thousandths $= \frac{3}{1,000}$
$0.0004 = 4$ ten thousandths $= \frac{4}{10,000}$

You can add zeros to the right of a decimal without changing its value. 0.1 and 0.10000 are equal. This is helpful when adding, subtracting, and dividing with decimals.

A decimal with numbers on both sides of the decimal point is called a *mixed decimal*. 264.03 is a mixed decimal. A decimal with numbers to the right of the decimal point only is called a decimal. A whole number is understood to have a decimal point to the right; the number 15, for example, could be written 15.0 or 15.00, etc.

To write a fraction as a decimal, divide the numerator by the denominator.

Example: Write $\frac{3}{4}$ as a decimal.

1. Divide the numerator by the denominator. $3 \div 4$

2. Rewrite the problem as a long division problem. You will have to add a decimal point and some zeros to the right of the number 3.

$$\begin{array}{r} .75 \\ 4\overline{)3.00} \\ \underline{2\,8} \\ 20 \\ \underline{20} \\ 0 \end{array}$$

3. The quotient is your answer. $\frac{3}{4}$ equals 0.75.

To change a decimal to a fraction, write the digits of the decimal as the numerator of a fraction and write the decimal's name as the denominator of the fraction. Reduce if possible.

Example: Rewrite 0.018 as a fraction.

1. Write 18 in the numerator of a fraction. $\frac{18}{?}$

2. Write the name of the fraction in the denominator. 0.018 is *eighteen one-thousandths*, so you should write 1,000 in the denominator of the fraction. $\frac{18}{1,000}$

3. Reduce. Both 18 and 1,000 are divisible by 2, so $\frac{18}{1,000}$ can be reduced: $\frac{18 \div 2}{1,000 \div 2} = \frac{9}{500}$

It is a good idea to memorize the decimal equivalent of the following common fractions:

$\frac{1}{5} = 0.2$

$\frac{1}{4} = 0.25$

$\frac{1}{3} = 0.3\overline{3}$

$\frac{2}{5} = 0.4$

$\frac{1}{2} = 0.5$

$\frac{3}{5} = 0.6$

$\frac{2}{3} = 0.6\overline{6}$

$\frac{3}{4} = 0.75$

The bar over the 3 and 6 in the decimal equivalents of $\frac{1}{3}$ and $\frac{2}{3}$ indicate that the decimal repeats infinitely. Decimals are not the most precise way to represent fractions whose denominators are not factors of a power of 10 (powers of 10 include 10; 100; 1,000; 10,000; etc.).

Comparing Decimals

Because decimals are easier to compare when they have the same number of digits after the decimal point, you should tack additional zeros onto the end of shorter decimals until the decimals you want to compare are of equal length. Then all you have to do is compare the numbers as though the decimal points weren't even there.

Example: Compare 0.08 and 0.1.

1. Tack one zero onto the end of 0.1 so that both decimals extend two places to the right of the decimal point. The result is the decimal 0.10.

2. Compare 0.08 and 0.10 as though the decimal points weren't there. Which is greater, 8 or 10? 10 is, so 0.1 is greater than 0.08.

Percentages

The word *percent* comes from the Latin words meaning "for every one hundred." A percent expresses the relationship between a part and a whole in terms of 100. When we say that 10% of the customers at a grocery store pay with cash, we are saying that 10 out of every 100 customers pay with cash. You encounter percentages every day. Sales tax, interest, discounts, and tips on meals are just a few of the percent calculations people make on a daily basis.

Changing a Percent to a Fraction and Vice Versa

A percent can easily be written as a fraction. Simply take the percent and put it in the numerator of the fraction. Then, write 100 in the denominator. That's all there is to it.

Example: Convert 75% to a fraction.

1. Write a fraction with 75 in the numerator.
2. Write 100 in the denominator.
3. Reduce if possible.

$$\frac{75}{?}$$
$$\frac{75}{100}$$
$$\frac{75 \div 25}{100 \div 25} = \frac{3}{4}$$

To write a fraction as a percent, multiply the fraction by $\frac{100}{1}$.

Example: Convert $\frac{1}{4}$ to a percent.
$\frac{1}{4} \times \frac{100}{1} = \frac{1 \times 100}{4} = \frac{100}{4} = 25$
$\frac{1}{4}$ equals 25%.

There is another way to convert a fraction to a percent: Divide the numerator by the denominator, and then move the decimal point two places to the right in your quotient.

$$4\overline{)1.00}^{\,.25} \qquad .25 = 25\%$$

It's a good idea to memorize the fraction equivalents of these common percents:

$10\% = \frac{1}{10}$

$20\% = \frac{1}{5}$

$25\% = \frac{1}{4}$

$30\% = \frac{3}{10}$

$33\frac{1}{3}\% = \frac{1}{3}$

$40\% = \frac{2}{5}$

$50\% = \frac{1}{2}$

$60\% = \frac{3}{5}$

$66\frac{2}{3}\% = \frac{2}{3}$

$80\% = \frac{4}{5}$

$100\% = 1$

Changing a Decimal to a Percent and Vice Versa

To change a decimal to a percent, move the decimal point two places to the right and tack on a percent sign (%). If there aren't enough places to move the decimal point two places to the right, add a zero to the right before moving the decimal.

Example: Write 0.247 as a percent.

1. Move the decimal two places to the right.   24.7
2. Add a percent sign.   24.7%

Example: Write 0.6 as a percent.

1. Because there aren't enough places to move the decimal two places to the right, add a zero to the far right of the decimal.   0.60
2. Move the decimal two places to the right.   60
3. Add a percent sign.   60%

To change a percent to a decimal, reverse the process. Delete the percent sign, and then move the decimal two places to the left. If there aren't enough places to move the decimal point two places to the left, add a zero to the left before moving the decimal.

Example: Write 28% as a decimal.

1. Delete the percent sign.   28
2. Move the decimal two places to the left.   0.28

28% equals 0.28.

Example: Write 4% as a decimal.

1. Delete the percent sign.   4
2. Because there aren't enough places to move the decimal two places to the left, add a zero to the far left of the number.   04
3. Move the decimal two places to the left.   0.04

4% equals 0.04.

Solving Percent Word Problems

Word problems involving percents generally take one of three forms.

- Find the percent of a whole.

  Example: What is 30% of 40?

- Find what percent one number is of another number.

  Example: 12 is what percent of 40?

- Find the whole when the percent of a number is given.

  Example: 12 is 30% of what number?

  Each can be solved using the translation techniques reviewed earlier in the chapter. Just remember that:

what	=	x, y, A (i.e., a variable)
what percent	=	$\frac{x}{100}$
is	=	equals (=)
of	=	multiplied by ($\times$)

  Let's see how to use the translation technique to solve each of the examples.

  Example: What is 30% of 40?

  Translate:

What	=	x
is	=	=
30%	=	$\frac{30}{100}$
of	=	$\times$
40	=	40

  "What is 30% of 40" translates to $= \frac{30}{100} \times 40$.

Now let's solve:

$= \frac{30}{100} \times 40$

$= \frac{30}{100} \times \frac{40}{1}$

$= \frac{30 \times 40}{100 \times 1}$

$= \frac{1,200}{100}$

$= 1,200 \div 100$

$= 12$

So 30% of 40 is 12.

Example: 12 is what percent of 40?

Translate:

12	=	12
is	=	=
what %	=	$\frac{x}{100}$
of	=	$\times$
40	=	40

"12 is what percent of 40" translates to $12 = \frac{x}{100} \times 40$.

Now let's solve:

$12 = \frac{x}{100} \times 40$

$12 = \frac{x}{100} \times \frac{40}{1}$

$12 = \frac{40x}{100}$

$12 \times 100 = \frac{40x}{100} \times \frac{100}{1}$

$1,200 = 40x$

$1,200 \div 40 = 40 \div 40$

$30 = x$

12 is 30% of 40.

Example: 12 is 30% of what number?

Translate:

12	=	12
is	=	=
30%	=	$\frac{30}{100}$
of	=	$\times$
what number	=	y

"12 is 30% of what number" translates to $12 = \frac{30}{100} \times y$.

Now let's solve:

$12 = \frac{30}{100} \times y$

$12 = \frac{30}{100} \times \frac{y}{1}$

$12 = \frac{30y}{100}$

$12 \times 100 = \frac{30y}{100} \times 100$

$1,200 = 30y$

$1,200 \div 30 = 30y \div 30$

$40 = y$

12 is 30% of 40.

The same techniques work for questions that ask about percent increase and percent decrease. Remember that after you calculate the percent, you must add (increase) or subtract (decrease) in order to determine the final result.

Example: A merchant usually sells hats for $20. He decides to have a sale during which he decreases the price of the hats by 25%. What is the price of the hats during the sale?

To answer this question, you must first answer the question "What is 25% of $20?" This is a question you can translate and solve. "What is 25% of $20" translates to:

$= \frac{25}{100} \times 20$

$= \frac{25}{100} \times \frac{20}{1}$

$= \frac{25 \times 20}{100 \times 1}$

$= \frac{500}{100}$

$= 5$

25% of $20 is $5. The merchant plans to decrease the price of the hat by 25%, so he plans to decrease the price by $5. That means the sale price of the hats will be $20 – $5, which equals $15.

A Quick Way to Find 10% of a Number

To find 10% of a number, simply move the decimal point one place to the left. The result equals 10% of the original number.

Example: Find 10% of 570.
Move the decimal point one place to the left.   57.0
10% of 570 is 57.

You can use this method to find multiples of 10% as well. If a question asks you to find 30% of a number, for example, first find 10%, and then multiply the result by 3 to get 30%.

Example: Find 30% of 570.
10% of 570 is 57.
$3 \times 57 = 171$
171 is 30% of 570.

Data and Statistics

Many civil service exams require you to read tables, charts, and graphs. Questions on these subjects ask you to identify key elements of a table or graph, retrieve data, and draw conclusions based on the data. This section reviews the different types of graphs and explains how to read them. It also discusses several basic concepts of statistics, including arithmetic mean (what most people call "the average" of a set of numbers) and range.

The simplest form of data presentation is a *reading table*. A reading table presents data in rows and columns. The following reading table shows the average weight of five different large animals.

AVERAGE WEIGHT, IN POUNDS, OF SELECT ANIMALS	
ANIMAL	WEIGHT IN POUNDS
Gorilla	200
Cow	1,000
Horse	1,500
Giraffe	2,600
Elephant	10,700

Each *column* of the table contains a type of data: The left column gives the names of the animals, while the right column gives weights. Each *row* of the table presents the data for a particular animal. The first row of the table tells you that an average gorilla weighs 200 pounds. The fourth row tells you that an average giraffe weighs 2,600 pounds.

A reading table is great for presenting data in a straightforward manner. Although some data benefits from graphic representation in a graph or pie chart, some data is perfectly clear in this simple reading table format. Reading tables are best for presenting a limited amount of data; when reading tables get too long, they are difficult to read and information can be hard to find. Anyone who has ever tried to pore over a long Excel spreadsheet knows this too well.

Often the data that appears in a reading table can also be represented in a *bar graph*. A bar graph is great for comparing values; because each number is graphically represented, it is easy to determine quickly which value in a data set is greatest, which value is least, etc. The bar graph that follows shows the number of lunch specials sold at a restaurant during a work week.

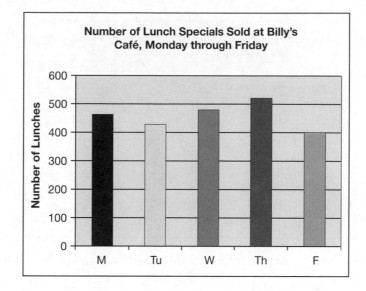

The bar graph makes it easy to determine that Billy's Café sold the most lunch specials on Thursday and that it sold the least on Friday. It makes it very easy to compare each day's sales with each of the other day's sales. It is not always easy to determine the precise value represented by a bar in a bar graph, however. We can tell that Billy's Café sold between 400 and 500 lunch specials on Monday, but it is not so easy to determine exactly how many lunch specials the restaurant sold on that day. Some bar graphs provide data labels to provide the exact value represented by each bar.

A bar graph has an *x-axis* and a *y-axis*. The *x*-axis is the horizontal axis; it usually represents the categories of data shown in the graph. A bar graph of the reading table titled "Average Weight, in Pounds, of Select Animals," for example, would list the names of the animals along the *x*-axis. The *y*-axis is the vertical axis. It usually shows the data scale; it tells you how many things are in each category. A bar graph of the reading table titled "Average Weight, in Pounds, of Select Animals" would have the weights shown on the *y*-axis.

Like a bar graph, a *line graph* represents data graphically, making it easy to compare values. A line graph is usually used to show changes in data over time. The line graph that follows shows changes to the population of Hardintown between 1995 and 2006.

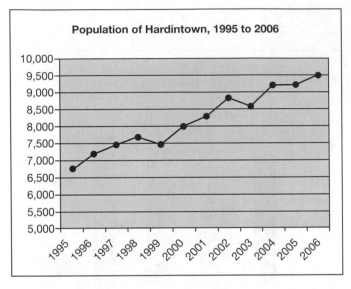

The line makes it easy to see the general trend toward growth in Hardintown's population. It also makes it easy to find the years in which population declined from the previous year (1999 and 2003). To determine the population of the town each year, find the dot corresponding to the year, and then look at the scale on the vertical axis (i.e., the *y*-axis) to find the value to which the dot corresponds. As in a bar graph, it is sometimes difficult to determine the exact value represented. We can tell that the population of Hardintown in 1998 was about 7,600, but we can't really say for sure whether it was 7,600; 7,601; 7,602, etc.

Sometimes a bar graph or a line graph will compare several sets of data. When they do, a *legend* is necessary to tell you how to read the graph. The bar graph that follows compares the responses of Democrats and Republicans to two survey questions.

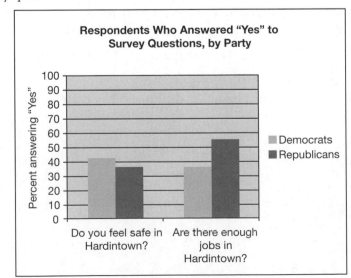

The legend of this bar graph tells you how to interpret the data. Democrats' responses are shown in light gray, while Republicans' responses are shown in dark gray.

A *pie chart* is best for showing how a whole is divided into parts. Each slice of the pie represents one part of the whole. The pie chart that follows shows how the city budget of Hardintown is divided among different expenses.

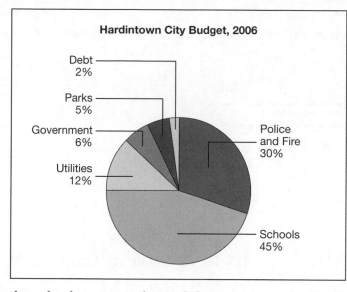

This pie chart shows that schools represent the single biggest expense for Hardintown, claiming 45% of the budget. Police and fire consume 30% of the budget, utilities 12%, etc.

Drawing Conclusions from Graph Data

Some questions will ask you to draw conclusions based on data presented in graphs. These questions do not ask you to draw subtle conclusions reached by reading between the lines or by making a lot of assumptions. On the contrary, the answers to these questions will be indisputably correct, and they will be fairly obvious. The incorrect answers are those that are not supported by the data or that require major assumptions to support the conclusion.

Let's look again at the pie chart titled Hardintown City Budget, 2006. Here's a typical "draw a conclusion" question based on that graph.

Example: Which of the following conclusions is best supported by data in the graph?
a. The people of Hardintown would like to reduce spending on education.
b. Hardintown would have more parks if the city increased its parks budget.
c. Schools and police and fire account for $\frac{3}{4}$ of the city's budget.
d. Hardintown's debt is too large.

You might be tempted to choose choice **a**; education is the single largest item on the city budget, so it is possible that people in Hardintown would like to reduce spending on education. However, it's also possible that the people of Hardintown would like to *increase* education spending. Because the graph provides no data on public opinion in Hardintown, it is impossible to say whether the people there would like to reduce spending on education. Choice **a** cannot be correct; eliminate it.

Choices **b** and **d** can be eliminated the same way. Each is based on an assumption that may or may not be correct. Only choice **c** is indisputably correct; because schools account for 45% of the budget and police and fire account for 30% of the budget, the two together account for 75% of the budget. 75% equals $\frac{3}{4}$, so choice **c** is the best answer.

Range and Arithmetic Mean

Some questions will ask you to find the range of a set of data. Others may ask you to calculate the average, or arithmetic mean, of a data set.

The *range* of a data set is the difference between the least and the greatest value in the set. Consider the following reading table:

JANE'S BOWLING SCORES	
Game 1	188
Game 2	215
Game 3	170

The greatest value in the data set is 215. The least value in the set is 170. The range of the data set is 215 – 170, which equals 45.

The *arithmetic mean* of a data set is what we sometimes refer to as the average of the set. It is calculated by adding all the data in the set and dividing the sum by the number of pieces of data in the set. In the previous table, there are three pieces of data, namely Jane's three bowling scores. The sum of the data is 188 + 215 + 170, which equals 573. To calculate the arithmetic mean, divide 573 by 3.

573 ÷ 3 = 191

The arithmetic mean of Jane's bowling scores is 191.

Strategy Review

Remember to employ these strategies to maximize your score on multiple-choice mathematics tests:

- Perform all work on paper.
- Skip questions that you find difficult or time consuming.
- Break questions down into component parts.
- Reread the question before you record your final answer.
- Use approximate values whenever you can.
- Before recording your answer, ask yourself if the answer is reasonable.
- Take advantage of the multiple-choice format of the test by working backwards whenever you can.

Follow these steps and complete the math review in this chapter. If you do, passing the math portion of your civil service exam should be as easy as 1, 2, 3!

Review Exercise

1. $\frac{2}{3} \times \frac{3}{4} =$
   a. $\frac{5}{8}$
   b. $\frac{1}{2}$
   c. $\frac{8}{9}$
   d. $\frac{9}{8}$

2. 73% of District voters approve of the job their congressperson is doing. If there are 410,000 voters in the district, how many approve of the job done by the congressperson?
   a. 5,616
   b. 287,000
   c. 299,300
   d. 320,000

3. Before leaving the fire station, Firefighter Sorensen noted that the mileage gauge on Engine 2 registered $4{,}357\frac{4}{10}$ miles. When he arrived at the scene of the fire, the mileage gauge registered $4{,}400\frac{1}{10}$ miles. What was the distance from the fire station to the scene of the fire?
   a. $42\frac{3}{10}$ miles
   b. $42\frac{7}{10}$ miles
   c. $43\frac{7}{10}$ miles
   d. $57\frac{3}{10}$ miles

4. $\frac{1}{4} + \frac{1}{3} =$
   a. $\frac{1}{12}$
   b. $\frac{3}{4}$
   c. $\frac{1}{7}$
   d. $\frac{7}{12}$

5. Reduce $\frac{18}{24}$ to lowest terms.
   a. $\frac{1}{24}$
   b. $\frac{2}{3}$
   c. $\frac{9}{12}$
   d. $\frac{3}{4}$

Study the following graph, and then use it to answer questions 6 to 8.

Number of sick days per year of employment

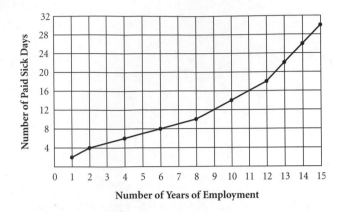

6. What is the range of the data displayed in the graph?
   a. 2
   b. 28
   c. 30
   d. 32

7. The average (arithmetic mean) number of paid sick days taken by employees who have been employed for 4, 5, 6, or 7 years is
   a. 6.5
   b. 7
   c. 7.5
   d. 9

8. Which of the following conclusions can be drawn from the data in the graph?
   a. The more years a person is employed, the more likely he or she is to take paid sick days.
   b. The rate of increase in paid sick days is constant from year to year for the first 15 years of a person's employment.
   c. The older a person is, the more likely he or she is to take paid sick days.
   d. Employees are not allowed to take more than eight sick days per year during their first siyears of employment.

9. As he drives away from his home, Jason notes that the gas tank of his car is $\frac{7}{8}$ full. When he returns home later in the day, he notes that his gas tank is $\frac{1}{4}$ full. How much gasoline did Jason usc during the day?
   a. $\frac{1}{4}$ tank
   b. $\frac{3}{8}$ tank
   c. $\frac{3}{4}$ tank
   d. $\frac{5}{8}$ tank

10. An automobile traveling at an average speed of 75 miles per hour travels for 40 minutes. How far does the automobile travel?
   a. 35 miles
   b. 40 miles
   c. 45 miles
   d. 50 miles

11. James spends 5% of each day watching television. How much time does James spend watching television each day?
   a. 61 minutes
   b. 72 minutes
   c. 120 minutes
   d. 144 minutes

12. Reduce $\frac{27}{108}$ to lowest terms.

   a. $\frac{1}{4}$

   b. $\frac{3}{11}$

   c. $\frac{1}{3}$

   d. The fraction cannot be reduced.

13. $2\frac{1}{12} \div 2\frac{1}{4} =$

   a. $\frac{25}{27}$

   b. $4\frac{11}{16}$

   c. $\frac{1}{3}$

   d. $\frac{1}{6}$

14. A savings bond yields 3.75% simple interest annually. If the bond is worth $8,000 on January 8, 2006, what is the value of the bond on January 8, 2007?

   a. $8,003.75

   b. $8,300

   c. $8,375

   d. $11,750

15. $1\frac{1}{7} - \frac{2}{3} =$

   a. $\frac{10}{21}$

   b. $\frac{19}{21}$

   c. $\frac{1}{4}$

   d. $\frac{4}{5}$

16. Randy earns an hourly wage of $12 for each of the first 40 hours he works in a week. For any hours he works in excess of 40 hours, Randy earns an hourly wage that is $1\frac{1}{2}$ times his standard wage. If Randy works a 50-hour week, how much does Randy earn?

   a. $600

   b. $480

   c. $660

   d. $900

17. A bus travels a route that runs $3\frac{3}{4}$ miles along Elm Street, and then turns right onto Palmetto Road. It then travels $2\frac{1}{2}$ miles along Palmetto Road before turning left on Main Street. The bus travels $5\frac{3}{4}$ miles along Main Street, completing its route. How many miles long is the bus route?

   a. 10 miles

   b. $11\frac{1}{2}$ miles

   c. 12 miles

   d. 15 miles

Study the following graph, and then use it to answer questions 18 to 20.

AVERAGE PRICE OF GROCERIES, 2009	
ITEM	**AVERAGE PRICE**
ground beef, 1 pound	$2.99
milk, $\frac{1}{2}$ gallon	$2.49
carrots, 5 pounds	$3.27
chicken noodle soup, 1 can	$1.82
oatmeal, 42 ounce box	$3.58

18. The data support which of the following conclusions?

   a. One can of chicken soup is not enough food to constitute a healthy meal.

   b. It is important to drink milk every day.

   c. Carrots are cheaper per pound than ground beef.

   d. Ground beef is too expensive for the quality of meat you receive.

19. What is the range of prices shown in the table?

    a. $1.82

    b. $2.49

    c. $2.99

    d. $1.76

20. The average (arithmetic mean) price of the items shown is

    a. $2.83

    b. $2.99

    c. $3.58

    d. $14.15

Answers

1. b. To multiply fractions, multiply numerator by numerator and denominator by denominator, then reduce if necessary. $\frac{2}{3} \times \frac{3}{4} = \frac{2 \times 3}{3 \times 4}$, which equals $\frac{6}{12}$. Divide both numerator and denominator by 6 to reduce $\frac{6}{12}$ to $\frac{1}{2}$.

2. c. The question asks you to find 73% of 410,000. There are a number of ways to solve this problem. One way is to multiply 410,000 by the fractional equivalent of 73%, which is $\frac{73}{100}$. $\frac{410,000 \times 73}{100} = \frac{29,930,000}{100}$, which reduces to 299,300.

3. b. This question asks you to subtract $4,357\frac{4}{10}$ from $4,400\frac{1}{10}$. To calculate $4,400\frac{1}{10} - 4,357\frac{4}{10}$, you will have to rewrite $4,400\frac{1}{10}$. Borrow 1, or $\frac{10}{10}$, from 4,400 to rewrite $4,400\frac{1}{10}$ as $4,399\frac{11}{10}$. Now calculate. $4,399\frac{11}{10} - 4,357\frac{4}{410} = (4,399 - 4,357) + (\frac{11}{10} - \frac{4}{10})$. The solution is $42\frac{7}{10}$.

4. d. To add fractions, rewrite them over a common denominator. 12 is divisible by 3 and 4, so 12 is a good common denominator for $\frac{1}{3}$ and $\frac{1}{4}$; $\frac{1}{3} \times \frac{4}{4} = \frac{4}{12}$ and $\frac{1}{4} \times \frac{3}{3} = \frac{3}{12}$, so $\frac{1}{3} + \frac{1}{4} = \frac{4}{12} + \frac{3}{12} = \frac{7}{12}$.

5. d. To reduce a fraction to its lowest terms, divide the numerator and the denominator by the largest value that divides evenly into both. 18 and 24 are both divisible by 6. $\frac{18 \div 6}{24 \div 6} = \frac{3}{4}$. If you selected choice **c**, you divided both numerator and denominator by 2. Your answer equals $\frac{18}{24}$, but it does not represent lowest terms for the fraction because both 9 and 12 are divisible by 3.

6. b. The least value shown on the graph is 2, representing the number of sick days for people who have been employed for one year. The greatest value is 30, representing the number of sick days for people who have been employed for 15 years. The range of the data is the difference between the greatest and least value, so the

range of this data set is $30 - 2$, which equals 28.

7. c. According to the graph, employees who have been employed for 4 years take an average of 6 sick days; for 5 years, 7 sick days; for 6 years, 8 sick days; and for 7 years, 9 sick days. To find the average (arithmetic mean), add the number of sick days and divide by 4, the number of time periods represented. $6 + 7 + 8 + 9 = 30$. 30 divided by 4 equals 7.5.

8. a. For each year a person is employed, the average number of sick days taken increases; thus, the statement "The more years a person is employed, the more likely he or she is to take paid sick days" is supported by the data in the graph. The rate of increase shown in the graph is constant between years 2 and 8, but after that, the rate increases; therefore, choice **b** is incorrect. The graph includes no information about age, so choice **c** is not supported by data in the graph. Choice **d** draws a conclusion about company policy; because no information about company policy is provided, this cannot be the correct answer.

9. d. This question asks you to subtract $\frac{1}{4}$ from $\frac{7}{8}$. To add or subtract fractions, you must rewrite them over a common denominator. Because 8 is divisible by 4, 8 would be a good common denominator. $\frac{1}{4} \times \frac{2}{2} = \frac{2}{8}$; $\frac{7}{8} - \frac{2}{8}$ equals $\frac{5}{8}$.

10. d. To solve rate problems, apply the equation $rt = d$, where r equals rate, t equals time, and d equals distance. This problem provides the rate (75 miles per hour) and the time (40 minutes). Before plugging the numbers into the formula, make sure your numbers are in common units. The rate is in miles per *hour*, but the time is measured in *minutes*. That's no good; you have to use all minutes or all hours. Rewrite 40 minutes in terms of hours; 40 minutes equals $\frac{40}{60}$ hours, or $\frac{2}{3}$ hours. Now, plug the values into the formula. $75(\frac{2}{3}) = t$. $\frac{75 \times 2}{3} = \frac{150}{3} = 50$.

11. b. This question asks you to calculate 5% of 24 hours. You can calculate percents easily using the 10% trick. To find 10% of a number, simply move the decimal point one place to the left. Therefore, 10% of 24 is 2.4. The question asks you to find 5% of 24 hours; 5% is half of 10%, so the answer is half of 2.4 hours, or 1.2 hours. Multiply 1.2 by 60 to determine that 1.2 hours equals 72 minutes.

12. a. To reduce a fraction to its lowest terms, divide the numerator and the denominator by the largest value that divides evenly into both. Both 27 and 108 are divisible by 27, so you can reduce $\frac{27}{108}$ to $27 \div \frac{27}{108} \div 27$, which equals $\frac{1}{4}$. If you don't recognize that 108 is divisible by 27 (most people don't), that's okay. Divide by something you do know goes evenly into 27 and 108, such as 3 or 9. Then, look at the result and see whether you can't reduce it again. Eventually you will wind up with the result $\frac{1}{4}$, which is the correct answer to this question.

13. a. To divide mixed numbers, first rewrite them as improper fractions. Rewrite $2\frac{1}{12}$ as $\frac{25}{12}$ and $2\frac{1}{4}$ as $\frac{9}{4}$. Next, multiply the dividend (the first fraction in the equation) by the reciprocal of the divisor (the second fraction in the equation). $\frac{25}{12} \times \frac{4}{9} = \frac{100}{108}$. Divide numerator and denominator by 4 to reduce $\frac{100}{108}$ to $\frac{25}{27}$.

14. b. The problem asks you to calculate 3.75% of $8,000. One way to solve this problem is to multiply $8,000 by 0.0375, the decimal equivalent of 3.75%. The result is $300. Add the $300 (interest) to the $8,000 (principal) to determine the bond's value of $8,300 after one year.

15. a. To add or subtract fractions, you must rewrite them over a common denominator. 21 is divisible by 7 and 3, so rewrite both

fractions with a denominator of 21. Rewrite the mixed number $\frac{11}{7}$ as the improper fraction $\frac{8}{7}$, and then multiply by $\frac{3}{3}$ to get $\frac{24}{21}$. Multiply $\frac{2}{3}$ by $\frac{7}{7}$ to get $\frac{14}{21}$; $\frac{24}{21} - \frac{14}{21}$ equals $\frac{10}{21}$.

16. c. Randy earns $12 per hour for each of the first 40 hours he works. Thus, he earns $480 for his first 40 hours of work. His overtime pay is $1\frac{1}{2}$ times his regular pay of $12. Half of $12 is $6, so Randy's overtime pay is $12 + $6 per hour, or $18 per hour. Randy works 10 hours of overtime, so he earns $18 × 10, which equals $180, in overtime pay. $480 + $180 equals $660, the correct answer.

17. c. This question asks you to add $3\frac{3}{4}$, $2\frac{1}{2}$, and $5\frac{3}{4}$. To do this, first add all the whole numbers: 3 + 2 + 5 equals 10. Next, add the fractions; this requires you to rewrite the fractions over a common denominator. Because 4 is divisible by 2, 4 is an excellent choice for common denominator. $\frac{3}{4} + \frac{2}{4} + \frac{3}{4} = \frac{8}{4}$, which equals 2. 10 + 2 equals 12, the correct answer.

18. c. According to the table, one pound of ground beef costs $2.99 and 5 pounds of carrots cost $3.27. Therefore, one pound of carrots costs $3.27 ÷ 5, or a little more than 65 cents per pound. The data in the table support the conclusion that a pound of carrots costs less than a pound of ground beef.

19. d. The range of the data is the difference between the greatest and least value, so the range of this data set is $3.58 – $1.82, which equals $1.76.

20. a. The average of a data set is the sum of the data divided by the number of pieces of data. In this case, there are 5 pieces of data. Their sum is $2.99 + $2.49 + $3.27 + $1.82 + $3.58, which equals $14.15. $14.15 ÷ 5 equals $2.83.

CHAPTER 6 ▶ WRITTEN COMMUNICATION SKILLS

All civil service exams test written communication skills in some form. Nearly all include a section testing your ability to read and understand extended passages. Many also include questions about grammar, vocabulary, and spelling.

There are good reasons for including these skills on civil service exams. To be an effective civil servant, you must be able to read and comprehend memos, policy statements, procedural instructions, documents, and reports. Similarly, most positions require you to communicate effectively in writing. You can't do that without some mastery of English grammar, vocabulary, and spelling.

The good news is that these exams test basic skills. No one is going to ask you to read a complicated novel and interpret its symbolism. Nor will a civil service test ask you to spell *Australopithecus* or to conjugate verbs in the future subjunctive tense (or even to know what the future subjunctive tense is, for that matter). All you need to do is to read a passage and answer some related questions, which will be pretty straightforward, and to recall some fundamental principles of grammar and spelling.

The chapter that follows reviews the basic skills necessary to pass the written communications portion of a civil service exam.

Reading Comprehension

You have probably encountered reading comprehension questions before. Many standardized tests, including the SAT and the ACT, include them. A reading comprehension section provides a reading passage, followed by a number of multiple-choice questions about the passage. There is an advantage to this question format:

> You do not need to know anything about the topic of the passage. All the information you need to answer the questions is contained within the passage itself.

The challenge, of course, is knowing where and how to find the information in a reasonable amount of time. The time element adds pressure, which causes some people to make careless mistakes. The test writers understand this and will phrase some incorrect answers in a way that makes them *seem* correct at first glance.

The best way to do well on reading comprehension questions is to be familiar with the types of questions that are typically asked, and to learn the defining characteristics of the correct and incorrect answers to each question type. The most common question types are those that ask you to:

1. describe the **main idea** of the passage
2. identify a **specific fact or detail** in the passage
3. draw an **inference or conclusion** based on information in the passage
4. define a **vocabulary word** that appears in the passage

On the following pages, we'll review each type of question and the characteristics of correct and incorrect answers for each. To do this, you'll first need to read a passage. All the sample questions that follow will be based on this passage.

Practice Passage

In television procedural dramas such as *Law & Order*, criminal defendants invariably stand trial for the crimes they commit. They enter a plea of "not guilty," the evidence against them is heard, and a jury decides their fate. Under the circumstances, the average American can be forgiven for assuming that this is the way our criminal justice system always works, but, in fact, it is hardly representative of the way that most criminal cases are resolved. In the real world, only a relatively small number of such cases ever reach trial. The majority are settled out of court, most often in a plea arrangement, sometimes referred to as a plea bargain or copping a plea.

There are numerous practical reasons that this practice is so <u>prevalent</u>. Prosecutors use plea arrangements to avoid costly trials that tie up prosecutors who could otherwise be working on other cases. Defendants avoid the risk of going to trial, where they might receive a more severe sentence than the prosecutor is willing to offer as part of a plea arrangement. They also elude the negative publicity a trial can bring. The uncertainty of a trial's result, in fact, is something that both prosecutors *and* defendants may wish to avoid; a plea arrangement achieves that end. The court system also benefits, as it can remove plea-bargained cases from its overbooked dockets.

While plea bargains are extremely common in American courts, they are not without their critics. Victims' rights groups believe that many plea arrangements result in overly lenient sentences. Defendants' rights groups argue that the system unfairly favors those defendants who can afford expensive, highly skilled lawyers. In this way, they say, the system actually favors big-time criminals over small-time criminals, quite the opposite of the way the system should work. Then there are those who say that the system subverts the intended function of the courts; they argue that in a truly just system every defendant would face his or her accusers.

Regardless of their drawbacks, plea arrangements are likely to remain a prominent fixture in our courts for the foreseeable future. Without plea arrangements, our courts would soon fall hopelessly behind their caseloads. If the United States wants to move away from a plea-arrangement dependent system, it must figure out a way either to reduce crime drastically or to increase dramatically its judiciary and its prosecutorial and public defense offices.

Main Idea Questions

The main idea of a passage or paragraph of a passage is what it is *mostly* about. When determining whether an answer choice could be the correct answer to a main idea question, ask yourself, "Does this statement apply to the *entire* passage or paragraph?" If your answer is yes, then the answer choice could be the correct answer to the question. If your answer is no and the answer choice applies only to one detail or one small portion of the passage/paragraph, then that answer choice cannot be the correct answer.

Sometimes the answer to a main idea question is stated clearly in the passage, frequently in the first or last sentence. The sentence that expresses the main idea is often described as the *topic sentence*. Other times, the main idea is not stated in a topic sentence but rather is *implied* by the overall content of the passage. In such circumstances, you'll need to deduce the main idea from the passage. In either circumstance, the rule remains the same.

> The correct answer to a main idea question describes the *entire* passage or paragraph. If it describes only one part or one detail, it is not the correct answer.

Just because an answer refers to the entire passage doesn't mean that it is correct. Although such answers are *usually* correct, occasionally an incorrect answer will refer to the entire passage or paragraph. What makes that answer incorrect is that it describes the content of the passage or paragraph inaccurately. Most often, it states a position stronger than the one the writer takes. Suppose, for example, the main idea of a passage is that Frank Sinatra is a great singer. An incorrect answer might state that Frank Sinatra is the greatest singer who ever lived. This answer is close to the author's main idea, but overstates it.

> Make sure that the answer to a main idea question *accurately* describes the content of the passage or paragraph.

Example:

Which statement from the passage best summarizes the main idea of paragraph 3?

a. While plea bargains are extremely common in American courts, they are not without their critics.

b. Defendants' rights groups argue that the system unfairly favors those defendants who can afford expensive, highly skilled lawyers.

c. Without plea arrangements, our courts would soon fall hopelessly behind their caseloads.

d. Victims' rights groups believe that many plea arrangements result in overly lenient sentences.

Let's consider each answer, applying the rules previously provided.

Choice **a** is the topic sentence of paragraph 3. This is the likely answer, but we should check all the other answers before we choose this one.

Choice **b** is a supporting detail from paragraph 3. It describes one of several groups who criticize plea bargains. It is not the main idea of the paragraph.

Choice **c** is taken from paragraph 4. Although it is possible that the main idea of one paragraph may be expressed by a sentence in another paragraph, it is not likely. Furthermore, this statement does not summarize paragraph 3, so it cannot be the correct answer.

Choice **d**, like choice **b**, is a supporting detail from paragraph 3. It describes one of several groups who criticize plea bargains. It is not the main idea of the paragraph.

The correct answer is choice **a**.

Example:

Which of the following best expresses the main idea of the passage?

a. Plea arrangements are unfair to poor defendants because they cannot afford to hire good lawyers.

b. Because plea arrangements are by definition unjust, American courts must find ways to hire more judges and lawyers so that all cases can be tried.

c. For a number of reasons, plea arrangements play a central role in the American justice system.

d. Prosecutors use plea arrangements when they are afraid that a jury might find a defendant "not guilty."

Let's consider each answer, applying the rules previously provided.

Choice **a** restates an idea from the third paragraph of the passage. It refers to one detail of the entire passage; it does not describe or summarize the passage as a whole. Therefore, it cannot be the correct answer to a main idea question.

Choice **b** overstates one of the points made in the passage. In paragraph 3, the writer observes that some people find the plea arrangement system unjust. In paragraph 4, he points out that the only way to address this problem is to hire more judges and lawyers. However, the author never states that he subscribes to this opinion. In fact, we never find out what the writer thinks about this subject. The purpose of this passage is to inform us about a subject, not to persuade us to take the author's position on that subject. This answer breaks the second rule. It overstates an idea expressed in the passage, and so it cannot describe the content of the passage accurately.

Choice **c** summarizes the passage well. In the first paragraph, the writer states that "The majority are settled out of court, most often in a plea arrangement . . ." In paragraph 2, he details the "numerous practical reasons that this practice is so prevalent." After discussing some people's objections to the practice in paragraph 3, he reasserts that "plea arrangements are likely to remain a prominent fixture in our courts for the foreseeable future," providing "a number of reasons" why that is so. Choice **c** is almost certainly the correct answer to the question. Even so, you *must* read choice **d** before you can be sure.

Choice **d** paraphrases one of the supporting details of paragraph 2. Like choice **a**, this answer fails to describe or summarize the passage as a whole. It is not the correct answer to this question.

The correct answer is choice **c**.

Detail Questions

Detail questions ask you to identify a specific piece of information from the passage. Detail questions often contain one of the following phrases:

> According to the passage . . .
> The passage states . . .

The correct answer to a detail question will be a direct quote or a paraphrase of information in the passage.

> On a detail question, any answer stating information that does not appear in the passage cannot be the correct answer.

Not all answers that repeat information from the passage are necessarily correct, however. The information must also be relevant to the question being asked. Some incorrect answers will contain irrelevant information from the passage.

> On a detail question, make sure that your answer not only can be found in the passage, but also addresses the question that is being asked.

To answer a detail question, first read the question to determine its subject. Next, determine where in the passage the subject of the question is discussed. Reread that portion of the passage before answering the questions.

Example:

According to the passage, defendants sometimes decide to accept a plea arrangement because they

  a. are in a hurry to begin serving their sentences.
  b. do not want to overburden prosecutors.
  c. do not want to appear in a television procedural drama.
  d. worry that a trial might result in a harsher sentence.

First, determine where in the passage this information is most likely to appear. Paragraph 2 of the passage discusses the reasons that prosecutors, defendants, and courts sometimes prefer plea agreements to trials. This is where the correct answer is most likely to be found. Reread the paragraph before reading the answer choices.

Let's consider each answer, applying the rules previously provided.

The passage never states or implies that defendants "are in a hurry to begin serving their sentences," so choice **a** cannot be correct.

Paragraph 2 mentions that prosecutors sometimes make a plea arrangement to keep their fellow prosecutors from being overburdened with cases. The passage does not suggest that defendants share this goal. Common sense should help you eliminate this answer: Why would defendants care about overburdening prosecutors? Choice **b** cannot be correct.

Television procedural dramas are mentioned in the first paragraph as part of rhetorical device, the purpose of which is to distinguish between the courts as they are portrayed on television and the way they actually function. These TV shows have nothing to do with why defendants sometimes decide to accept a plea arrangement. Paragraph 2 notes that defendants sometimes wish to avoid the negative publicity of a trial; it does not, however, state or suggest that such negative publicity would be the result of the defendant's appearing on a television drama. Again, common sense should help you here. Actors appear on television dramas, not actual courtroom defendants. Choice **c** is not correct.

Choice **d** paraphrases the following sentence from the paragraph 2: "Defendants avoid the risk of going to trial, where they might receive a more severe sentence than the prosecutor is willing to offer as part of a plea arrangement."

The correct answer is choice **d**.

Inference Questions

Inference questions are not all that different from detail questions. Detail questions ask you to restate information from the passage, often in the form of a paraphrase. Inference questions ask you to find information in the paragraph, and then use it to draw an inference that is necessarily, or deductively, true. Inference questions often begin with one of the following phrases.

It can be inferred from the passage . . .
The passage suggests . . .
Which of the following conclusions is best supported . . .

For example, suppose the passage states that all voters in a city are either Democrats or Republicans and that the majority of voters in the city are Democrats. The correct answer to an inference question may state that a minority of voters in a city are Republicans. This is an inference because the passage does not state directly that the minority of voters in the city are Republicans; even so, it is necessarily true Republicans constitute a minority if the majority of voters are Democrats.

When answering an inference question, do not choose an answer that requires you to make a major assumption or to use outside knowledge. Look for answers that are fully supported by information in the passage.

Example:
It can be inferred from the passage that groups that safeguard the rights of victims worry that the plea arrangement system

a. is biased against poor defendants.
b. allows criminals to go free too soon.
c. overloads the dockets of criminal courts.
d. contributes to an increase in the crime rate.

First, determine where in the passage this information is most likely to appear. Groups that criticize the plea arrangement system are discussed in paragraph 3. That is where the answer to this question is likely to appear.

Let's consider each answer, applying the rules previously provided.

Defendants' rights groups worry that the plea arrangement system is biased against poor defendants. This question asks about victims' rights groups, however, not defendants' rights groups. Choice **a** is not the correct answer to this question.

Choice **b** is a good paraphrase of the following sentence from the passage: "Victims' rights groups believe that many plea arrangements result in overly lenient sentences." Note that this is the only sentence in the entire passage that discusses "groups that safeguard the rights of victims." The correct answer must, therefore, be contained in this sentence. There is a slight inference involved in connecting the sentence to choice **b**. It requires you to infer that "overly lenient sentences"—i.e., sentences that are not long enough—result in sentences that "allow criminals to go free too soon." Notice that the jump from statement to inference is a tiny one, not a huge leap. That's the way correct answers to inference questions are.

Choice **c** refers to a concern expressed by the courts, not by victims' rights groups. Furthermore, that concern is expressed in favor of the system of plea arrangements, not in opposition to it. This cannot be the correct answer.

Choice **d** is an example of a huge inference, one much too big to be the correct answer. One might be tempted to think that because victims' rights groups "believe that many plea arrangements result in overly lenient sentences" that this, therefore, means that they believe these arrangements "contribute to an increase in the crime rate." However, the crime rate is never mentioned in the passage; therefore, there is no basis

on which to draw any inferences about it or about how a particular group feels about it. Second, in order for choice **d** to be a correct answer, choice **b** must also be correct, because choice **d** relies on an assumption stated directly in choice **b**. The reverse is not true; choice **b** can be correct without choice **d** also being correct. Therefore, choice **b** is the correct answer, and choice **d** is incorrect.

Vocabulary

Questions designed to test vocabulary are really trying to measure how well you can figure out the meaning of an unfamiliar word from its context. *Context* refers to the words and ideas surrounding a vocabulary word. If the context is clear enough, you should be able to substitute a nonsense word for the one being sought and still be able to find the correct answer, because you will be able to determine meaning strictly from the sense of the sentence. Consider the following sentence:

> The scholarship recipient was quite *exbobulated* when she learned that her award would cover the entire cost of her tuition, room, and board.
> In the sentence, *exbobulated* most likely means
> **a.** disappointed.
> **b.** confused.
> **c.** thrilled.
> **d.** concerned.

The context of the sentence makes clear that the correct answer is choice **c**, thrilled. No one would be disappointed, confused, or concerned to receive such a generous award.

The tested word itself may contain a context clue. Look for familiar prefixes and suffixes. Look to see whether the word shares a common root with some other word you know.

As in all reading comprehension questions, use the answer choices to guide your work. Replace the vocabulary word with each of the answer choices and ask yourself, does the sentence make sense this way? If an answer turns the sentence into nonsense, eliminate the answer choice. It cannot be correct.

> Test each answer choice by rereading the sentence with the answer choice in place of the vocabulary word. Eliminate answers that don't make sense.

Example:

As used in the passage, the word *prevalent* most nearly means

    a. expensive.
    b. popular.
    c. uncertain.
    d. moral.

First, consider the context. Read the sentence in which the word *prevalent* appears ("There are numerous practical reasons that this practice is so prevalent"), and then think about the purpose of the paragraph in which it appears. The sentence mentions "practical reasons," suggesting that the tone of the sentence and paragraph is favorable toward plea arrangements. The paragraph goes on to list reasons that prosecutors, defendants, and courts sometimes favor plea arrangements. Again, the tone is favorable.

Would plea arrangements meet with such favorable responses if they were *expensive* (choice **a**) or *uncertain* (choice **c**)? No, these are negative words, and the tone of this paragraph is positive. Eliminate choices **a** and **c**. The correct answer is either *popular* (choice **b**) or *moral* (choice **d**). The practice of plea arrangements is clearly popular; many cases are settled in plea arrangements, and prosecutors, defendants, and courts

all have their reasons for using them. The morality of plea arrangements, however, is not discussed in paragraph 2. It is hinted at later in the passage, in paragraph 3, but for the purposes of this question, we are interested only in paragraph 2.

The correct answer is choice **b**.

Strategies for All Reading Comprehension Questions

You can improve your performance on reading comprehension questions by employing a few simple strategies.

Learn to skim passages for information. Because the passages are relatively short, you will probably have time to read them carefully before answering questions. You don't want to answer questions from memory, though; you want to return to the passage, find the part that addresses the subject of the question, and reread it before choosing your answer. That's where skimming comes in. If you can't figure out where the answer to a question is found, try skimming the passage for a key word or words. For example, if the question is about defendants' rights groups, skim the passage for the words *defendants*, *rights*, and *groups*. Skimming is especially helpful in finding the answers to questions about proper nouns (e.g., people's names, place names) because capital letters are especially easy to skim for.

Take advantage of the multiple-choice format of the test by using process of elimination. Multiple-choice tests give you the correct answer. Of course, they bury the answer among three incorrect choices. Even so, the fact that the correct answer already appears in the test means that you do not have to come up with the choices on your own. A good way to find the correct answer on multiple-choice tests is to look at all the choices and eliminate all those that you know are incorrect. Quite often you will be able to eliminate every choice except the correct one.

When nonnative speakers of English have trouble with reading comprehension tests, it is often because they lack the cultural, linguistic, and historical frame of reference that native speakers enjoy. People who have not lived in or been educated in the United States often don't have the background information that comes from reading American newspapers, magazines, and textbooks.

The second and much more significant problem for nonnative English speakers is the difficulty in recognizing vocabulary and idioms (i.e., expressions such as *chewing the fat*) that assist comprehension. In order to read with good understanding, you need to have an immediate grasp of as many words as possible in the text. Test takers need to be able to recognize vocabulary and idioms immediately so that the ideas those words express are clear.

The Long View

Read newspapers, magazines, and other periodicals that deal with current events and matters of local, state, and national importance. Pay special attention to articles related to the career you want to pursue.

Be alert to new or unfamiliar vocabulary or terms that occur frequently in the popular press. Use a highlighter pen to mark new or unfamiliar words as you read. Compile a list of those words and their definitions. Review your list for 15 minutes each day. Although at first you may find yourself looking up a lot of words, don't be frustrated—as time progresses, you will be looking up fewer and fewer words, and your vocabulary will quickly expand.

During the Test

While you are taking the test, make a picture in your mind of the situation being described in the passage. Remain focused on the main idea; ask yourself, what is it that is most important to the writer? What is the most major point that the writer is trying to make?

Locate and underline the topic sentence of the passage. Remember that it does not necessarily have to be the first sentence of the passage or of any of the paragraphs. If there is no clear main idea sentence, try to summarize the main idea in a few words of your own. Remember, most of the correct answers will reflect the main idea in some way, and none of the correct answers will contradict the main idea.

Skip questions that you find difficult. Remember that you need only to pass this test; you do not need a perfect score. Therefore, you do not have to answer every question. If you can't answer a question, skip it and move on. There will be other questions ahead that you can answer, and you want to make sure to get to them. Also, because your final score will be based on the number of questions you answer correctly, you do not want to work on difficult questions until you have answered every easy question that you can answer quickly. Circle questions that you skip to make them easier to locate if and when you return to them. When you have finished answering all the questions you know you can answer correctly for a particular passage, take one more look at the difficult questions. You may be surprised to find that the question seems much easier now. Often a question seems difficult when your mind gets stuck on one way of thinking. Skipping a question and returning to it later is a good way to get unstuck.

Spelling and Vocabulary

Spelling and vocabulary are tested on many civil service exams. Both are necessary to communicate effectively, and many civil service jobs require strong communication skills.

Vocabulary is seen as a measure of one's ability to express ideas clearly and precisely. For almost any job, you must know the working vocabulary of the profession or have the tools needed to acquire that vocabulary quickly. Spelling is regarded as a measure of a person's accuracy in presenting information. Most civil service jobs require you to write correctly in order to communicate clearly. In addition, accurate spelling and a rich, varied vocabulary both indicate someone who is thoughtful and well educated, desirable qualities in any job candidate.

Vocabulary

Many civil service exams test vocabulary. There are two basic types of questions:

1. Synonyms and antonyms: These questions provide a word and ask you to identify an answer that has the same or opposite meaning.
2. Complete the sentence: These questions provide a sentence with a crucial word missing and ask you to select the best option for the missing word.

All are multiple-choice questions, meaning that you will never have to come up with an answer on your own. All you will need to do is determine which of the answer choices is the best option.

Synonym and Antonym Questions

Two words are *synonyms* if they have the same meaning or nearly the same meaning. *Antonyms* are words that have opposite meanings. Synonym and antonym questions ask you to find an answer choice that has the same or opposite meaning as an underlined word in the question stem. The word is often part of a phrase or sentence so that some context is provided. Sometimes the context is helpful, but at other times, context alone is not enough to help you determine which answer is correct.

Regardless of whether a question asks for a synonym or an antonym and regardless of whether it provides context clues, you should always take advantage of the multiple-choice format of the exam by using process of elimination. Look critically at each answer choice and get rid of those that cannot be the correct answer.

Example:

Select the answer that is closest in meaning to the underlined word.

a <u>substantial</u> novel

a. meaningless
b. weighty
c. alleged

If you know the word *substantial*, you know that it means *considerable* or *significant*. You would probably also realize that *weighty* is closest in meaning and that choice **b** is the correct answer.

If you did not know the word *substantial*, you would still have a chance to answer this question correctly if you recognized that *substantial* is a form of the word *substance*. Substance is something that is solid and dependable. It is not *meaningless*, nor is it *alleged*. It is *weighty*; therefore, choice **b** would be your best guess.

Example:
Find the answer that is most nearly the opposite of the underlined word.

such <u>exorbitant</u> prices

a. expensive
b. mysterious
c. reasonable

Note that the question asks for the opposite, or antonym, of exorbitant. The most common careless mistake on antonym questions involves choosing a synonym instead of the antonym.

Sure enough, choice **a** is a synonym for *exorbitant*. If this were a synonym question, choice **a** would be the correct answer. However, this is an antonym question, so this answer is incorrect.

Choice **b**, *mysterious*, is unlikely to be the correct answer. The opposite of *mysterious* is *straightforward*. Could prices be straightforward? Not really. Choice **b** is unlikely to be correct.

The opposite of *reasonable* is *unreasonable*, and prices certainly can be unreasonable. In fact, that's exactly what *exorbitant* prices are. The correct answer is choice **c**.

Complete the Sentence Questions

Complete the sentence questions provide a sentence with a single word missing. Your job is to figure out which of the answer choices is the missing word.

To answer a complete the sentence question, you must study the context of the missing word. Context is the text surrounding the missing word. You can use context to determine the meaning of an unfamiliar

word provided that the context offers enough hints. If you read that a *pusillanimous* boxer trembled in his corner and refused to fight, you could probably figure out that *pusillanimous* means *cowardly* even if you've never seen the word *pusillanimous* before. The context clues strongly suggest the meaning of the word. You will use context clues in exactly this way to answer complete the sentence questions.

As always, take advantage of the multiple-choice format of the exam by using process of elimination. Look critically at each answer choice and get rid of those that cannot be the correct answer.

Example:
Professor Hardison's _____ was amply demonstrated by the references to ancient scholarly texts throughout his address.

a. erudition
b. discipline
c. indecency

The context clues in the sentence include the phrase "ancient scholarly texts," which indicates that Professor Hardison is a learned man. Which of the words is closest in meaning to *learned*? Choice **a**, *erudition*, means *learned*. Suppose you don't know that, though. What should you do? The first thing you should do is look at the other answer choices without eliminating choice **a**. If you don't know the meaning of an answer, you cannot eliminate it.

Choice **b**, *discipline*, is tempting. A scholar must certainly be *disciplined* to master a field of study. But *disciplined* does not have the same meaning as *learned*; one can be disciplined in many ways without being a highly educated individual. Choice **b** is not likely to be the correct answer.

Choice **c**, *indecency*, should be easy to eliminate. Someone who is *indecent* is cruel or morally deficient.

If English Isn't Your First Language

If your native language is a Romance language (e.g., Spanish, French, or Italian), look for roots of words. Many English words have etymologies that trace back to Romance languages, meaning that a number of English words share roots with words in Spanish, French, and Italian. You may recognize a shared root, and that may be enough to tell you the meaning of the English word.

Also, as you read a word, imagine how it would sound spoken. Some nonnative English speakers find it easier to recognize words they hear than words they read on a page.

Indecency has nothing to do with scholarship, so choice **c** cannot be the correct answer.

At this point, if you did not know the meaning of *erudition*, you would be forced to guess between choices **a** and **b**. Because we've determined that choice **b** is unlikely to be the correct answer, you should guess choice **a**, which is, in fact, the correct answer.

Spelling

Spelling questions provide you with three answer choices. Typically, one is spelled correctly and two are spelled incorrectly. Occasionally a question will offer two correctly spelled answer choices and one incorrectly spelled answer choice; it will ask you to identify the word that is *not* spelled correctly.

The best way to prepare for a spelling test is to review spelling fundamentals so that you will recognize when common spelling rules are violated. Remember, though, that the English language is full of exceptions in spelling. You have to develop a good eye to spot spelling errors.

Even though there are many variant spellings for English words, civil service exams focus primarily on a few areas. Mostly these exams want to ensure that you know and can apply some basic rules, such as:

- *i* before *e* except after *c*, or when the word makes the long *a* sound (i.e., rhymes with *way*).

  Examples: *piece, receive, neighbor*

- *gh* can replace *f* or be silent.

  Examples: *enough, night*

- When you add an ending to a word that ends in a consonant, double the consonant.

  Examples: *forget/forgettable, shop/shopping*

- When you add a suffi to a word that ends in *e*, don't drop the *e*.

  Examples: replace/replacement/replaceable, peace/peaceful/peaceable

- Drop the *e* when you add *-ing*.

  Examples: *hope/hoping, dive/diving*

- The spelling of prefixes and suffixes generally doesn't change.

  Examples: *project, propel, proactive*

- When writing the plural of a word that ends in a consonant and a *y*, drop the *y* and add *ie*.

  Examples: *baby/babies, filly/fillies*

- When writing the plural of a word that ends in a vowel and a *y*, just add *s*.

  Examples: *monkey/monkeys, day/days*

You should also learn common roots and the words in which they are found.

WORD ELEMENT	MEANING	EXAMPLES
ama/amo	love	amateur, amorous
ambi	both	ambivalent, ambidextrous
aud	hear	audition, audible
bell	war	belligerent, bellicose
bene	good	benefactor, benediction
cid/cis	cut	homicide, scissors
cogn/gno	know	cognitive, recognize
curr	run	current
flu/flux	flow	fluid, fluctuate
gress	to go	congress, congregation
in	not, in	ingenious, integral
ject	throw	inject, reject
luc/lux	light	lucid, translucent
neo	new	neophyte, neoconservative
omni	all	omnivorous, omnipotent
pel/puls	push	impulse, propeller
pro	forward	project, produce
pseudo	false	pseudonym, pseudoscientific
rog	ask	interrogate
sub	under	subjugate, subterranean
spec/spic	look, see	spectator, spectacles
super	over	superfluous, supercede
temp	time	contemporary, temporal
un	not, opposite	uncoordinated, uninvited
viv	live	vivid, vivacious

Finally, compile spelling lists. Some test writers will give you a list to study before you take the test. If you receive such a list:

- Divide the list into smaller groups of words. Study them one smaller batch at a time. Make flash cards for the words that give you difficulty.
- Highlight or circle troublesome elements in each word.

- Cross out or discard words that you know for certain. Don't waste time studying words you already know how to study.
- Say the words aloud as you read them. Spell them out in your mind so you can "hear" the spelling.

Following is a sample spelling list. These words are typical of the words that appear on exams. Study this list if the people administering your test do not provide you with a spelling list.

achievement	doubtful	ninety
allege	eligible	noticeable
anxiety	enough	occasionally
appreciate	enthusiasm	occurred
asthma	equipped	offense
arraignment	exception	official
autonomous	fascinate	pamphlet
auxiliary	fatigue	parallel
brief	forfeit	personnel
ballistics	gauge	physician
barricade	grieve	politics
beauty	guilt	possess
beige	guarantee	privilege
business	harass	psychology
bureau	hazard	recommend
calm	height	referral
cashier	incident	recidivism
capacity	indict	salary
cancel	initial	schedule

circuit	innocent	seize
colonel	irreverent	separate
comparatively	jeopardy	specific
courteous	knowledge	statute
criticism	leisure	surveillance
custody	license	suspicious
cyclical	lieutenant	tentative
debt	maintenance	thorough
definitely	mathematics	transferred
descend	mortgage	warrant

Grammar

Grammar questions, like spelling and vocabulary questions, typically have only three answer choices. Thus, grammar questions greatly reward those who use process of elimination. Eliminate one answer choice and you have a 50-50 chance of guessing correctly; eliminate two answer choices and you will have found the correct answer by process of elimination.

Grammar questions typically present three variations of a single sentence and ask you to determine which is written correctly. Each of the incorrect answers will contain at least one identifiable error.

In order to perform well on the grammar section, you must know a few basic grammatical principles. Master them and you will be able to distinguish correctly written sentences from poorly written sentences. The section that follows reviews all the concepts that are tested frequently on civil service exams.

Complete and Incomplete Sentences

The sentence is the basic unit of written language. Written communication typically uses complete sentences (there are a few exceptions, but they are rare), so it is important to know when a sentence is complete and when it is not complete. Incomplete sentences are called *sentence fragments*.

A complete sentence expresses a complete, independent thought. If a group of words can stand alone and have an understandable meaning, that group is a sentence. Consider the following examples.

Fragment:	The dog walking down the street.
Sentence:	The dog was walking down the street.
Fragment:	Exploding from the bat for a home run.
Sentence:	The ball exploded from the bat for a home run.

These examples show that a sentence must have a subject and a verb to complete its meaning. The first fragment has a subject (*dog*) but not a verb. Although *walking* looks like a verb, it is not a verb in this fragment; it is an adjective describing *dog*. By adding *was* to *walking*, the sentence transforms it from an adjective to a verb. In the second example, the fragment has neither a subject nor a verb. Again, *exploding* may look like a verb, but it is, in fact, an adjective in this fragment.

When distinguishing between sentences and fragments, be especially aware of answer choices that begin with a subordinating conjunction. What follows is a list of subordinating conjunctions:

after	that
although	though
as	unless
because	until
before	when
if	whenever
once	where
since	wherever
than	while

Answer choices that begin with these words are often sentence fragments. That's because these words indicate that more information is required to complete the thought being expressed.

Example: Unless you want to travel by automobile.

The preceding example is a sentence fragment. It suggests that something will happen *unless you want to travel by automobile*, but it never tells us what that something is. The thought expressed is incomplete. Here are some ways to complete the sentence.

Examples: We will go to the park by bus unless you want to travel by automobile.
Unless you want to travel by automobile, we should take our bikes to the park.

The second example shows that it is possible to write a complete sentence that begins with a subordinating clause. So, do not eliminate answer choices just because they start with subordinating clauses. Be aware, however, that many incorrect answers to complete sentence questions begin with subordinating clauses, and read such answer choices carefully.

Occasionally, a complete sentence question will ask you to identify and eliminate a *run-on sentence* from among the answer choices. A run-on sentence contains more than one *independent clause*, which is a group of words that would form a sentence if they stood alone. The sentences are run-on sentences because the independent clauses are not properly connected. To connect two independent clauses properly, you must use either a conjunction or appropriate punctuation (either a semicolon or a colon). Here is a run-on sentence:

Example: I went to the store I bought some food.

The clauses *I went to the store* and *I bought some food* are both independent, so they must be connected appropriately. A conjunction, such as *and*, *but*, or *or*, is the most common way to connect independent clauses.

Example: I went to the store, *and* I bought some food.

You can also use a preposition to turn one of the independent clauses into as prepositional phrase.

Example: I went to the store, where I bought some food.

To determine whether a sentence is complete and correctly formulated, check to make sure that:

- the sentence has both a subject and a verb
- the sentence is not a run-on sentence

Capitalization

You may encounter questions that test your ability to capitalize correctly. Here is a quick review of the most common capitalization rules:

- Capitalize the first word of a sentence. If the first word is a number, write it as a word.
- Capitalize the first word of a complete quotation, as in:
  Roger said, "I think I'll go to the ball game tonight."
- Don't capitalize the first word of a partial quotation, as in:
  Roger may go to the ball game tonight, but for now he's "still thinking about it."
- Capitalize proper nouns and proper adjectives.

The following table provides examples.

CAPITALIZATION	
CATEGORY	**EXAMPLES (PROPER NOUNS)**
days of the week, months of the year	Friday, Saturday; January, February
holidays, special events	Christmas, Halloween; Two Rivers Festival, Dilly Days
names of individuals	John Henry, Zora Neale Hurston
names of structures, buildings	Lincoln Memorial, Chrysler Building
names of trains, ships, aircraft	Queen Elizabeth, the Orient Express
product names	Corn King hams, Dodge Intrepid
cities and states	Des Moines, Iowa; Juneau, Alaska
streets, highways, roads	Grand Avenue, Interstate 29, Roxboro Road
landmarks, public areas	Continental Divide, Grand Canyon, Glacier National Park
bodies of water	Atlantic Ocean, Mississippi River
ethnic groups, languages, nationalities	Asian American, English, Arab
official titles	Mayor Daley, President Johnson
institutions, organizations, businesses	Dartmouth College, Lions Club, Goya Foods
proper adjectives	English muffin, Polish sausage

To answer capitalization questions, eliminate answers that include capitalization errors.

Example: Select the sentence that is written most correctly.

a. Abraham Adams made an appointment with Mayor Burns to discuss the building plans.
b. Abraham Adams made an appointment with Mayor Burns to discuss the Building Plans.
c. Abraham Adams made an appointment with mayor Burns to discuss the building plans.

To find the correct answer, compare the answer choices. Note that they are mostly the same. Choice **c**, however, is different because it does not capitalize the word *mayor*. In this example, the word *mayor* is used as a person's official title, so it should be capitalized. Eliminate choice **c**. Choices **a** and **b** are different because choice **b** capitalizes the phrase *Building Plans*. This phrase is not a proper noun, however, so it should not be capitalized. Eliminate choice **b**. The correct answer is choice **a**.

Punctuation

The English language uses many punctuation marks, but fortunately civil service exams focus on just a few: periods, commas, apostrophes, and quotation marks. Let's review the rules for using each.

Periods

Use a period:

- at the end of a sentence that is not a question or an exclamation
- after an initial in a name, e.g., Millard T. Fillmore
- after an abbreviation (e.g., Mrs., Dr., etc.), unless the abbreviation is an acronym (e.g., UNICEF, NASA)

When a sentence ends in an abbreviation, use only one period (e.g., We brought food, tents, sleeping bags, etc.).

Commas

Using commas correctly can make the difference between presenting information clearly and obscuring the meaning of a sentence. Study the following chart to see how commas clarify meaning.

COMMAS AND MEANING	
Number of people unknown	My sister Diane John Carey Melissa and I went to the fair.
Four people	My sister Diane, John Carey, Melissa and I went to the fair.
Five people	My sister, Diane, John Carey, Melissa and I went to the fair.
Sipeople	My sister, Diane, John, Carey, Melissa and I went to the fair.

Here are the rules covering the most common uses of commas.

■ Use a comma before *and*, *but*, *or*, *for*, *nor*, and *yet* when they separate two independent clauses.

> **Example:** The coaches laid out the game plan, and the team executed it to perfection.

■ Use a comma to separate items in a series.

> **Example:** Careful drivers use the IPDE method in which they identify, predict, decide, and execute a plan for safe driving.

■ Use a comma to separate two or more adjectives modifying the same noun.

> **Example:** The hot, black, rich coffee tasted great after an hour in below-zero weather.

■ Use a comma after introductory words, phrases, or clauses in a sentence.

> **Examples:** Usually, the class begins with a short writing assignment.
> Racing down the street, the yellow car ran a stoplight.
> After we found the source of the noise, we relaxed and enjoyed the rest of the evening.

■ Use a comma after a name followed by Jr., Sr., or some other abbreviation.

> **Example:** The class was inspired by the speeches of Martin Luther King, Jr.

■ Use a comma to separate items in an address.

> **Example:** The car stopped at 1433 West G Avenue, Orlando, Florida 36890.

■ Use a comma to separate a day and a year, as well as after the year.

> **Example:** I was born on July 21, 1954, during a thunderstorm.

■ Use a comma after the greeting of a friendly letter and after the closing of any letter.

> **Example:** Dear Uncle Jon,
> Sincerely yours,

■ Use a comma to separate contrasting elements in a sentence.

> **Example:** Your essay needs strong arguments, not strong opinions, to convince me.

■ Use commas to set off an appositive (a word or phrase that explains or identifies a noun).

> **Example:** My cat, a Siamese, is named Ron.

Apostrophes

Apostrophes communicate important information in written language. There are two main rules governing the use of apostrophes:

■ Use an apostrophe to show that letters have been omitted from a word to form a contraction.

> **Examples:** do not = don't; I will = I'll; it is = it's

■ Use an apostrophe to show possession.

> **Examples:** Bob's guitar; Linda's new car

APOSTROPHES TO SHOW POSSESSION		
SINGULAR NOUNS (ADD 'S)	**PLURAL NOUNS ENDING IN S (ADD ')**	**PLURAL NOUNS NOT ENDING IN S (ADD 'S)**
boy's	boys'	men's
lion's	lions'	children's
lady's	ladies'	women's

There's one important exception that you should remember, because it often turns up on tests: The possessive of *it* is *its*, not *it's* as many people mistakenly think. *It's* only means *it is*; *its* means *belonging to it*.

Quotation Marks

Quotation marks are generally used to indicate that someone's exact words are being reproduced. There are other uses for quotation marks (to indicate irony, for example), but for the purposes of this test, you need to know only about their primary use.

Here are the rules for using quotation marks:

- Quotes that are complete sentences are preceded by a comma and begin with a capital letter. End punctuation appears inside the quotes.

    Examples: The reporter asked the governor, "Do you have any plans to increase the education budget this year?"
    The governor said, "I would love to find a way to increase the education budget."

- Quotations that are not complete sentences begin with a lowercase letter and include end punctuation only if they appear at the end of the sentence.

    Examples: The governor added that he would "look into the matter further."
    The governor added that he would "look into the matter further" before reaching a decision.

- Use single quotation marks instead of double quotation marks for a quotation that appears within a quotation.

    Example: The head of the teacher's union told reporters that "The governor told me 'I will do everything I can to increase the education budget,' and I see no reason to doubt her."

Subject-Verb Agreement

For a sentence to be grammatically correct, its subject and verb must agree in number. This means that if the subject is singular, the verb must be singular; if the subject is plural, the verb must also be plural.

Generally speaking, the third person singular form of a verb (i.e., the form used with the words *he* or *she*) ends in the letter *s*.

    Examples: He walks; she sings; Jane dances; Robert cooks

The first and second person forms of a verb (i.e., the forms used with the words *I*, *you*, and *we*) generally do not end in the letter *s*.

    Examples: I relax; you read; we visit

Pronoun Subjects

Pronoun subjects can make things a little tricky, even for expert English speakers. Some pronouns are always singular, others are always plural, and still others can be both singular and plural.

These pronouns are always singular:

anybody
anyone
each
either
everybody
everyone
neither
no one
nobody
one
somebody
someone

The indefinite pronouns *each*, *either*, and *neither* are most often misused. You can avoid a mismatch by mentally adding the word *one* after the pronoun and removing the other words between the pronoun and the verb.

Examples: Each **of the men** wants his own car.
Each **one** wants his own car.

Although these sentences may sound awkward, they are written correctly (they sound awkward because you are used to hearing these pronouns used incorrectly).

Some pronouns are always plural and require a plural verb. They include:

both
few
many
several

Some pronouns can be either singular or plural. The verb they take depends on the words or prepositional phrases that follow them.

all
any
most
none
some

Examples: All of the milk **is** gone.
All of the students **are** gone.

Subjects joined by the word *and* are called *compound subjects*. They always take a plural verb.

Examples: He and she want to buy a new house.
Roger and George sing nicely together.

Subjects joined by the words *or* or *nor* agree with the noun or pronoun closest to the verb.

Examples: He or she wants to buy a house.
Either the Wilsons or the Johnsons plan to buy the house.

Verb Tense

The tense of a verb tells readers when the action occurs. Present tense verbs tell the reader to imagine that the action is happening right now, as they are reading the words. Past tense verbs tell readers that the action has already happened. Future tense verbs tell readers that the action will happen at a later time.

This table shows the three basic verb tenses:

VERB TENSE		
PRESENT TENSE (TODAY I . . .)	**PAST TENSE** (YESTERDAY I . . .)	**FUTURE TENSE** (TOMORROW I . . .)
drive	drove	will drive
think	thought	will think
rise	rose	will rise
catch	caught	will catch

When a sentence describes two or more actions that occur at the same time, both tenses must be described in the same tense. The sentence "Terry opens the door and saw the crowd" contains a confusing and grammatically incorrect verb tense shift. Because both actions occurred at about the same time, both should be described using the same tense. Either "Terry opens the door and sees the crowd" or "Terry opened the door and saw the crowd" are acceptable.

That does not mean that it is impossible to use more than one verb tense in a sentence, however. A sentence that describes actions that occur at different times, for example, must use more than one verb tense. For example, the sentence "The game warden sees the fish that you caught" is correctly formulated. The verb *sees* is in the present tense, because the sentence indicates that the warden is seeing the fish right now. The fish was caught earlier; that's why *caught* is in the past tense, to indicate that it happened before the warden saw the fish.

Pronoun Case

In most cases, a single pronoun in a sentence is easy to use correctly. Most English speakers can identify the errors in the sentences that follow.

Errors: Me went to the movie with he.
My teacher gave she a ride to school.

In the first sentence, *me* should be *I* and *he* should be *him*. In the second sentence, *she* should be *her*. These are errors in pronoun case; they use the subject form of the pronoun when they should use the object form, or vice versa. As previously noted, such errors are relatively easy to spot when the pronoun stands alone. They are more difficult to spot, however, when the pronoun is paired with another pronoun or a noun. Consider the following sentences:

Errors: The director rode with Jerry and I.
Belle and him are going to the arena.

Both of these sentences contain pronoun case errors. Did you find them? The trick to finding these errors is to turn each sentence into two sentences.

Errors: The director rode with Jerry.
The director rode with I.

Belle is going to the arena.
Him is going to the arena.

By isolating each noun or pronoun in its own sentence, you can check pronoun case more easily. This will help you determine that the sentences should read *The director rode with Jerry and me* and *Belle and he are going to the arena.*

Pronoun Agreement

Like subjects and verbs, pronouns must agree in number with the nouns they represent. If a pronoun replaces a singular noun, the pronoun must also be singular. If the pronoun replaces a plural noun, the pronoun must also be plural.

> **Examples:** A doctor should take a break whenever *she* gets tired.
> Doctors should take a break whenever *they* get tired.

If a pronoun replaces another pronoun, the same rule applies: They must agree in number.

> **Examples:** One of the girls misplaced *her* purse.
> *All* of the girls misplaced *their* purses.

If two or more nouns or pronouns are joined by *and*, use a plural pronoun to represent them.

> **Example:** Ben and Jerry built an ice cream company that made *them* rich and famous.

If two or more singular nouns or pronouns are joined by *or* or *nor*, use a singular pronoun to represent them.

> **Example:** Matthew or Jacob will loan you *his* calculator.

If a singular and plural noun or pronoun are joined by *or* or *nor*, choose a pronoun that agrees with the one that comes after *or* or *nor*.

> **Examples:** Neither the soldiers nor the sergeant was sure of *his* location.
> Neither the sergeant nor the soldiers were sure of *their* location.

Passive Voice

Verbs have an *active voice* and a *passive voice*. A verb is in the active voice when the subject performs the action. A verb is in the passive voice when the subject receives the action.

> **Active:** Roger kicked the ball.
> **Passive:** The ball was kicked by Roger.

In the sentence written in active voice, *Roger* is the subject and he performs the action: He *kicks* the ball. In the sentence written in the passive voice, *the ball* is the subject and it receives the action: It *is kicked*.

The active voice is more precise than the passive voice; it clarifies what has happened and who is responsible. (Note that when the government or a corporation admits to something embarrassing, it uses the passive voice. It says *mistakes were made* in the passive voice rather than *we made mistakes* in the active voice.) Therefore, the active voice is preferred in most instances. There are times when the passive voice is appropriate and clear (e.g., *I was paid reasonably for my work*), but generally answers written in the passive voice are incorrect. When given the choice between two answers—one active, one passive—the active answer is much more likely the correct one.

Remember that regardless of the voice used, voice must remain consistent throughout a sentence. It is almost always incorrect to shift from the active to passive voice, or vice versa, in a sentence.

> **Incorrect:** The swimmer won the race, and a medal was received by her.
> **Correct:** The swimmer won the race and received a medal.

Modifiers

A modifier is a descriptive word, clause, or phrase. Modifiers are like adjectives. They help describe nouns (people, places, things, and concepts) by adding useful information.

A modifier must be clearly attached to the word or words it is describing; if it is not, it creates confusion. It can even result in an unintended (and often comical) meaning to the sentence.

Errors: Nailed to the tree, Cedric saw a "No Hunting" sign.
Waddling down the road, we saw a skunk.

Both *nailed to the tree* and *waddling down the road* are examples of *misplaced modifiers*. They are called misplaced modifiers because their placement makes it difficult to determine which noun they modify. The first sentence incorrectly suggests that it was Cedric and not the sign that was nailed to the tree; the second suggests that the people, rather than the skunk, were waddling down the road.

Here's how to correct the errors:

Corrected: Cedric saw a "No Hunting" sign nailed to a tree.
We saw a skunk waddling down the road.

Sometimes a modifier does not refer to any word or phrase in the sentence; rather, it refers to a concept that is implied but not stated. This is a grammatical error called a *dangling modifier*. Here are some examples:

Errors: After teaching all day, relaxing with a book is always a nice way to spend the evening.
Having received a letter, a reply was necessary.

The modifiers *after teaching all day* and *having received a letter* suggest a person who taught all day or received the letter. No such person is mentioned in the sentence, however; that's why the modifiers are called

dangling modifiers. These modifiers are metaphorically dangling in space, attached to nothing.

Here's how to correct the errors:

Corrected: The teacher feels that, after teaching all day, relaxing with a book is always a nice way to spend the evening.
Having received a letter, Bill realized that a reply was necessary.

Unnecessary Words

Good writing is clear and concise. Extra words take up valuable time and space, and they create opportunities for misunderstanding.

A *redundant* sentence is one that repeats an idea unnecessarily. Here are some examples of redundant sentences.

Examples: They refunded our money back to us.
We can proceed ahead with the plan we made ahead of time.
The car is red in color.

Consider the first example. To *refund* money is to give it back; therefore, it is unnecessary to say that the money was refunded *back to us*. The words *back to us* repeat an idea already expressed by the word *refund* without adding any new information. Similarly, *proceed* means *to go ahead* and a plan must, by definition, be made *ahead of time*; thus, *ahead* and *ahead of time* are redundant in the second example. Because *red* is a color, it is unnecessary and redundant to say the car is *red in color*. Simply write *The car is red*.

Other common examples of redundancy include:

actual experience
cheap price
connected together
consensus of opinion

final end
5 A.M. in the morning
join together
past experience
postponed until later
proven conclusively
the reason is because
unanimous consensus
true facts

A *wordy* sentence contains unnecessary words. When an idea can be expressed more concisely, it should be.

Examples:
Error: Bill is as good as or better than Marty.
Corrected: Bill is at least as good as Marty.

Error: It appears to me that it is starting to rain.
Corrected: It is starting to rain.

Error: It is the purpose of the encyclopedia to provide information on all topics.
Corrected: The encyclopedia's purpose is to provide information on all topics.

Additional Resources

Here are some good ways to build your vocabulary, reading, and grammar skills so that you can do your best on the written communication section of a civil service test.

- If you have Internet access, search for articles related to the career you'd like to pursue. Find bulletin boards related to your career and use them to exchange views with others on the Internet. These strategies will help you expand your knowledge of job-related material that may appear on the test while they help you develop your communication skills.

- Use the library. Many public libraries have sections, sometimes called "Lifelong Learning Centers," that contain materials for adult learners. In these sections, you will find books with exercises for reading and study skills. It's also a good idea to enlarge your base of information by reading related books and articles. Many libraries have computer systems that allow you to access information quickly and easily. Library personnel will show you how to use the computers and microfilm and microfiche machines.

- Begin now to build a broad knowledge of your potential profession. Get in the habit of reading articles in newspapers and magazines on job-related issues. Keep a clipping file of those articles. This will help keep you informed of trends in the profession and familiarize you with relevant vocabulary.

- Consider reading or subscribing to professional journals. They are usually available for a reasonable annual fee. Your public library may have copies you can read for free.

- If you need more help building your reading skills and taking vocabulary tests, consider *Reading Comprehension in 20 Minutes a Day* and *501 Reading Comprehension Questions*, both by LearningExpress. If you need more help with spelling, consult *Vocabulary and Spelling in 20 Minutes a Day* by LearningExpress.

- Nonnative English speakers should consider *English Made Simple* by Arthur Waldhorn and Arthur Ziegler or *Errors in English and Ways to Correct Them* by Harry Shaw. Other good grammar reviews include *501 Grammar and Writing Questions* and *Writing Skills in 20 Minutes a Day*, both by LearningExpress.

Review Exercise

Reading Comprehension

Read the following passage. Then, answer questions 1 to 5.

Although not admissible as evidence in most courts of law, polygraph tests play an important role in modern law enforcement. Commonly referred to as a "lie detector," a polygraph is an electronic instrument that monitors certain involuntary biological reactions. By tracking heart rate, blood pressure, respiratory rate, and sweat secretion on the subject's fingertips, the polygraph detects biological indicators of the type of stress associated with lying.

A polygraph test is typically broken up into four stages. The first is the pretest, during which the subject engages in a casual interview with his or her interrogator. This portion of the exam, during which the matter under investigation is discussed in detail, can take up to an hour to complete. The second stage is the design stage, during which examiners confer to design a series of questions about the matter under investigation; these are the questions to be asked during the actual polygraph exam. After the questions have been formulated, the actual exam is administered.

During the actual exam, the interrogator asks a series of questions, only a few of which have to do with the matter under investigation. The other questions are control questions, general questions designed to get the subject to lie, such as "Have you ever lied to get out of trouble with the police?" Most people will answer no to this question even though most people have, in fact, lied to get out of trouble with the police; this lie provides the examiner with a baseline response with which to compare other responses, allowing him to determine when the sub-

ject is lying. A polygraph exam concludes with a posttest, during which the polygraph operator examines the results and determines whether the subject has lied and, if so, when.

Polygraph test results are not universally accepted. Even champions of the test concede that it cannot indicate whether a person is lying; rather, it detects symptoms and reactions that are indicative of lying in most people. Detractors argue that the test is stress-inducing, causing some people to register a "false positive" (a test result indicating that they are lying even though they are telling the truth), and that this is an uncorrectable flaw in the procedure. For this reason, some people are skeptical that polygraph tests will ever be reliable enough to gain universal acceptance in the courtroom.

1. According to the passage, which of the following occurs during the pretest segment of a polygraph test?
   a. The examiners ask the subject control questions.
   b. The examiners design questions to ask the subject.
   c. The examiners engage the subject in a casual interview.
   d. The subject's heart rate and blood pressure fluctuate.

2. As used in the passage, the word *skeptical* most nearly means
   a. doubtful.
   b. irate.
   c. intolerant.
   d. enthusiastic.

3. Which of the following best summarizes the author's purpose in writing the passage?
   a. to convince readers that polygraph tests are accurate
   b. to inform readers about how polygraph tests work
   c. to praise police forces that rely on polygraph tests
   d. to propose new methods for conducting polygraph tests

4. Critics would most likely argue that the biggest problem with polygraph tests is that
   a. too few polygraph operators are skilled enough to read test results accurately.
   b. the test is susceptible to power surges and power outages.
   c. their flaws cannot be fixed through redesign.
   d. a polygraph test takes too long to complete.

5. According to the passage, lie detectors monitor which of the following biological functions?
   a. brain waves
   b. saliva production
   c. eye movement
   d. breathing rate

Read the following passage. Then, answer questions 6 to 10.

The year 2005 was a watershed for school nutrition. That's because 2005 was the year that 42 state legislatures considered major revisions to policies concerning vending machines and cafeteria offerings in public schools; many passed legislation that imposed sweeping reforms. For many public school students, that meant the end of access to potato chips, candy bars, and high-sugar soft drinks.

This revolution was slow in coming and for a predictable reason: money. Schools are chronically underfunded, and as a result, they are always looking for ways to increase revenue in order to fund such "luxuries" as arts programs, athletic teams, field trips, and extracurricular clubs. Over the years, vending machines stocked with junk food became a reliable source of this much-needed income. Schools were understandably <u>dubious</u> about any new nutrition regulations. They wanted to promote healthy eating, but they also relied on vending machines for cash, and they knew that the most successful vending machines in schools sold junk food.

Then came an avalanche of reports on childhood obesity. The consensus: that anywhere between 10% and 33% of all American children were either overweight or in danger of becoming overweight. This is no small problem: Childhood obesity carries with it a number of potential complications, including high blood pressure, sleep disorders, liver disease, and Type 2 diabetes. Psychological effects can include depression and learning difficulties. Under the circumstances, state legislatures had little choice. When the media began reporting regularly on childhood obesity, citizens began to demand that the government take action.

It's too early to determine what, if any, effect these changes have had on childhood obesity. As for school revenues, reports are mixed. Philadelphia schools report no drop in income since they stopped stocking machines with soda and started stocking them with juice, milk, and water. Chicago schools, on the other hand, report a loss in income. Miami-Dade County public schools actually report a notable increase in income since making the switch. Public health expert Damien Seip notes, "Regardless of the impact on revenue, it's clear to everyone that junk food has got to go from our schools. We simply cannot participate in the fattening of America's youth. It's unconscionable."

6. Which of the following best summarizes the main idea of the passage?
   a. Somewhere between 10% and 33% of American children today are overweight.
   b. In Miami-Dade County, public schools saw an increase in vending machine revenue when they switched from junk food to healthy snacks.
   c. Type 2 diabetes is especially dangerous in young people, as it can lead to lifelong health problems and even premature death.
   d. Increased awareness of childhood obesity has led many states to enact new school food-service regulations.

7. According to the passage, changes to school food policies have so far resulted in

   a. a measurable decrease in obesity among public school students.
   b. an increase in truancy as students leave campus to buy junk food off school premises.
   c. a variety of positive and negative effects on school income from food sales.
   d. a decrease in the incidence of depression among high school students.

8. According to the passage, schools resisted changes to nutrition policies because they
   a. relied on vending machine sales to fund extracurricular activities.
   b. believed the changes didn't go far enough in banning junk food.
   c. felt that such decisions should be made by school boards, not state legislatures.
   d. worried that the changes would require an increase in cafeteria staff, which the schools could not afford.

9. The writer most likely puts the word *luxuries* in quotes to indicate that he is
   a. repeating what someone else said.
   b. using the word ironically.
   c. uncertain about the meaning of the word.
   d. introducing an unfamiliar technical term.

10. As used in the passage, the word *dubious* most nearly means
   a. uncertain.
   b. opposed.
   c. excited.
   d. misinformed.

Spelling and Vocabulary

Select the best answer choice for each question.

11. Chester's _____ table manners drove me to leave the dinner early.
   a. apaling
   b. apalling
   c. appalling

12. Shaniqua bought a snow globe as a _____ of her skiing vacation.
   a. momento
   b. memento
   c. mimento

13. Find the word that is closest in meaning to the underlined word below.

   a person of remarkable <u>composure</u>
   a. calm
   b. skill
   c. humor

14. Find the word that is closest in meaning to the underlined word below.

a <u>potent</u> drug

a. ineffective
b. powerful
c. illegal

15. Find the word that best completes the sentence below.

Engineers speak in a technical _____ I simply cannot understand.

a. dialect
b. jargon
c. vigilance

Grammar

Select the best answer choice for each question.

16. Select the sentence that is written most correctly.
   a. The Henderson family plans to visit the Grand Canyon some time in february.
   b. the Henderson Family plans to visit the Grand canyon some time in February.
   c. The Henderson family plans to visit the Grand Canyon some time in February.

17. Select the sentence that is written most correctly.

   a. Neither of the salespeople seems to know how much this item costs.
   b. Neither of the salespeople seem to know how much this item costs.
   c. Neither of the salespeople seems to know how much this item cost.

18. Select the sentence that is written most correctly.
   a. It's time to check the automobile to see whether its paint job has dried.
   b. Its time to check the automobile to see whether it's paint job has dried.
   c. It's time to check the automobile to see whether it's paint job has dried.

19. Select the sentence that is written most correctly.
   a. Eaten as a delicacy in France for centuries, American diners are only now beginning to enjoy the culinary pleasures of escargot.
   b. Eaten as a delicacy in France for centuries, escargot are only now beginning to bring culinary pleasure to American diners.
   c. Escargot have been eaten as a delicacy in France for centuries, American diners are only now beginning to enjoy them.

20. Select the sentence that is written most correctly.
   a. Some people say that jury duty is a nuisance that takes up their precious time and that we don't get paid enough.
   b. Some people say that jury duty is a nuisance that takes up your precious time and that they don't get paid enough.
   c. Some people say that jury duty is a nuisance that takes up one's precious time and that one doesn't get paid enough.

Answers

1. **c.** The pretest is discussed in paragraph 2 of the passage. The passage states: "The first [stage] is the pretest, during which the subject engages in a casual interview with his or her interrogator." Thus, choice **c** is correct. Choice **a** describes the actual polygraph exam; choice **b** describes the design stage of the test; and choice **d** refers to information from a different part of the passage. Because the passage never states that the subject's heart rate and blood pressure fluctuate during the pretest, this cannot be the correct choice to an "According to the passage . . ." question.

2. **a.** *Skeptical* means *uncertain* or *doubtful*. *Irate* (choice **b**) means *angry*. *Intolerant* (choice **c**) means *unwilling to accept another's beliefs or customs*. *Enthusiastic* (choice **d**) means *excited*.

3. **b.** Use the process of elimination to answer this question. The tone of the passage is informative, not persuasive; furthermore, the author points out serious flaws in the polygraph test. Therefore, choice **a** cannot be correct. The author never discusses police forces, so choice **c** cannot be correct. Finally, the author reviews polygraph methods but does not suggest any new methods for improving the test; therefore, choice **d** cannot be correct.

4. **c.** In the final paragraph, the author reports: "Detractors argue that the test is stress-inducing, causing some people to register a 'false positive' (a test result indicating that they are lying even though they are telling the truth), *and that this is an uncorrectable flaw in the procedure.*" The final part of the sentence supports the conclusion drawn in choice **c**. None of the other answer choices is men-

tioned or alluded to in the passage, so none of them can be correct.

5. **d.** The first paragraph states that polygraph tests measure respiratory rate. Choice **d**, *breathing rate*, is a good paraphrase of that information. Reread the first paragraph to see that the passage does not mention choices **a**, **b**, or **c**.

6. **d.** Of the answer choices, only choice **d** refers to the entire passage; the others refer to specific details from one portion of the passage. The answer to a main idea question must address the passage as a whole, not merely one section of the passage.

7. **c.** In the final paragraph, the passage states: "As for school revenues, reports are mixed." This, and the details that follow, support the conclusion that new school food policies have resulted in "a variety of positive and negative effects on school income from food sales." Choices **b** and **d** refer to data that is not provided in the passage and, therefore, cannot be correct; choice **a** is contradicted by the first sentence of the final paragraph.

8. **a.** Choice **a** is supported by paragraph 2, which explains how schools have become dependent on vending machine sales to pay for sports, arts programs, and other extracurricular activities. None of the other answers is mentioned in the passage and, therefore, cannot be correct.

9. **b.** The writer is indicating that he does not truly think that arts programs, sports, field trips, and extracurricular clubs are luxuries. He is being ironic. Irony is often indicated in writing by quotation marks.

10. **a.** Use context clues to answer this question. The sentence that follows the sentence in which *dubious* appears helps define the term. The schools "want to promote healthy eating," but "also relied on vending machines for cash." Their desires were at cross purposes and, therefore, the schools were *dubious*, or *uncertain*, about proposed changes.

11. **c.** The correct spelling is *appalling*.

12. **b.** The correct spelling is *memento*. Think of the words *memory* or *meme* to remember that *memento* starts with the letters *me*.

13. **a.** *Composure* means *a peaceful state of mind*. Of the three answer choices, *calm* (choice **a**) is closest in meaning.

14. **b.** *Potent* means *powerful*. *Ineffective* (choice **a**) is the opposite, or antonym, of *potent*.

15. **b.** *Jargon* means *technical language*. A *dialect* (choice **a**) is *a regional variation of a language*. *Jargon* is the better of the two choices because *jargon* is specifically associated with the technical specificity of engineers' conversation. *Vigilance* (choice **c**) means *watchfulness*.

16. **c.** Each incorrect answer contains capitalization errors. In choice **a**, the word *February* should be capitalized. In choice **b**, the word *family* should not be capitalized and the word *Canyon* should be capitalized (because it is part of a proper noun).

17. **a.** *Neither* takes a singular verb. Therefore, choice **b** is incorrect because it incorrectly states that *neither . . . seem* instead of *neither . . . seems*. Choice **c** is incorrect because *item* is singular and, therefore, must also take the singular verb *costs* instead of the plural verb *cost*.

18. **a.** The possessive form of *it* is *its*, not *it's*. The contraction *it's* means *it is*. Choice **b** uses the incorrect form of the word twice. Choice **c** incorrectly uses *it's paint job* when *its paint job* would be grammatically correct.

19. **b.** Choice **a** incorrectly states that *American diners* have been *eaten as a delicacy in France for centuries* when, in fact, it is *escargot*, not *American diners*, that have been eaten as delicacies there. Choice **c** contains two independent clauses but no conjunction or punctuation to connect them properly, making choice **c** a confusing run-on sentence.

20. **c.** Choices **a** and **b** contain ungrammatical pronoun shifts. Choice **a** uses *their* and *we* to describe the same group of people; choice **b** uses *your* and *they* similarly. Only choice **c** remains grammatically consistent, using *one* in both instances.

7

C H A P T E R

CIVIL SERVICE SKILLS

Many civil service exams include skill tests specific to the job for which they are designed. Clerical exams, for example, may contain sections on alphabetizing and filing. Police exams often include sections on face recognition skills. The U.S. postal exam contains a section on address checking.

Three skill sets pop up most frequently on civil service exams: customer service, memory, and coding. These skills, and the questions used to test them, are the subject of this chapter.

Customer Service

Customer service questions on civil service exams ask about a variety of situations and scenarios, but most can be answered by remembering a few basic principles.

- The top priority of customer service is a satisfied customer. Good customer service makes things as easy and comfortable for the customer as is reasonably possible.
- Always be polite to customers; any action that will upset the customer (e.g., telling the customer that he or she is being rude) is bad.
- Respect customers' right to privacy, especially when recording or handling personal information (e.g., Social Security numbers, addresses, birth dates, etc.).
- Try to resolve the customer's problem yourself, but if you can't, find someone who can. Whenever possible, resolve problems during a single visit or contact.
- Express regret when you cannot resolve the customer's problem.
- Handle complaints professionally.

Most customer service questions test these principles in one way or another.

Example: A customer asks you which form she must complete in order to apply for a certain government program. You are not sure of the answer. Which of the following should you do?

a. Give the customer the answer you think is most likely correct.
b. Direct the customer to another employee.
c. Inform the person that you are not sure but will find the answer for her.
d. Tell the customer that she must figure it out on her own.

Consider each answer choice. Choice **a** creates the real possibility that you will give the customer incorrect information. She may then fill out and submit the incorrect form, which will result in a delay in resolving

her matter and which may require her to make a return visit to your office. This is not a good answer choice; eliminate it.

Choice **b** suggests that you dump your problem onto another employee. This is not only poor customer service, but also the sort of workplace etiquette that will make you many enemies among your coworkers. Eliminate this answer choice.

Choice **c** looks good. You honestly inform the customer that you do not know the answer to her question, but you promise to find the answer for her. You are showing the customer the proper respect by telling her the truth, and you are attempting to resolve the problem in a single visit or contact. This is probably the correct answer, but we must look at choice **d** to be sure.

Choice **d** violates most of the basic principles tested by customer service questions. The response will certainly not result in a satisfied customer; it's not a polite response; it represents a failure on your part to try to resolve the customer's issue and it's unprofessional. This is definitely not the correct answer.

The correct answer to this question is choice **c**.

The Citizen Service Levels Interagency Committee (CSLIC) Report

In October 2005, the federal government released *The Citizen Service Levels Interagency Committee (CSLIC) Report*, a study commissioned by President Bush. The report contains "proposed performance measures, practices, and approaches for government-wide citizen contact activities" that focus on making government services "market-based, citizen-centric, and customer-focused." Simply put, the *CSLIC Report* is the federal government's official policy on what constitutes good customer service. Its recommendations have certainly had an impact on state and local governments as well. Because this report has become the government standard by which customer service is measured, you should be familiar with its contents. A summary of its most important points follows (those wishing to read the entire 36-page report will find it online by searching for *CSLIC Report*).

The report studies five areas: telephone service, e-mail service, traditional service such as walk-in and postal mail, cross-channel issues (e.g., customer complaints, multilingual service), and developing technologies (e.g., instant messaging, virtual meetings). Here's what it has to say about each.

In All Areas

Customer service must focus on ease of use for the customer, timely response, respect for privacy, quality service, consistency in service, and convenience for the customer. Applied to specific cross-function areas, this means that:

- **Customer complaints** should be counted and evaluated regularly in order to determine whether improvement in overall service is necessary. Customers should have a variety of options to choose from in registering complaints (in person, by telephone, via the Internet) and should be given a choice as to whether they would like a response. Complaints should be acknowledged promptly.

- **Queries should be resolved during first contact** whenever possible.

- **Plain language** (i.e., language that is easy for the general public to understand) should be used in all documents for the public and in all interactions with the public. Avoid using technical terms and acronyms. Prepared scripts for common queries should be prepared; they should utilize plain language.

- **Privacy policies** should be clearly posted and available in print, online, and e-mail form. Customers should be informed whenever their interactions are being recorded or otherwise

monitored, whether for training or quality assurance purposes. Customers should be informed that information they provide will be recorded for future reference in order to make future interactions with the customer easier, i.e., they will not have to repeat the process of providing name, birth date, Social Security number, etc.

- **Continuously available channels of contact** such as 24-hour help lines, web chat, and Internet sites should be made available and should be promoted in order to inform customers of their availability. Promotion should include placards and pamphlets displayed at customer service sites, recorded messages on government telephone lines, and reminders by agents at the conclusion of an interaction.

- **Language translation** services should be provided for customers with limited English skills. Quality of translation should be emphasized over quantity of available languages. In other words, it is better to have a great Spanish translator than a translator who translates Spanish, French, and Portuguese poorly. When used, auto translators should be checked regularly for accuracy and functionality.

- **Interagency contact information** (e.g., telephone extensions) should be updated regularly to ensure that agents always have the most current information.

- **Correspondences** should conform to an agency style guide that is regularly reviewed and updated. Styles should include a standard greeting and closing and sample instructions to customers.

- **Creative scheduling**, including flextime, should be used to meet customer needs by expanding hours of customer support. Hours of operation should be set to meet the needs and preferences of customers, and should be reevaluated regularly to ensure that customer needs continue to be met.

- **Supervisors** should be available to speak with customers in a timely manner when customers request such contact.
- **Overall customer satisfaction** should be regularly evaluated, with formal reviews at least once per year. Customers should be asked to assess their satisfaction with such services and to record their assessment on a uniform customer satisfaction survey, the results of which should be used to evaluate agency performance. Customer feedback should be incorporated into trainings and manuals.

Telephone Service

Even as options for contacting the government increase, the telephone remains the means of communication preferred by most of the government's customers. This is true across all age groups, not just for older citizens.

Contacting the government by telephone can be an unpleasant experience. Customers complain of prolonged hold times, repeated transfers among different agents within and between agencies, faulty automated answering and interactive voice response systems, unreturned voicemail and the delivery of inaccurate information by government agents. The *CSLIC Report* looks for ways to address these problems. Its recommendations:

- **Incoming calls during business hours** should be answered quickly. At least 80% of calls should be handled within 60 seconds. The abandonment rate—the rate at which customers hang up before they get to speak to a representative—should be kept below 4% annually.
- **Audio provided during hold time** should provide answers to frequently asked questions. If hold time is expected to be longer than 30 seconds, the customer should be periodically informed of the projected wait time.

- **Toll-free numbers** should be available to people calling from within the United States.
- **Interactive voice response (IVR) systems** should be used to free staff for other tasks and to allow customers to navigate their own way to the appropriate assistance. Speech recognition technology should be included in a government IVR system, allowing customers to navigate by voice as well as by keypad (e.g., "If you are calling to check on the status of your refund check, press or say 'one.'").
- **A common voice** should be used for all recorded messages. The voice should be calm; the speaker should speak slowly and clearly.
- **Recorded messages for those who call after business hours** should state the agency's hours of operation and should encourage callers to use online resources.
- **Return calls** for voicemail messages should be made no later than the next day. Agents should attempt to return the call three times at three different times of day before giving up.
- **Call transfers** should not be made until the customer is told to whom he or she is being transferred, the reason for the transfer, and the telephone number and extension of the person to whom he or she is being transferred.

E-mail and Internet

E-mail and Internet connection are preferred slightly over telephone contact by customers who have easy access to high-speed Internet connections (e.g., a cable modem). Customers who use these channels complain most often that e-mails are not always returned, requiring multiple submissions before a response arrives. Many agencies do not even generate an auto-reply confirming receipt, meaning that the customer cannot even be certain that his or her e-mail has reached its destination.

To address these issues, the CSLIC recommends:

- **Agency e-mail addresses** should be easy to find, both on the Internet and at the agency office. Accounts should be monitored throughout office hours.

- **Use of agents' individual e-mail accounts should be minimized** to reduce the likelihood that customer response will be delayed because of vacation or attrition.

- **An auto-reply** should be sent to a customer upon receipt of his or her query to confirm that the e-mail has been received. Auto-replies should suggest alternative means of resolution (telephone, walk-in visit, website) if such alternatives would yield a faster response.

- **Mandatory fields in customer e-mail submissions** should be kept to a minimum. In most instances, name, street address, e-mail address, and nature of query should provide enough information for the agent to identify and contact the customer.

- **Simple queries** should be answered within two business days. More complequeries should be answered within five business days; the customer should be informed of the approximate wait anticipated for response. Extremely complequeries may take longer; customers should be notified of the progress made toward resolution every five to ten business days.

- **E-mail responses should be concise** and should be written in plain language.

- **When an e-mail is not successfully delivered**, the agent should make at least two subsequent attempts to resend. This is not necessary when the e-mail is not delivered because the customer has incorrectly entered his or her e-mail address.

- **Misdirected e-mail**, which is e-mail sent to the wrong agency, should be sent to the U.S. General Services Administration's (GSA) USA Services center for redirection. Senders of misdirected e-mail should be notified and told that their inquiry is being forwarded to the appropriate office via USA Services. They should be advised to follow up on their inquiries if they do not receive a response within a reasonable amount of time.

- **Web response forms should be used whenever possible** to minimize spam. Such forms should include links to FAQs (frequently asked questions) and drop-down menus that allow the customer to categorize his or her query. Date and time of transmission should be automatically recorded.

Postal Mail, Fax, and Walk-In Service

Government employees must handle copious amounts of postal mail each day. Customers often prefer to use mail for urgent matters, compleinquiries, and issues that require them to disclose personal information. Civil servants must also interact with numerous walk-in customers and manage daily fatransmissions.

The CSLIC studied these matters and rendered the following recommendations:

- **Postal mail** should be acknowledged with an immediate response; the response should include an estimate of the time required to resolve the query if an answer cannot be delivered within 15 working days. Incoming mail should be logged, with topic, date of receipt, and date of response recorded. Agencies should have a clearly established policy for routing letters addressed to an agency's leadership.

- **Fatransmissions** should receive responses by postal mail for fax; rules for response are the same as those previously outlined for postal mail.

- **Walk-in customers** should be able to speak with a receptionist (or an employee serving the same function) immediately upon arrival at the office.

This greeter should inform the customer of the approximate wait time to see an agent and should inform the customer of the information required to address the query. Some sort of queuing system—take a number or electronic self-registration, for example—should be in operation in offices where more than a few customers are left waiting at any given time.

- **Appointments should be offered** by agencies whose walk-in customers typically wait more than 15 minutes to meet with an agent.
- **Extended hours of operation**, with possible extension into evening hours and Saturdays, should be considered by offices whose customers have difficulty visiting the office during regular business hours.

Web Chat, Etc.

Modern technology is rapidly changing the way citizens interact with the government. Websites allow citizens to retrieve information instantaneously, expediting transactions and freeing government employees to perform more important tasks. RSS (Really Simple Syndication) technology allows citizens to be notified immediately whenever a government webpage is updated. Other technologies—web chat, instant messaging, and videoconferencing to name a few—are being developed and adapted for use in government-citizen interactions.

The incorporation of new technology hasn't been a completely smooth ride for the government. Citizens have complained that some government websites are poorly organized, making it difficult to find important information. FAQs are not updated often enough to serve their purpose effectively.

To address these issues, the CSLIC recommends:

- **BOTs** (response software programmed to answer certain customer queries automatically) should

be reviewed at least once every three months to ensure that they work properly and provide accurate information.

- **Contact pages at websites** should include numerous options: telephone number(s), e-mail address(es), postal address(es), etc.
- **Links to other agencies' websites** should be provided, as appropriate.
- **FAQs** should be reviewed regularly for accuracy and relevance. Customers should have the option of having FAQs e-mailed to them.
- **RSS feeds** should be made available; feeds should include descriptions of updated material. Instructions should be provided to explain how to link to the agency's RSS feed. Agencies should inform USA.gov (a website that provides official information and services from the U.S. government; formerly FirstGov) when they establish a new RSS feed so the feed can be included in the government-wide RSS library.
- **Web chat** should be available for as many hours a day as possible. If 24-hour service is impossible, hours of operation should be clearly posted.
- **Websites should be designed** with low load times and minimal required scrolling; page layout should be kept clear and simple. Spelling should be carefully checked, as misspellings impede web searches; common misspellings of words appearing on a webpage should be included among the page's meta key words.

Memory

Questions that test memory appear on a number of civil service exams. Practically all police exams include a memory section. Qualifying exams for most postal positions include them as well. Many other exams at the federal, state, and local level test memory.

The reason for this should be fairly obvious: Most jobs require you to remember procedures and protocols, and some jobs require you to remember a great deal more. Memory is certainly a more important skill in some jobs than in others—police officers, for example, rely on memory to solve crimes and, later, to testify accurately at criminal trials, making a good memory a crucial asset for their work—but nearly every job requires some ability to remember important facts and principles.

The most common format for memory questions asks you to study a picture for a fixed amount of time (typically five minutes). The image is then removed from view (on a computer test, the image simply disappears from the screen; on a paper-and-pencil test, you will be asked to close the "memory book" and turn to the test booklet), after which you must answer a number of questions about the image.

There are no shortcuts to finding the correct answers to memory questions; unfortunately, either you remember or you don't, and if you don't, you can only make your best guess and move on. Fortunately, there are several tricks for improving memory. We'll discuss two methods that are well suited to quick memorization:

- the **story** method
- the **peg** method

We will also discuss how to use each method to memorize details of an image or items on a list.

Story Method

To use the story method of memorization, take the items you are trying to memorize and weave a simple, memorable story out of them. The story method is well suited to memorizing images because an image helps suggest a narrative. Consider the image on page 150; it is the sort of image you might see on a memory test.

Before we can use the story method to remember this image, we have to decide what we are going to memorize from this picture. It's a busy picture with lots of detail; we must choose the details that we think the exam is most likely to test, and then memorize them. You should figure that the more prominent a detail, the more likely it is to be tested. Tiny details are least likely to be tested.

So what are the prominent features of this photograph?

People
   A bald white man in sunglasses (or shades) and an Artie's Deli T-shirt
   A dark-haired man in a short-sleeve shirt with a bag across his shoulder
   A black woman carrying a purse

Stores
   Salon & Spa
   Newsstand (selling cigarettes, magazines, cold drinks, and phone cards)
   Photo shop
   Jeweler
   Japanese restaurant (Sushi-Time)

Other details
   Phone booth
   Billboard (automobile advertisement)
   Sign that reads "Podiatry"
   Jewelry sale, 20% to 60% off

That's about it. Yes, there are other details in the photograph, but they are pretty small and difficult to make out; they are unlikely to be the subject of a memory question. Now, let's write a story that incorporates the items we listed.

A <u>bald</u> man named <u>Artie Shades</u> took <u>photographs</u> of <u>jewelry</u> from <u>Japan</u> to sell to the <u>newspaper</u>. He went to the <u>salon and spa</u> to make a <u>phone</u> call to a <u>dark-haired man</u> who told him he would put the photos in his <u>shoulder bag</u> and deliver them by <u>automobile</u>. Artie would have rather walked, but his <u>podiatrist</u> told him he should reduce his walking by <u>20% to 60%</u>. His podiatrist was a <u>black woman</u> who <u>pursed</u> her lips while she talked.

Yes, the story is a little strange. It's certainly not the best story you ever heard. However, it is the sort of story you can write and memorize in five minutes. It contains memory cues (sometimes called *mnemonics*) for every item on the list we created. The fact that the story is ridiculous is good; the more ridiculous the story, the more likely you are to remember it. And although it doesn't repeat every item from the list word for word, it does contain key words that should trigger your memory (e.g., Artie Shades will trigger your memory that the bald man is wearing sunglasses and an "Artie's Deli" T-shirt).

Example: The dark-haired man walking past the newsstand is carrying a

a. briefcase.
b. shoulder bag.
c. suitcase.
d. basket.

If your mnemonic story works, you will remember that the man with the dark hair is carrying a shoulder bag (in the story, he puts the photos in it). If you can't remember the shoulder bag, you still might realize that your story does not mention a briefcase, a suitcase, or a basket; therefore, they are probably not the correct answers. The correct answer to this question is choice **b.**

Peg Method

The peg method of memorization works by associating, or pegging, the items you wish to memorize with items on a list you have already memorized. The most commonly used peg list uses rhymes for the numbers 1 through 10:

1–gun
2–shoe
3–tree
4–door
5–hive
6–bricks
7–Kevin
8–gate
9–wine
10–hen

To use the peg method, you would first memorize this list. This would become, in effect, your permanent "peg board." Whenever you want to memorize a list of ten or fewer items, you would then be able to do so by pegging the item to your list. Say, for example, you wanted to memorize the following grocery list:

apples
lettuce
ground beef
cola
potato chips
napkins
paper plates

You would memorize this list by associating each item on the list with an item on the peg list. Imagine and form a solid mental image of:

a gun that shoots apples

a pair of shoes made of lettuce (or filled with lettuce)

a tree that grows ground beef

a door that is blocked by cases of cola piled on top of one another

bees returning to their hive carrying potato chips

bricks wrapped in napkins

Kevin having a picnic and eating off paper plates

Suppose you want to memorize more than ten items. You would have to memorize a longer peg list. The alphabet provides a good model for a 26-item peg list. Create a list that works best for you. For most people, a list of words beginning with the corresponding letter works best. Make up your own if you like or use this example:

A–ape
B–bee
C–car
D–dog
E–egg
F–frog
G–gold
H–hat
I–ice
J–jail
K–kangaroo
L–log
M–monkey
N–nose
O–owl
P–pig
Q–queen
R–rock
S–sun
T–truck
U–umbrella
V–vest
W–wig
X–X-ray
Y–yogurt
Z–zoo

The peg method is best suited to memorizing lists or charts, diagrams, tables, etc., that can be turned into lists. You might use it when a memory question asks you to study a table such as the one that follows. It lists the alternate side of the street parking regulations for streets surrounding a municipal office. If you work at this office and drive to work, you'll need to memorize this table if you don't want to get lots of parking tickets!

ALTERNATE SIDE OF THE STREET PARKING REGULATIONS	
STREET NAME	ALTERNATE SIDE PARKING IN EFFECT
Branson Street	Monday and Wednesday, 8 A.M. to noon
Franklin Avenue	Tuesday and Friday, 8 A.M. to noon
Park Row	Monday and Thursday, 8 A.M. to 11 A.M.
Water Street	Monday and Wednesday, noon to 4 P.M.
Independence Avenue	Tuesday and Friday, noon to 4 P.M.
Elm Street	Monday and Thursday, 11 A.M. to 2 P.M.

At first, this may seem like a lot of information to memorize. Before you start trying to commit it all to memory, however, study the table for a few moments. Note that two of the streets have alternate side parking on Monday and Wednesday, one in the morning and one in the afternoon. The same is true for Tuesday and Friday. Alternate side parking for the two Monday and Thursday streets is in effect for different hours (8 A.M. to 11 A.M. and 11 A.M. to 2 P.M.) rather than 8 A.M. to noon and noon to 4 P.M.).

Under the circumstances, it would be better for you to rearrange the information in the table this way:

Monday–Wednesday
Branson (early)
Water (late)

Tuesday–Friday
Franklin (early)
Independence (late)

Monday–Thursday
Park (early)
Elm (late)

The peg system requires you to memorize items in a list, so you'll really be memorizing:

Monday
Wednesday
Branson
Water
Tuesday
Friday
Franklin
Independence
Monday
Thursday
Park
Elm

The only information missing from this list is that the hours for alternate side of the street parking for Park and Elm are different from the hours for the other four streets. By listing them last, you should be able to remember that they are the two streets that are different from the other four.

To memorize the list, peg each item to one of your peg words. Because the list contains more than ten items, let's use the alphabet peg list. For each item, try to form a vivid mental picture. To peg "Monday," the first item on the list you want to memorize, to "ape," the first item on your peg list, picture an ape-faced monster in your mind. To peg "Wednesday" to "bees," imagine two bees having a wedding.

Here's how you might finish out your peg list. Remember to choose dramatic images; they will be easier to remember than mundane images.

An ape-faced monster
Two bees having a wedding
A car driving to Branson, Missouri, for vacation
A dog swimming through lots of water
An egg with lots of twos written on it (twos = Tuesday)
A fried frog
A statue of Benjamin Franklin made entirely of gold
A hat tossed in the deep end of a pool (in deep end = Independence; believe it or not, the wackier the mnemonics, the easier they will be to remember)
A monkey crawling on a tree made of ice
A thirsty man in jail (thirsty = Thursday)
A kangaroo parked at a parking meter
Michael Jordan sitting on a log

You can try other mnemonic techniques if the story method and the peg method don't seem right for you. Search for *mnemonics* online or look for books on memory at your local library.

Coding

Government offices use a variety of coding systems to record information in shorthand. As a result, many government jobs require coding skills. Therefore, civil service exams include coding questions.

Also, coding questions test your ability to follow directions, an ability required in all government jobs. To answer a coding question correctly, you must read instructions carefully and follow them accurately.

Example: An office uses a code to record the e-mails it receives from citizens during the day. A code is assigned to each e-mail and logged on a spreadsheet; one spreadsheet is created for each day. The code is assigned according to the following rules:

Characters one through four
The time, in military-time format (e.g., 9:00 A.M. = 0900, 3:00 P.M. = 1500)

Characters five through eight
The first three letters of the sender's last name, and the sender's first initial (e.g., Bob Harris = HARB)

Example: An e-mail arrives at 4:25 P.M. from Catherine McDonald. Which of the following is the correct code for the e-mail?
  a. 1625MCDC
  b. 1625CATM
  c. 0425MCDC
  d. 0425CATM

There are two possible strategies for answering a coding question. The first is to create the correct code according to the information in the question, and then check your code against each of the answer choices until you find the one that matches. Try writing the proper code for the e-mail now.

This approach is certainly one alternative, but it is not without drawbacks. First, it requires you to create the code accurately. Then, it requires you to match your answer accurately with the corresponding answer choice. The problem with this strategy, then, is that it creates two opportunities for a careless mistake. Did you write the code 1625MCDC? Unless you did, there is no way you could answer this question correctly using this approach. And you would still have to match your code to the correct answer without making a careless mistake.

A better strategy is to check each rule, one at a time, against the answer choices, eliminating any answer that breaks the rule. Continue this process until you have eliminated three incorrect choices. The remaining choice must be the correct answer. You will have found the answer by process of elimination.

For example, you might first look at the rule stating that the final four characters should be the first three letters of the sender's first name, followed by the sender's first initial. The first three letters of this sender's last name are MCD; her first initial is C. Therefore, the correct answer must end MCDC. Check the answers and eliminate choices **b** and **d**, which end with CATM.

Now check the other rule, which states that the time should be recorded in military format. The time 4:25 P.M. is written "1625" in military format, meaning you can eliminate choice **c**. The correct answer, by process of elimination, is choice **a**.

Coding questions are typically more elaborate than the example we just studied. Usually they contain at least three rules and often several more than that. The more elaborate the rules for the code, the more effective the strategy of checking rules and eliminating incorrect answers, because you are more likely to make a careless mistake on a question with elaborate instructions.

Let's look at a more complicated example.

Example: All teachers in a state receive a license. The license is coded to reflect the duration of the license, the academic level for which the teacher is licensed, and the primary subject in which the teacher is licensed. The license code is generated according to the following rules.

First and second characters (type of license)
00—Teaching assistant
01—One-year license
02—Two-year license
03—Three-year license
04—Four-year license
05—Five-year license

Third and fourth characters (level)
10—Preschool
11—Elementary
12—Middle school
13—High school
14—All levels

Fifth, sixth, and seventh characters (primary subject)
200—Agriculture
201—Business
202—Computer science
203—Family education
204—Foreign language
205—Health science
206—Language arts
207—Mathematics
208—Natural science
209—Physical education
210—Social science
211—Special education
212—Technical education
213—Theater, music, and/or art

Eighth, ninth, and tenth characters (last name)
First three letters of license holder's last name (e.g., Fong = FON)

Example: A school principal receives notification that the school will soon have a new teacher and that the teacher's license number is 0212207JAC. Which of the following statements about the new teacher could be true?

  a. She is a middle school teacher whose name is Jacqueline Richardson.
  b. She holds a two-year license and teaches physical education.
  c. She is an elementary school teacher who teaches mathematics.
  d. She is a middle school teacher whose name is Mary Jackson.

This question asks you to look at a code and determine to whom it could belong. Once again, the best approach is to check the rules one by one, eliminating answer choices that break the rules.

Let's check the first two digits first. The digits 02 in the first two slots tell us that the teacher has a two-year license. This information tells us that choice **b** might be correct. Unfortunately, it does not allow us to eliminate any answer choices. Let's move on.

The second two digits are 12. These digits tell us that the teacher is a middle school teacher. This is enough information to eliminate choice **c**, which says the teacher is an elementary school teacher.

The fifth, sixth, and seventh digits are 207; they tell us that the teacher is a mathematics teacher. Therefore, she is not a physical education teacher; eliminate choice **b**. The answer must be choices **a** or **d**.

The final three letters of the code tell us that the teacher's last name begin with the letters JAC. This information allows us to eliminate choice **a**. The correct answer, by process of elimination, is choice **d**.

Review Exercise

Customer Service—Questions 1 through 4

Select the best answer choice for each question.

1. A customer approaches you and immediately begins to list his many complaints with your agency's service. What should you do?
   a. Make a note of his complaints and check into their accuracy.
   b. Figure that the customer is having a bad day and listen patiently but ignore the complaints.
   c. Assume the complaints are accurate and take immediate action to remedy the indicated problems.
   d. Direct the customer to a complaint desk in another building.

2. Which of the following statements is most accurate?
   a. It is better to give a customer incorrect information than to admit that you do not know the answer to his question.
   b. When in doubt, you should instruct a customer that he or she should return to the line and wait for an employee who can answer his or her question.
   c. If you do not know the answer to a customer's question, write it down and tell him or her you will send your response within three weeks.
   d. When you cannot answer a question, find someone who can answer the question and make sure the answer is clearly conveyed to the customer.

3. A customer indicates her concerns about providing personal information. You should
   a. explain to the woman that the government handles thousands of people's personal information every day, so the odds of her privacy being compromised are low.
   b. assure her that the government respects and protects privacy, showing her the appropriate policy statements if she asks to see them.
   c. agree that her concerns are legitimate and advise her that she may want to reconsider seeking service from the government.
   d. advise her not to share any information she does not want to share and hope that her query is processed without the missing information.

4. When writing a letter to a customer, you should
   a. use an informal tone in order to make the customer comfortable.
   b. include as many technical terms and acronyms as you can.
   c. tell the customer to resolve future matters via the Internet.
   d. conform to the style mandated by agency policy.

Memory—Questions 5 through 12

Take five minutes to study the following picture. Then, answer questions 5 to 8 without looking back at the picture.

5. Based on the photo, the number of people crossing the street in front of the train is

a. one.

b. two.

c. three.

d. undeterminable from the photo.

6. Based on the photo, the number of people who are crossing the street while wearing a personal music device is

a. one.

b. two.

c. three.

d. undeterminable from the photo.

7. Other than those seen crossing the street in front of the train, how many other people or nontransit vehicles can be observed in the photo?

a. one person and no vehicles

b. one person and one vehicle

c. two persons and no vehicle

d. two persons and one vehicle

8. What is the total number of people seen in the photo?

a. three

b. four

c. five

d. six

Take five minutes to study the following flow chart. Then, answer questions 9 to 12 without looking back at the picture.

A government office used the flow chart below to determine which documents to save and where to save them.

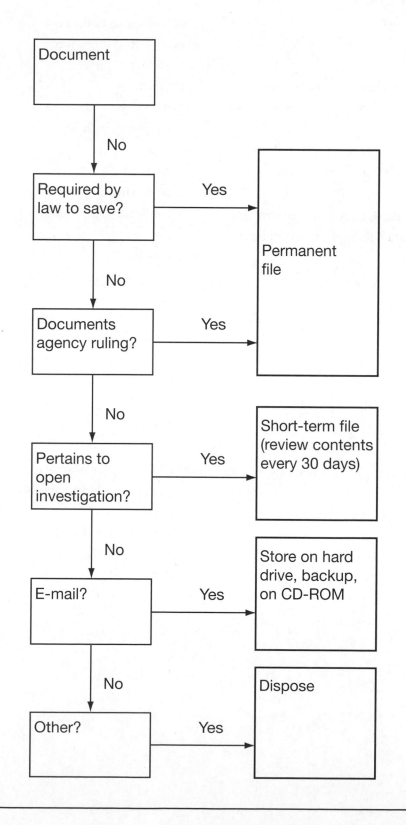

9. Documents that pertain to an open investigation should be

a. filed in the permanent file.

b. filed in the short-term file.

c. stored on computer.

d. thrown away.

10. The permanent file includes

a. only documents that the agency is required by law to save.

b. documents that the agency is required by law to save and documents that pertain to an open investigation.

c. documents that the agency is required by law to save and documents that relate to an agency ruling.

d. all documents that the agency creates.

11. Documents stored in the short-term file should be reviewed once a

a. day.

b. week.

c. month.

d. year.

12. Andrew Distefano contacts the agency by e-mail. His correspondence is

a. saved on a hard drive and CD-ROM.

b. saved in the permanent file.

c. saved in the short-term file.

d. destroyed after it has been read.

Coding—Questions 13 to 20

To answer questions 13 through 20, refer to the following scenario.

A government office uses the following code to log every e-mail it receives:

First letter

A = received in the A.M.

P = received in the P.M.

Four digits

First two digits = month (e.g., February = 02)

Second two digits = date (e.g., February 4 = 0204)

Four letters

First three letters = first three letters of sender's last name

Fourth letter = first letter of sender's first name

Thus, an e-mail received at 10:45 A.M. on October 18 from Henry Watson would be coded:

A1018WATH

13. At 1:38 P.M. on March 16, the office received an e-mail from Janet Dubois. The e-mail should be coded

a. 0138P0316JAND.

b. P0316JAND.

c. P316DUBJ.

d. P0316DUBJ.

14. At 11:57 A.M. on December 14, the office received an e-mail from Martin Anderson. The e-mail should be coded
  a. A1214ANDM.
  b. A1157ANDM.
  c. A1214MARA.
  d. A1157MARA.

15. The office received an e-mail from David Levitsky at 9:38 A.M. on June 1. The e-mail should be coded
  a. DAVLA0601.
  b. LEVDA0601.
  c. A0601LEVD.
  d. A0938LEVD.

16. On August 30, the office received an e-mail from Sharon Douglas at 2:15 P.M. The e-mail should be coded
  a. 0830SHADP.
  b. P0830DOUS.
  c. P0215DOUS.
  d. P0830SHAD.

17. The code A1105FARB could represent an e-mail sent by
  a. Andrew Farber.
  b. Farley Benson.
  c. Frank Arbuckle.
  d. Betty Farmer.

18. The code P0311JANA represents an e-mail that arrived
  a. at 3:11 P.M.
  b. on the afternoon of November 3.
  c. on the afternoon of March 11.
  d. on the afternoon of January 11.

19. Which of the following people might have sent the e-mail coded P1010ANDR?
  a. Rachel Anderson
  b. Parker Andrews
  c. Andrea Rivera
  d. Annette Dreiser

20. An e-mail arrives at 2:48 P.M. on November 3 from Lorraine Drew. An employee codes the e-mail P113DREL. What error does the code contain?
  a. The date is incorrectly coded.
  b. The sender's last name is incorrectly coded.
  c. The time of day at which the e-mail arrived is incorrectly coded.
  d. The employee recorded the time of arrival where the date of arrival should be recorded.

Answers

1. a. The customer's complaints may or may not be accurate; the only way to find out is to note and investigate them. You shouldn't figure that the customer is having a bad day, choice **b**, and you certainly shouldn't dismiss complaints without first determining whether they are accurate. You also shouldn't assume the complaints are accurate (choice **c**), because they may not be. Sending the complainant to another building (choice **d**), will probably make him angry, which is a big no-no.

2. d. Use process of elimination to get rid of incorrect answers. Giving a customer incorrect information (choice **a**) may get rid of him or her in the short term, but it almost guarantees that he or she will return, and when this person does, he or she will be angry because his or her time has been wasted. Instructing a customer to return to the line because you do not know the answer to his or her question (choice **b**) is unfair to the customer; this person is your responsibility, so you must find the answer for him or her. Three weeks is a long time to wait for resolution to a problem, choice **c**, and while such a wait may be appropriate in resolving compleproblems, it is not universally appropriate. Choices **a**, **b**, and **c** are all poor answers; the correct answer must be choice **d**. Indeed, the proper course of action is to find the answer to the customer's question, even if that requires you to get assistance from a coworker.

3. b. The best course of action is to assure the customer that the government has strict policies in place to safeguard her privacy. Suggesting that it is unlikely that her personal information will be compromised (choice **a**) indicates that it *might* be compromised and so is unlikely to satisfy the customer; in addition, it presumably contradicts government policies that ensure privacy. Citizens should be able to seek government services with confidence and should not be discouraged from seeking those services; thus, choice **c** is incorrect. An incomplete submission to a government agency will not be processed; therefore, choice **d** is poor advice.

4. d. Letters should be written in accordance with agency policy. They should be written in plain language, but that is not the same as writing a letter in an informal tone (choice **a**); letters should still assume a tone appropriate for business. The plain language policy mandates that letters include as few technical terms and acronyms as possible; therefore, choice **b** is incorrect. A letter may suggest that the customer use other channels for future queries but should not tell him or her to do so (choice **c**); if this person wishes to continue to correspond via postal mail, he or she should not be discouraged from doing so.

5. c. Three people are seen crossing the street in the photo.

6. a. The woman in the center of the photo closest to the viewer is wearing headphones that appear to be connected to a personal music device.

7. d. On the left-hand side of the photo, two people are in the corner of the photo, one partially hidden by a wall and the other crouched in front of the wall. One vehicle can be seen in the background moving in the direction opposite the train.

8. c. Three people are seen crossing the tracks, and two people are visible in the left-hand portion of the photo.

9. b. According to the flow chart, if the answer to the question "Pertains to open investigation?" is "Yes," then the document is to be filed in the short-term file.

10. c. Arrows point to the permanent file for documents that the government is "required by law to save" and documents that "relate to agency rulings."

11. c. The flow chart states that the agency should "review contents [of the short-term file] every 30 days."

12. a. According to the flow chart, e-mails are stored on a computer hard drive and backed up on a CD-ROM.

13. d. The first letter of a correct code must be A or P; this information allows you to eliminate choice **a**. The code for the date must be four digits long; this information allows you to eliminate choice **c**. The code for the name of the sender must start with the first three letters of the sender's last name (in this case, DUB); this information allows you to eliminate choice **b**. The correct answer must be choice **d** by process of elimination.

14. a. The four digits following A or P in the code represent the date on which the e-mail was sent (in this case, 1214), not the time at which it was sent (1157). Use this information to eliminate choices **b** and **d**. The code for the name of the sender must start with the first three letters of the sender's last name (in this case, AND); this information allows you to eliminate choice **c**. The correct answer must be choice **a** by process of elimination.

15. c. The first letter of a correct code must be A or P; this information allows you to eliminate choices **a** and **b**. The four digits following A or

P in the code represent the date on which the e-mail was sent (in this case, 0601), not the time at which it was sent (0938). Use this information to eliminate choice **d**. The correct answer must be choice **c** by process of elimination.

16. b. The first letter of a correct code must be A or P; this information allows you to eliminate choice **a**. The four digits following A or P in the code represent the date on which the e-mail was sent (in this case, 0830), not the time at which it was sent (0215). Use this information to eliminate choice **c**. The code for the name of the sender must start with the first three letters of the sender's last name (in this case, DOU); this information allows you to eliminate choice **d**. The correct answer must be choice **b** by process of elimination.

17. d. Look at the final four letters of the code. The first three (FAR) represent the first three letters of the sender's last name. This information allows you to eliminate choices **b** and **c**. The fourth letter (B) is the sender's first initial; use this information to eliminate choice **a**. The correct answer must be choice **d** by process of elimination.

18. c. The four numbers following A or P represent the date on which the e-mail was received. Thus, this e-mail was received on March 11 (03 = March, so 0311 = March 11).

19. a. Look at the final four letters of the code. The first three (AND) represent the first three letters of the sender's last name. This information allows you to eliminate choices **c** and **d**. The fourth letter (R) is the sender's first initial; use this information to eliminate choice **b**. The correct answer must be choice **a** by process of elimination.

20. a. The date must be recorded with a four-digit code; thus, it should be recorded 1103, not 113.

III ▶ PRACTICE EXERCISES

8 ▶ CIVIL SERVICE PRACTICE EXAM 1

T his is the first of three practice exams designed to prepare you for your civil service exam. As you read in Chapter 3, many state and local government jobs have a written exam as part of the selection process. The type of test varies greatly from job to job and from location to location, but most exams include at least some basic reading, writing, and sometimes math skills. The practice exams in this book also test spelling, vocabulary, grammar, civil service skills, memory, and coding.

The test that follows was created not to be identical to one particular civil service exam, but to allow you to practice the kinds of questions you may encounter on your exam. You can hone your skills in commonly tested areas by taking the practice exams and thoroughly reviewing the answers and explanations provided at the end of the chapter.

Civil Service Practice Exam 1

1.	ⓐ	ⓑ	ⓒ	ⓓ	36.	ⓐ	ⓑ	ⓒ	ⓓ	71.	ⓐ	ⓑ	ⓒ ⓓ
2.	ⓐ	ⓑ	ⓒ	ⓓ	37.	ⓐ	ⓑ	ⓒ	ⓓ	72.	ⓐ	ⓑ	ⓒ ⓓ
3.	ⓐ	ⓑ	ⓒ	ⓓ	38.	ⓐ	ⓑ	ⓒ	ⓓ	73.	ⓐ	ⓑ	ⓒ ⓓ
4.	ⓐ	ⓑ	ⓒ	ⓓ	39.	ⓐ	ⓑ	ⓒ	ⓓ	74.	ⓐ	ⓑ	ⓒ ⓓ
5.	ⓐ	ⓑ	ⓒ	ⓓ	40.	ⓐ	ⓑ	ⓒ	ⓓ	75.	ⓐ	ⓑ	ⓒ ⓓ
6.	ⓐ	ⓑ	ⓒ	ⓓ	41.	ⓐ	ⓑ	ⓒ	ⓓ	76.	ⓐ	ⓑ	ⓒ ⓓ
7.	ⓐ	ⓑ	ⓒ	ⓓ	42.	ⓐ	ⓑ	ⓒ	ⓓ	77.	ⓐ	ⓑ	ⓒ ⓓ
8.	ⓐ	ⓑ	ⓒ	ⓓ	43.	ⓐ	ⓑ	ⓒ	ⓓ	78.	ⓐ	ⓑ	ⓒ ⓓ
9.	ⓐ	ⓑ	ⓒ	ⓓ	44.	ⓐ	ⓑ	ⓒ	ⓓ	79.	ⓐ	ⓑ	ⓒ ⓓ
10.	ⓐ	ⓑ	ⓒ	ⓓ	45.	ⓐ	ⓑ	ⓒ	ⓓ	80.	ⓐ	ⓑ	ⓒ ⓓ
11.	ⓐ	ⓑ	ⓒ	ⓓ	46.	ⓐ	ⓑ	ⓒ	ⓓ	81.	ⓐ	ⓑ	ⓒ ⓓ
12.	ⓐ	ⓑ	ⓒ	ⓓ	47.	ⓐ	ⓑ	ⓒ	ⓓ	82.	ⓐ	ⓑ	ⓒ ⓓ
13.	ⓐ	ⓑ	ⓒ	ⓓ	48.	ⓐ	ⓑ	ⓒ	ⓓ	83.	ⓐ	ⓑ	ⓒ ⓓ
14.	ⓐ	ⓑ	ⓒ	ⓓ	49.	ⓐ	ⓑ	ⓒ	ⓓ	84.	ⓐ	ⓑ	ⓒ ⓓ
15.	ⓐ	ⓑ	ⓒ	ⓓ	50.	ⓐ	ⓑ	ⓒ	ⓓ	85.	ⓐ	ⓑ	ⓒ ⓓ
16.	ⓐ	ⓑ	ⓒ	ⓓ	51.	ⓐ	ⓑ	ⓒ	ⓓ	86.	ⓐ	ⓑ	ⓒ ⓓ
17.	ⓐ	ⓑ	ⓒ	ⓓ	52.	ⓐ	ⓑ	ⓒ	ⓓ	87.	ⓐ	ⓑ	ⓒ ⓓ
18.	ⓐ	ⓑ	ⓒ	ⓓ	53.	ⓐ	ⓑ	ⓒ	ⓓ	88.	ⓐ	ⓑ	ⓒ ⓓ
19.	ⓐ	ⓑ	ⓒ	ⓓ	54.	ⓐ	ⓑ	ⓒ	ⓓ	89.	ⓐ	ⓑ	ⓒ ⓓ
20.	ⓐ	ⓑ	ⓒ	ⓓ	55.	ⓐ	ⓑ	ⓒ	ⓓ	90.	ⓐ	ⓑ	ⓒ ⓓ
21.	ⓐ	ⓑ	ⓒ	ⓓ	56.	ⓐ	ⓑ	ⓒ	ⓓ	91.	ⓐ	ⓑ	ⓒ ⓓ
22.	ⓐ	ⓑ	ⓒ	ⓓ	57.	ⓐ	ⓑ	ⓒ	ⓓ	92.	ⓐ	ⓑ	ⓒ ⓓ
23.	ⓐ	ⓑ	ⓒ	ⓓ	58.	ⓐ	ⓑ	ⓒ	ⓓ	93.	ⓐ	ⓑ	ⓒ ⓓ
24.	ⓐ	ⓑ	ⓒ	ⓓ	59.	ⓐ	ⓑ	ⓒ	ⓓ	94.	ⓐ	ⓑ	ⓒ ⓓ
25.	ⓐ	ⓑ	ⓒ	ⓓ	60.	ⓐ	ⓑ	ⓒ	ⓓ	95.	ⓐ	ⓑ	ⓒ ⓓ
26.	ⓐ	ⓑ	ⓒ	ⓓ	61.	ⓐ	ⓑ	ⓒ	ⓓ	96.	ⓐ	ⓑ	ⓒ ⓓ
27.	ⓐ	ⓑ	ⓒ	ⓓ	62.	ⓐ	ⓑ	ⓒ	ⓓ	97.	ⓐ	ⓑ	ⓒ ⓓ
28.	ⓐ	ⓑ	ⓒ	ⓓ	63.	ⓐ	ⓑ	ⓒ	ⓓ	98.	ⓐ	ⓑ	ⓒ ⓓ
29.	ⓐ	ⓑ	ⓒ	ⓓ	64.	ⓐ	ⓑ	ⓒ	ⓓ	99.	ⓐ	ⓑ	ⓒ ⓓ
30.	ⓐ	ⓑ	ⓒ	ⓓ	65.	ⓐ	ⓑ	ⓒ	ⓓ	100.	ⓐ	ⓑ	ⓒ ⓓ
31.	ⓐ	ⓑ	ⓒ	ⓓ	66.	ⓐ	ⓑ	ⓒ	ⓓ				
32.	ⓐ	ⓑ	ⓒ	ⓓ	67.	ⓐ	ⓑ	ⓒ	ⓓ				
33.	ⓐ	ⓑ	ⓒ	ⓓ	68.	ⓐ	ⓑ	ⓒ	ⓓ				
34.	ⓐ	ⓑ	ⓒ	ⓓ	69.	ⓐ	ⓑ	ⓒ	ⓓ				
35.	ⓐ	ⓑ	ⓒ	ⓓ	70.	ⓐ	ⓑ	ⓒ	ⓓ				

Section 1: Mathematics

Select the best choice for each question.

1. *The Daily Newspaper* asked its 16 salespeople to divide into four sales teams for a competition. Team Hurricane, with Barb, Peter, Boris, and Jason won the competition by selling 1,500 subscriptions. Barb was responsible for 20% of the subscription sales, Peter sold 325 subscriptions, and Boris sold $\frac{7}{5}$ of what Peter sold. How many subscriptions must Jason have sold?
   a. 275
   b. 420
   c. 455
   d. 1,355

2. A stock begins the day at the price $28\frac{3}{8}$ and ends the day at the price $26\frac{3}{4}$. Which choice best describes the change in the stock's price?
   a. The stock lost exactly $1 in value.
   b. The stock lost exactly $1\frac{1}{4}$ in value.
   c. The stock lost exactly $1\frac{5}{8}$ in value.
   d. The stock gained $1\frac{1}{2}$ in value.

3. Find the percent equivalent of $\frac{18}{25}$.
   a. 18%
   b. 43%
   c. 7%
   d. 72%

4. Jeanette went shopping with $100 and returned home with only $18.42. How much money did she spend?
   a. $81.58
   b. $72.68
   c. $72.58
   d. $71.68

5. Lynn was moving and decided to sell $\frac{3}{5}$ of her CD collection. Her neighbor Jim bought $\frac{1}{3}$ of the CDs on sale. What fraction of Lynn's original CD collection did Jim purchase?
   a. $\frac{1}{5}$
   b. $\frac{4}{15}$
   c. $\frac{1}{3}$
   d. $\frac{4}{5}$

6. $\frac{1}{2} + 4\frac{3}{4} + 2\frac{5}{6} =$
   a. $7\frac{3}{4}$
   b. $8\frac{1}{12}$
   c. $1\frac{1}{4}$
   d. $6\frac{3}{4}$

7. Harold wishes to leave a 15% tip for a restaurant meal. If the meal cost $16.80, how much money should Harold leave for the tip?
   a. $2.52
   b. $2.40
   c. $1.68
   d. $1.50

8. $8\frac{1}{5} =$
   a. $\frac{81}{5}$
   b. $\frac{5}{81}$
   c. $\frac{13}{5}$
   d. $\frac{41}{5}$

9. $7\frac{1}{10} - 5\frac{2}{3} =$
   a. $2\frac{1}{3}$
   b. $1\frac{13}{30}$
   c. $1\frac{2}{13}$
   d. $2\frac{2}{7}$

10. A farmer plants 75 rows of cabbage. Each row contains 40 cabbages. How many cabbages does the farmer plant?

a. 115

b. 1,150

c. 1,500

d. 3,000

Study the following graph, and then use it to answer questions 11 to 13.

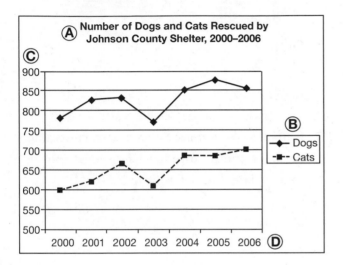

11. Which letter corresponds to the legend of the graph?

a. A

b. B

c. C

d. D

12. Which letter corresponds to the *y*-axis of the graph?

a. A

b. B

c. C

d. D

13. Which letter corresponds to the title of the graph?

a. A

b. B

c. C

d. D

14. A help line receives calls from people with legal questions. The automated voice service can handle simple calls, while challenging calls are directed to a live operator. Challenging calls account for $\frac{3}{5}$ of total calls, and among the challenging calls, 25% require a specialist. How many calls require a specialist on a day when there are 60 total calls?

a. 9

b. 15

c. 21

d. 27

15. Mr. Stone commutes 15 miles from home to work. After driving $\frac{2}{5}$ of the way from home to work, Mr. Stone stops to buy some breakfast. How far is Mr. Stone from work when he stops for breakfast?

a. $14\frac{3}{5}$ miles

b. 6 miles

c. 4 miles

d. 9 miles

16. $14 \div \frac{3}{4} =$

a. $18\frac{2}{3}$

b. $10\frac{1}{2}$

c. $13\frac{1}{4}$

d. $20\frac{1}{4}$

17. What is the decimal equivalent of $\frac{7}{8}$?
   a. 0.75
   b. 0.78
   c. 0.875
   d. 0.888

18. Three teaspoons of water equal 1 tablespoon of water; 2 tablespoons of water equal 1 ounce of water. How many teaspoons of water are there in a pint of water (1 pint = 16 ounces)?
   a. 23 teaspoons
   b. 32 teaspoons
   c. 96 teaspoons
   d. 192 teaspoons

Study the following table, and then use it to answer questions 19 and 20.

AVERAGE LIFE SPAN AND WEIGHT OF DOGS, BY BREED		
BREED	**AVERAGE LIFE SPAN IN YEARS**	**AVERAGE WEIGHT IN POUNDS**
Jack Russell Terrier	13.6	15
Chihuahua	13	5
Corgi	11.2	25
Weimaraner	10	75
Rhodesian Ridgeback	9.1	80
Great Dane	8.4	160

19. The range of weights shown in the table is
   a. 160 pounds.
   b. 145 pounds.
   c. 80 pounds.
   d. 155 pounds.

20. Which of the following conclusions is best supported by the data in the table?
   a. Small dogs tend to live longer than large dogs.
   b. No dog has ever lived past the age of 15.
   c. A chihuahua is an excellent house pet.
   d. A great dane weighs more than most humans.

21. During a sale, the price of a suit is reduced by 30%. If the suit sold for $350 before the sale, what is the sale price of the suit?
   a. $105
   b. $175
   c. $245
   d. $320

22. Fred burns 60 calories a mile when he walks. How many miles must Fred walk to burn 400 calories?
   a. $1\frac{1}{2}$ miles
   b. 6 miles
   c. $6\frac{1}{3}$ miles
   d. $6\frac{2}{3}$ miles

23. $\frac{12}{9} =$
   a. $1\frac{1}{3}$
   b. $\frac{3}{4}$
   c. $12\frac{1}{3}$
   d. $1\frac{1}{9}$

24. Reduce $\frac{42}{51}$ to lowest terms.
   a. $\frac{4}{5}$
   b. $\frac{14}{17}$
   c. $\frac{21}{25}$
   d. $\frac{1}{9}$

25. A community survey asked voters if they would or would not support the building of a new school. All respondents answered that either they would or would not. It was discovered that a total of 40% of respondents would support the building of a new school. If 12,800 people responded that they would support the building of a new school, how many total people responded to this survey?

a. 17,920
b. 19,200
c. 30,500
d. 32,000

Study the following graph, and then use it to answer questions 26 and 27.

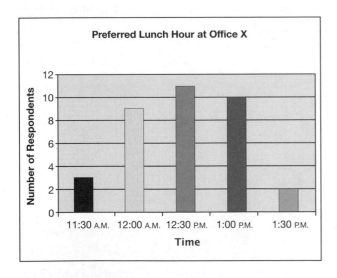

26. The workers at Office X were asked to choose their preferred time to start their lunch hour. The results of the survey are shown in the graph above. How many workers responded to the survey?

a. 11
b. 21
c. 35
d. 50

27. What is the range of the data shown?

a. 9
b. 10
c. 11
d. 35

28. Heather worked an eight hour day. She discovered that $\frac{6}{15}$ of her time was spent reviewing reports. How many minutes did she spend reviewing reports?

a. 180 minutes
b. 192 minutes
c. 240 minutes
d. 288 minutes

29. Linda walks 15 miles in 4 hours. What is Linda's average speed during her walk?

a. 3 miles per hour
b. 3.5 miles per hour
c. 3.75 miles per hour
d. 4 miles per hour

30. Three of every 25 customers at a grocery store pays for his or her groceries with a check. What percentage of the customers pay for groceries with a check?

a. 3%
b. 12%
c. 28%
d. 75%

31. New office filing cabinets can hold a maximum of $8\frac{1}{4}$ training manuals. Which of the following equals $8\frac{1}{4}$ training manuals?

a. $\frac{1}{8}$ training manuals?
b. $\frac{8}{4}$ training manuals
c. $\frac{33}{4}$ training manuals
d. 16 training manuals

Study the following graph, and then use it to answer questions 32 and 33.

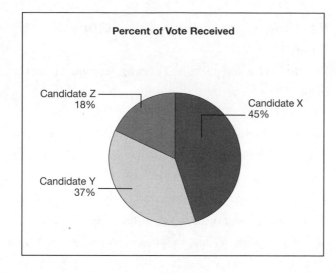

Percent of Vote Received

Candidate Z 18%

Candidate X 45%

Candidate Y 37%

32. The pie graph supports which of the following conclusions?

    a. More than 50% of eligible voters participated in the election.

    b. Two candidates each received more than 40% of the vote.

    c. Candidate X received the greatest number of votes.

    d. Voters would have preferred to vote for Candidate W, but she was not running.

33. If 600 voters voted in the election, how many votes did Candidate Z receive?

    a. 60

    b. 108

    c. 222

    d. 260

34. A ream of paper weighs $5\frac{2}{5}$ pounds. Sturdy Paper Company sells reams of paper by the box. If each box contains 8 reams, how much does one of these boxes weigh?

    a. $40\frac{2}{5}$ pounds

    b. $40\frac{8}{5}$ pounds

    c. $43\frac{1}{5}$ pounds

    d. $43\frac{2}{5}$ pounds

35. Of 300 consumers polled, 180 reported that they purchase household cleaning products at least once per week. Based on these results, approximately how many consumers out of 1,000 could be expected to buy household cleaning products at least once per week?

    a. 480

    b. 600

    c. 720

    d. 880

36. $\frac{7}{10} \times 2\frac{1}{5} =$

    a. $\frac{49}{50}$

    b. $1\frac{3}{5}$

    c. $\frac{7}{50}$

    d. $1\frac{11}{25}$

37. In 2009, a certain government agency employed 1,660 people. In 2010, the number of employees at the agency decreased by 15% and no additional employees were hired. How many people were employed by the agency in 2010?

    a. 1,367

    b. 1,395

    c. 1,411

    d. 1,645

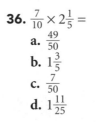

38. An airplane flight takes exactly 4 hours to complete. If the airplane travels at an average speed of 480 miles per hour, how many miles long is the flight?

   a. 1,920 miles
   b. 2,000 miles
   c. 2,080 miles
   d. 2,400 miles

Study the following table, and then use it to answer questions 39 and 40.

PRICE OF LEADING DVD PLAYERS	
Ultrabo4000	$89
Vizzione MR-1	$74.50
Clara 718	$95
Abomino 1	$61.50

39. What is the average (arithmetic mean) price of the leading DVD players?

   a. $61.50
   b. $76.00
   c. $80.00
   d. $95.00

40. What is the range of prices shown in the table?

   a. $28.50
   b. $27.50
   c. $32.50
   d. $33.50

Section 2: Written Communication

Reading Comprehension—Questions 41–60

Read the following passage. Then, answer questions 41 to 44.

We generally think of libraries as publicly managed facilities offering books on a wide range of subjects, but, in fact, public libraries are only one highly visible facet of the library universe. Many offices—including many government offices—maintain large collections of reference materials, historical documents, and other relevant resources. In other words, such offices maintain libraries.

Any sizeable library collection must be organized in order to be useful. Librarians may organize a collection in any way they choose, but they generally choose between two options: the Dewey decimal classification system, which assigns a number between 000 and 999 to books based on their subject matter; and the Library of Congress classification system, which assigns an initial letter to books based on subject matter.

What are the differences between the two systems? The Dewey decimal system contains fewer subject classifications, with only ten general subject categories as opposed to the Library of Congress's 21. The latter system not only uses more general subject categories, but also subdivides each category into more, and more specific, subcategories. In the area of specificity, it is generally agreed that the Library of Congress system is more efficient.

When it comes to ease of use, however, the Dewey decimal system is typically the favorite. Users searching for books about dogs, for example, almost always find it easier to remember the Dewey code for such books (636) than the Library of Congress code (SF427). Furthermore, there is an internal logic to the entire Dewey system; the principles of code assignment are consistent throughout all ten subjects. Each Library of Congress subject category, on the other hand, was developed independently of the others, so each follows its own unique set of rules.

The differences between the two systems means that they are suited to <u>diverse</u> purposes. Ease of use makes the Dewey decimal system the system of choice for general public-use libraries. Research institutions, archives, and government agencies cataloging a great deal of highly specific or technical material, on the other hand, tend to prefer the Library of Congress system.

41. Which sentence best summarizes the main idea of the passage?
   a. The Library of Congress classification system is better than the Dewey decimal classification system.
   b. The differences between two cataloging systems makes each more appropriate for a particular purpose.
   c. More libraries should consider cataloging their collections alphabetically by the authors' last names, without regard to subject matter.
   d. There is an urgent need for librarians to develop a new classification system, because the two most common systems are deeply flawed.

42. In the passage, the word *diverse* is closest in meaning to
   a. unlike.
   b. unimportant.
   c. scientific.
   d. illogical.

43. The passage supports which of the following conclusions?
   a. Libraries that use the Dewey system typically contain more books about dogs than do libraries that use the Library of Congress system.
   b. Libraries must pay a licensing fee to use either the Dewey or the Library of Congress system, so they typically choose whichever system is cheaper.
   c. The Library of Congress system is more difficult to memorize than is the Dewey system.
   d. Books with certain subjects cannot be classified within the Dewey system because the system makes no place for them.

44. According to the passage, in comparison to the Dewey decimal system, the Library of Congress system is
   a. appropriate only to collections owned by the U.S. Congress.
   b. more likely to be used by public libraries.
   c. easier for casual library users to master.
   d. more specific in its categorization of books.

Read the following passage. Then, answer questions 45 to 48.

Throughout the years, many professions have realized the importance of a college education as a prerequisite to employment, but this has not necessarily been true of U.S. police departments. For police, an educational requirement as a prerequisite for employment or promotion has been a topic of considerable controversy, dating back to the 1900s. One hundred years later, there still does not appear to be an agreement among police professionals as to whether the benefits of requiring higher educational standards outweigh the costs. Previous research findings have pointed to the beneficial effects of higher education on policing. Education correlates with a <u>myriad</u> of favorable factors including less authoritarian attitudes, fewer citizen complaints, more mature candidates, a greater understanding of constitutional rights, greater empathy for minorities and the effects of racial discrimination, greater understanding of diverse cultural values, and better communication skills. Police officers are often required to make difficult decisions, and they face ethical challenges throughout their careers. Research shows that higher education is positively related to sound ethical and moral decision making. College requires a commitment of time, effort, money, and motivation, but often results in many positive outcomes. If police departments do not recognize this, they risk losing potentially valuable college educated officers. Based on extant research, it appears that a college educated officer is a more effective officer.

45. Which of the following would be the best title for this passage?
   a. *Professionalizing the Police: Is Effectiveness Achieved Through Education?*
   b. *Losing College-Educated Officers: A Tragedy for U.S. Police Departments*
   c. *Strained Relationships: How to Improve Community and Police Relations*
   d. *College and the Preservation of Constitutional Rights*

46. According to this passage, education benefits police in all of the following ways EXCEPT
   a. fewer citizen complaints.
   b. better ethical decision making.
   c. better understanding of diverse values.
   d. more authoritarian attitudes.

47. According to this passage, what topic remains controversial?
   a. teaching officers to respect the rights of minority citizens
   b. ensuring that officers make sound moral decisions
   c. requiring college credits for police applicants
   d. helping officers to communicate more effectively

48. As used in the passage, the word *myriad* is closest in meaning to
   a. a bad decision.
   b. a rare condition.
   c. almost none.
   d. a great number.

Read the following passage. Then, answer questions 49 to 52.

Some scholars believe that all roads in American criminology eventually lead to issues of race. Some available statistics show that African-Americans are disproportionately represented at every point in the criminal justice system. Considering the impact of the criminal justice system on minorities, the issue of race and crime is clearly integral to the study of criminal justice. Surprisingly, given the importance of race and ethnicity, criminal justice educators have often been reluctant to confront the issue directly. Some go so far as to declare that race has been virtually ignored in the area of criminal justice education. It would appear then that it is the responsibility of criminal justice educators to build a foundation of knowledge that integrates diverse multicultural perspectives.

Previous research examining race and crime education focused on undergraduate teaching. One survey of introductory criminal justice textbooks found that issues of race and ethnicity received inadequate coverage. Moreover, when African-American doctoral students were asked, 50% said that they regarded their professors as insensitive to issues of race; at the same time, 25% of white students described their professors as insensitive to issues of race. Furthermore, while it is widely recognized that race and ethnicity must be incorporated into any effective criminal justice or criminology program, there is no consensus on the best method to do so. Some scholars suggest that a segment of the core knowledge must involve a multicultural perspective, while others emphasize the importance of recognizing the work of African-American scholars, and note how their work has been historically ignored by the mainstream.

49. What is the primary purpose of this passage?
    a. to review how race is presented in criminal justice textbooks
    b. to establish the extent to which race and ethnicity are taught to students
    c. to argue that the work of African-American scholars should be studied by students
    d. to teach students about how race and ethnicity should be taught

50. According to the passage, who believes that teaching race and ethnicity to criminal justice students is important?
    a. the police
    b. students
    c. some scholars
    d. doctoral students

51. According to the passage, why is race and ethnicity ignored by criminal justice scholars?
    a. The topic is omitted from textbooks.
    b. Some teachers are reluctant to discuss the topic.
    c. Some students are not interested in the topic.
    d. Doctoral students do not believe the topic is important to their teachers.

52. According to the passage, why is it important to study issues of race and ethnicity?
    a. Racial differences appear at each stage of the criminal justice system.
    b. African-American scholars believe the topic has been ignored.
    c. Undergraduate students have asked for it to be taught.
    d. Criminal justice educators believe it may be important.

Read the following passage. Then, answer questions 53 to 56.

The political activity of federal employees presents policy makers with a double-edged sword of a problem. On one hand, the integrity of the federal government requires that employees not pursue personal political goals through their offices; therefore, some restrictions on the political activities of federal employees seem <u>prudent</u> and even necessary. On the other hand, individual liberty and the right to participate in the political process are two bedrock principles of American government. Surely we cannot deny our government's employees rights so fundamental to the nation's identity.

Government leaders have been visiting and revisiting this question since the beginning of the republic. Thomas Jefferson issued an executive circular in 1801 advising federal employees to abstain from campaigning and electioneering. The Pendleton Act of 1883, which created a merit-based system for awarding civil service jobs, further codified proscribed political behavior.

These measures were deemed inadequate to check political coercion and patronage in the 1930s, when the massive expansion of the federal government created many new opportunities for the abuse of power. In response, Congress passed the Hatch Act of 1939, which prohibited a wide range of political activities by federal employees. The law made it illegal for federal civil servants to endorse candidates, seek political contributions, or run for office with the endorsement of a political party. Not all political activity was forbidden; Hatch allowed federal employees to vote, discuss politics privately, and contribute money to political parties.

The constitutionality of the Hatch Act has been challenged several times, with two such cases reaching the Supreme Court; in both instances, the court ruled that the Hatch Act was indeed constitutional. Nonetheless, discontent ultimately led to a 1993 amendment that allowed federal employees to participate in elections so long as their activity occurred outside their place of work. At the same time, the amendment increased penalties for those who abused the powers of their offices for political gain. At the signing ceremony, President Bill Clinton observed that "People who devote their lives to public service should not be denied the right to participate more fully in the democratic process. This law moves us in a more sensible direction."

53. As used in the passage, the word *prudent* is closest in meaning to
    a. optional.
    b. ill-advised.
    c. sensible.
    d. counterproductive.

54. The author's main purpose in writing this passage is to
    a. report the historical developments of a particular issue in American government.
    b. argue that the 1993 amendment to the Hatch Act had a destructive impact on good governance in the United States.
    c. describe the conditions under which the Hatch Act of 1939 was passed.
    d. propose the repeal of both the Pendleton Act of 1883 and the Hatch Act of 1939.

55. According to the passage, Thomas Jefferson did which of the following?
    a. oversaw the massive expansion of the federal government
    b. suggested to federal employees that they refrain from public politics
    c. signed an amendment to the Hatch Act
    d. endorsed the Pendleton Act

56. The passage supports which of the following conclusions?

   a. Under the Hatch Act, federal employees were prohibited from engaging in all political activity, including voting.

   b. Thomas Jefferson believed that there was no conflict in holding a federal office and engaging in such political activity as campaigning for candidates.

   c. The amendment to the Hatch Act aimed to preserve integrity in government while freeing federal employees to become more politically active as private citizens.

   d. Under the Hatch Act, federal employees could actively promote political parties but not individual candidates.

Read the following passage. Then, answer questions 57 to 60.

Community policing has frequently been touted as the best way to reform urban law enforcement. The idea of putting more officers on foot patrol in high crime areas, where relations with the police have frequently been strained, was most famously implemented in Houston in 1983 under then-Commissioner Lee Brown. Brown believed that officers should be accessible to the community at the street level. If officers were assigned to the same area over a period of time, those officers would eventually build a network of trust with neighborhood residents. As a result, merchants and residents in the community would be more likely to inform officers about criminal activities in the area and support police intervention.

Since Brown's <u>initiative</u>, many large cities have experimented with community-oriented policing services (COPS), with somewhat mixed results. Some have found that police and citizens are grateful for the opportunity to work together. Others have found that unrealistic expectations by citizens and resistance from officers have combined to hinder the effectiveness of COPS.

Overall, however, the verdict on community policing is positive, as the concept has evidently yielded notable successes. Since the federal government began funding COPS programs, national crime rates have declined measurably. Although this drop in crime rates has occurred nationwide (including areas that receive no federal assistance), the drops have been more pronounced in those locations that receive substantial COPS funding.

Unfortunately, stress on the federal budget in the post–9/11 era has resulted in a sharp decrease in federal assistance to local police. This decrease comes at a time when the federal government is expecting local law enforcement to contribute more to the national fight against terror, further increasing the strain on state and city government law enforcement budgets. As a result, many have had to reduce or even eliminate their COPS programs. The debate over the effectiveness of COPS programs might once and for all be settled as a result; if crime rates increase as COPS programs disappear, that would certainly provide a strong indicator that the programs are effective in reducing crime.

57. Which of the following best summarizes the main idea of the passage?

   a. Opponents of community policing correctly argue that such programs cause more problems than they solve.

   b. Community policing is a promising concept, but implementation of effective community policing programs faces several problems.

   c. Many local police forces lack the funding necessary to support community policing programs.

   d. Lee Brown is an innovative law enforcement leader whose talents should be utilized by the federal government.

58. As used in the passage, the word *initiative* most nearly means
   a. misfortune.
   b. blunder.
   c. victory.
   d. decision.

59. In paragraph 3, the author suggests that
   a. community policing programs have helped to reduce crime rates.
   b. community policing programs have had no effect on crime rates.
   c. community policing programs have resulted in an increase in crime rates.
   d. the government does not accurately track crime rates, making it impossible to determine the effectiveness of community policing programs.

60. According to Commissioner Brown, community policing is effective because
   a. criminals are less likely to commit crimes if they are familiar with their local police officers.
   b. community policing emphasizes the need for street patrols late at night, the time at which most crimes occur.
   c. community policing deputizes members of the community, allowing them to make arrests without an actual police officer present.
   d. citizens are more likely to cooperate with police if they have a closer relationship with local officers.

Spelling—Questions 61 to 65
Select the choice that is spelled correctly.

61. The shopkeeper was known for selling the best _____ in town.
   a. merchandise
   b. merchendise
   c. merchindise

62. The carpenter tied a red _____ around her forehead to keep the sweat out of her eyes.
   a. bandanner
   b. banndana
   c. bandanna

63. Jim's outburst was not planned; on the contrary, it was entirely _____.
   a. spontaneous
   b. spontainious
   c. spontaineus

64. Which of the following words is spelled incorrectly?
   a. frivolous
   b. embelish
   c. confound

65. Which of the following words is spelled incorrectly?
   a. lunar
   b. scapegoat
   c. retalliate

Vocabulary—Questions 66 to 70

Select the best answer for each question.

66. Find the word that is closest in meaning to the underlined word below.
    attest to the truth
    a. contradict
    b. verify
    c. inquire

67. Find the word that is closest in meaning to the underlined word below.
    a consumate performer
    a. expert
    b. novice
    c. strange

68. Find the word that is most nearly the opposite of the word below.
    the virtuoso musician
    a. amateur
    b. experimental
    c. unpopular

69. Find the word that best completes the sentence below.
    The _____ window shades kept the hotel room nice and dark well into the late morning.
    a. malfunctioning
    b. flimsy
    c. opaque

70. Find the word that best completes the sentence below.
    Minimum wage is poor _____ for a fry cook's hard work.
    a. reprisal
    b. retribution
    c. remuneration

Grammar—Questions 71 to 80

Select the best answer for each question.

71. Which of the following is a complete sentence?
    a. The onset of the cold war, having been brought on by natural tensions between the communist and free worlds and the end of World War II.
    b. Natural tensions between the communist and free worlds, the end of World War II, bringing on the onset of the cold war.
    c. The onset of the cold war was brought on by natural tensions between the communist and free worlds and the end of World War II.

72. Select the sentence that is written most correctly.
    a. Genetically modified to increase yield and reduce disease, many consumers do not trust crops developed recently by agricultural scientists.
    b. Genetically modified to increase yield and reduce disease, crops developed recently by agricultural scientists are distrusted by many consumers.
    c. Crops developed recently by agricultural scientists have been genetically modified to increase yield and reduce disease that consumers do not trust.

73. Select the sentence that is written most correctly.
  a. Last Thursday, my Mother, my Aunt Barbara, and I went to the museum to see an exhibit of African art.
  b. Last Thursday, my mother, my Aunt Barbara, and I went to the museum to see an exhibit of African art.
  c. Last Thursday, my mother, my aunt Barbara, and I went to the Museum to see an exhibit of african art.

74. Select the sentence that is written most correctly.
  a. The Band we saw last night consisted of two guitarists, a bass player, a drummer a keyboardist and two percussionists.
  b. The band we saw last night consisted of two, guitarists, a bass player, a drummer, a keyboardist, and, two percussionists.
  c. The band we saw last night consisted of two guitarists, a bass player, a drummer, a keyboardist, and two percussionists.

75. Select the sentence that is written most correctly.
  a. The perpetrator was stopped by the police officer, and he struck him with a stick.
  b. The perpetrator, striking him with a stick, was stopped by the police officer.
  c. The police officer stopped the perpetrator, who then struck the officer with a stick.

76. Select the sentence that is written most correctly.
  a. Billy wasn't going to join us at the park, but he couldn't refuse the invitation after I told him there is a basketball court there.
  b. Billy was'nt going to join us at the park, but he could'nt refuse the invitation after I told him there is a basketball court there.
  c. Billy wasnt going to join us at the park, but he couldnt refuse the invitation after I told him there is a basketball court there.

77. Select the sentence that is written most correctly.
  a. Make sure that everyone in the office have turned off their desk lights before leaving for the day.
  b. Make sure that everyone in the office has turned off his or her desk light before leaving for the day.
  c. Make sure that everyone in the office has turned off their desk lights before leaving for the day.

78. Select the sentence that is written most correctly.
  a. The benefits of this therapy far outweigh its potential drawbacks.
  b. The positive benefits of this therapy far outweigh its potentially negative drawbacks.
  c. The benefits of this therapy far outweigh their potentially negative drawbacks.

79. Select the sentence that is written most correctly.
   a. After completing the obstacle course Renee proceeded to the shooting range.
   b. After completing the obstacle course, Renee proceeded to the shooting range.
   c. After completing the obstacle course, Renee proceeded, to the shooting range.

80. Select the sentence that is written most correctly.
   a. David asked me "whether I wanted to attend the baseball game with him tonight?"
   b. David asked me "whether I wanted to attend the baseball game with him tonight."
   c. David asked me whether I wanted to attend the baseball game with him tonight.

Section 3: Civil Service Skills

Customer Service— Questions 81 to 85
Select the best answer for each question.

81. Records of an office's prior contacts with a customer should be maintained in order to
   a. document the amount of work done by the office so that staffing will not be reduced.
   b. make sure that no one customer overuses the office's facilities and services.
   c. minimize the need for the customer to provide the same basic information (e.g., address, Social Security number) repeatedly.
   d. prevent customers from asking for and receiving services that have already been provided.

82. When one is creating a recorded message to be heard by customers calling a government agency after hours of operation, which of the following pieces of information is least important?
   a. the agency's hours of operation
   b. the street address of the agency
   c. instructions on how to access the agency's website
   d. instructions on how to leave a message

83. An agency's phone system offers the capacity for audio during a customer's hold time. The agency would be best served to use this capacity to provide
a. music to entertain customers while they are waiting.
b. live programming from a local talk-radio station.
c. live audio, transmitted via speaker phone, of the office with which they are waiting to speak.
d. a recorded message providing choices to commonly asked questions.

84. The term *abandonment rate* refers to the
a. frequency with which customers calling an office hang up before reaching a representative.
b. number of times a customer must contact an office before receiving final resolution to an inquiry.
c. average amount of time a customer visiting an office must wait on a service line before speaking with a representative.
d. speed at which a government agent can redirect a telephone inquiry to the appropriate recipient.

85. An agency serving walk-in customers should consider offering appointments whenever
a. customers cannot begin resolving their inquiry upon arrival.
b. average wait times for customers exceed one hour.
c. average wait times for customers exceed 15 minutes.
d. such a policy would result in fewer visitors to the agency's office.

Memory—Questions 86 to 90

Take five minutes to study the following picture. Then, answer questions 86 to 87 without looking back at the picture.

86. The number of destinations other than Broadway Station that are shown in the photo is

a. one.

b. two.

c. three.

d. zero; no other destinations are shown in the photo.

87. Based on the directional arrows on the signage at Broadway Station, a rail rider could correctly assume that the train will be heading _____ from Broadway Station to Union Station.

a. south

b. north

c. east

d. west

Take five minutes to study the following text. Then, answer questions 88 through 90 without looking back at the text.

A city is divided into five sectors. In each sector, garbage is collected twice a week and recycling is scheduled once a week, according to the schedule that follows:

SECTOR	GARBAGE	RECYCLING
1	Monday, Thursday	Friday
2	Tuesday, Saturday	Wednesday
3	Wednesday, Saturday	Thursday
4	Tuesday, Friday	Saturday
5	Monday, Friday	Tuesday

88. Recycling is collected in sector 2 on

    a. Monday.

    b. Tuesday.

    c. Wednesday.

    d. Saturday.

89. Garbage is collected Monday through Saturday. On which day is recycling NOT collected?

    a. Monday

    b. Wednesday

    c. Friday

    d. Saturday

90. In three of five sectors, the second garbage collection of the week occurs exactly three days after the first. In which two sectors is this NOT the case?

    a. 1 and 2

    b. 1 and 4

    c. 2 and 5

    d. 3 and 4

Coding—Questions 91 to 100

To answer questions 91 through 95, refer to the following scenario.

A municipal agency uses a code to log each visitor to its office. Each code is five characters long and is assigned according to the rules that follow. Each code is preceded by the time of the visit (format: 10:00 A.M.).

Gender

M = Male

F = Female

Citizenship

C = Citizen

N = Noncitizen

Age

1 – under age 18

2 – age 18 to 30

3 – age 31 to 65

4 – over age 65

Residence

V = northeast quadrant of city

W = southeast quadrant of city

X = northwest quadrant of city

Y = southwest quadrant of city

Z = outside the city

Purpose of Visit

5 = responding to summons

6 = filing complaint

7 = applying for employment

8 = other

91. A male citizen, age 38, who resides in the north-west quadrant of the city visits the office at 11:46 A.M. to file a complaint. How should this visit be coded?
    a. MC3X6
    b. MC38 11:46 A.M. X6
    c. 11:46 A.M. MC3X6
    d. MC 11:46 A.M. V6

92. A female citizen, age 67, who resides outside the city visits the office at 4:00 P.M. to solicit charitable contributions from employees. How should this visit be coded?
    a. FC67Z 4:00 P.M.8
    b. FC67X8 4:00 P.M.
    c. 4:00 P.M. FC67Z8
    d. 4:00 P.M. FC4Z8

93. A male noncitizen who resides in the southeast quadrant of the city visits the office at 10:45 A.M. to respond to a summons. He is 16 years old. How should the visit be coded?
    a. 10:45 A.M. MN1W5
    b. 10:45 A.M. MC1Z8
    c. MNW 11:45 A.M. 168
    d. MNW168 11:45 A.M.

94. Which of the following describes the visitor whose visit was coded 12:00 P.M. FC3Y6?
    a. The visitor was a noncitizen residing in the southwest quadrant of the city.
    b. The visitor was a female who filed a complaint.
    c. The visitor was a male citizen over the age of 65.
    d. The visitor was a female under the age of 18.

95. The visitor whose visit was coded 9:10 A.M. MC2Z7 visited the office in order to
    a. respond to a summons.
    b. file a complaint.
    c. apply for employment.
    d. none of the above

To answer questions 96 through 100, refer to the following scenario.

A state assigns numbers to the fishing licenses it issues using the following code:

2 letters = first two letters of county of residence
8 digits = license recipient's date of birth (e.g., September 30, 1957 = 09301957)
2 letters = license recipient's initials (e.g., Robert Sims = RS)
2 digits = license recipient's height in inches (rounded to nearest whole number)
3 letters = randomly assigned

96. Danielle Valenzuela receives a fishing license. She resides in Ardmore County and is 62 inches tall. Her date of birth is May 11, 1973. Which of the following could be her fishing license number?
    a. AR05111973DV62
    b. DV05111973AR62MPY
    c. DV051173AR62
    d. AR05111973DV62XLE

97. Milton Mazur, a resident of Hazelton County, receives a fishing license. His date of birth is December 7, 1948. He is 70.4 inches tall. Which of the following could be his fishing license number?
    a. HA12071948MM70EEE
    b. HA12071948MM70.4WQA
    c. MM12071948HA70LBD
    d. MMHC120714870.4

98. Jerome Fielding, a resident of Buncomb County, is 75 inches tall. His date of birth is August 26, 1980. The number assigned to his license, BU26081980JF75RBC, is incorrectly assigned. What error does his license number contain?

a. His height was incorrectly recorded.

b. His height and date of birth have been transposed.

c. The three randomly assigned letters have been omitted.

d. His date of birth is incorrectly recorded.

99. A fishing license with the number TR11151938WE72DVA could belong to an individual named

a. Toni Rouse.

b. Warren Evers.

c. David Van Allen.

d. Victoria Andrews.

100. A fishing license with the number LA08081967MU66ABO belongs to someone

a. born in 1967.

b. born in 1966.

c. who lives in Munroe County.

d. named Linda Almonte.

Civil Service Practice Exam 1 Answers

Section 1: Mathematics

1. b. To answer this question, you must first determine how many subscriptions were sold by Barb, Peter, and Boris, and then take the sum of those subscriptions and subtract it from the total of 1,500 to determine how many Jason sold. Barb sold 20% of the total (1,500), which equals $1,500 \times .20 = 300$. It is given that Peter sold 325 subscriptions. Boris sold $\frac{7}{5}$ of what Peter sold. To determine this multiply 325 by the numerator (7), and divide the product by the denominator (5). So, $325 \times 7 = 2,275$; $2,275 \div 5 = 455$. Thus, $1,500 - 300$ (Barb) $- 325$ (Peter) $- 455$ (Boris) $= 420$. Therefore, Jason sold 420 newspaper subscriptions.

2. c. To determine the change in the stock's price, first determine whether the price of the stock increased or decreased. Because the price decreased, you can immediately eliminate choice **d**. Next, subtract the smaller value from the larger value. You will have to rewrite the fractions $\frac{3}{8}$ and $\frac{3}{4}$ in common terms as $\frac{3}{8}$ and $\frac{6}{8}$. Because $\frac{6}{8}$ is larger than $\frac{3}{8}$, you will have to borrow to rewrite $28\frac{3}{8}$ as $27\frac{11}{8}$. Now you can subtract $\frac{6}{8}$ from $\frac{11}{8}$ and 26 from 27 to get the correct choice, $1\frac{5}{8}$.

3. d. To rewrite a fraction as a percent, create an equation that allows you to rewrite the fraction with a denominator of 100. Here's the equation you should write: $\frac{18}{25} = \frac{x}{100}$. Next, cross multiply to create the equation $1,800 = 25x$. Finally, divide both sides of the equation by 25 to produce the result $72 = x$. Because a percent is the numerator of a fraction when it is written with a denominator of 100, this is the correct choice.

4. a. To determine how much money Jeanette spent, subtract the amount of money she returned home with ($18.42) from the amount of money she left the house with ($100). The result, $81.58, is the correct choice. If you chose any of the incorrect choices, you probably miscalculated. You should practice carrying and borrowing to avoid such careless errors in the future.

5. a. To determine the fraction of CDs Jim bought you must multiply the $\frac{1}{3}$ he purchased by $\frac{3}{5}$, the fraction of the total that was on sale. To multiply fractions, multiply the numerators and then the denominators, and reduce if necessary. $\frac{1}{3} \times \frac{3}{5} = \frac{3}{15}$. Then reduce to get the correct answer of $\frac{1}{5}$.

6. b. To answer this question, you must rewrite the fractions over a common denominator; 12 is a good common denominator because it is divisible by 2, 4, and 6, the denominators in the problem. Rewrite the problem as $\frac{6}{12} + 4\frac{9}{12} + 2\frac{10}{12}$. Next, add the fractions; $\frac{6}{12} + \frac{9}{12} + \frac{10}{12} = \frac{25}{12}$, which can be rewritten as the mixed number $2\frac{1}{12}$. Add $4 + 2 + 2\frac{1}{2}$ to get $8\frac{1}{12}$.

7. a. To calculate 15% of $16.80, multiply $16.80 by 0.15. The product, $2.52, is your correct answer. You might also try this shortcut: Find 10% of $16.80 by moving the decimal point one place to the left. Thus, 10% of $16.80 is $1.68. Immediately eliminate choices **c** and **d**, because 15% of $16.80 must be greater than 10% of $16.80. Next, find 5% of $16.80 by dividing $1.68 (10% of $16.80) in half. Half of $1.68 is $0.84. Therefore, 15% of $16.80 equals $1.68 + $0.84 = $2.52.

8. d. This question asks you to rewrite the mixed number $8\frac{1}{5}$ as an improper fraction. To do this, multiply the whole number 8 by the denominator 5 to get the product 40. Add 40 to the numerator 1 and rewrite the fraction $\frac{41}{5}$. Choices **a**, **b**, and **c** all represent results achieved by incorrect procedures; if you chose one of these, review the correct procedure for rewriting mixed numbers as improper fractions.

9. b. There are several ways to answer this question. One way is to rewrite each mixed number as an improper fraction, and then find a common denominator for the two fractions and subtract. By this method, you would rewrite $7\frac{1}{10}$ as $\frac{71}{10}$ and $5\frac{2}{3}$ as $\frac{17}{3}$. You would then rewrite the improper fractions over the common denominator of 30 as $\frac{213}{30}$ and $\frac{170}{30}$. Finally, you would subtract $\frac{213}{30} - \frac{170}{30}$ to get $\frac{43}{30}$, which equals the mixed number $1\frac{13}{30}$.

10. d. The farmer plants 40 cabbages in each of 75 rows; therefore, he plants 40×75 cabbages, which equals 3,000 cabbages.

11. b. The legend of a graph shows which line represents which set of data. In this graph, the legend tells you which line represents the number of dogs and which line represents the number of cats.

12. c. The *y*-axis is the vertical axis of a graph.

13. a. The title tells you what information is contained in the graph. Choice **d** corresponds to the *x*-axis of the graph.

14. a. To answer this question, convert the percentage of challenging calls (25%) to a fraction, which is $\frac{1}{4}$. Next, multiply the fraction of challenging calls ($\frac{3}{5}$) by the fraction representing challenging calls that require a spe-

cialist ($\frac{1}{4}$). $\frac{3}{5} \times \frac{1}{4} = \frac{3}{20}$. Lastly, multiply the total number of calls (60) by the numerator (3) and divide by the denominator (20) to determine the number of calls that required a specialist. $60 \times 3 = 180$; $180 \div 20 = 9$.

15. d. To find the choice, first find $\frac{2}{5}$ of 15, the distance from Mr. Stone's home to his work, by multiplying $\frac{2}{5}$ and 15. $\frac{2}{5}$ of 15 equals 6, meaning that Mr. Stone has driven 6 miles when he stops for breakfast. The question asks how far Mr. Stone is from work, however, so you must subtract 6 (the distance traveled so far) from 15 (the entire distance of the trip) to determine how much distance remains in his trip. Thus, the correct choice to the question is 9.

16. a. To divide fractions, multiply the dividend (the first fraction in the equation) by the reciprocal of the divisor (the second fraction in the equation). Thus, $14 \div \frac{3}{4}$ should be rewritten as $14 \times \frac{4}{3}$, which equals $\frac{56}{3}$. Rewrite $\frac{56}{3}$ as $18\frac{2}{3}$ to identify the correct answer.

17. c. To find the decimal equivalent of a fraction, divide the numerator by the denominator: $7 \div 8 = 0.875$.

18. c. Because 3 teaspoons of water equal 1 tablespoon of water and 2 tablespoons of water equal 1 ounce of water, 3×2 teaspoons of water equal 1 ounce of water. Therefore, there are 6 teaspoons of water in 1 ounce of water, and there are 6×16 teaspoons of water in a pint of water; $6 \times 16 = 96$, so 96 is the correct answer to this question.

19. d. The range of a data set is the difference between the greatest and least values in the set. The greatest value in this set is 160 and the least value is 5, so the range of the data is $160 - 5$, which equals 155.

20. a. The data in the table show a correlation between weight and expected life span. In general, smaller dogs tend to live longer than larger dogs. Choice **b** cannot be correct because the table tells us about the average age for an entire breed of dogs only, not the lifespan of any individual member of that breed. Choice **c** cannot be correct because the table does not contain any information about how good or bad a house pet each breed makes. Choice **d** cannot be correct because the table does not include any information about the weight of an average human.

21. c. You can solve this problem by finding 30% of $350 and subtracting the result from $350, the original price of the suit. Or, you can find 70% of the price of the suit, because a suit discounted by 30% will sell for 70% of its original price. Calculate 70% of $350 by finding 10% of $350 and multiplying the result by 7; 10% of $350 is $35, and $35 × 7 = $245.

22. d. You can solve this problem by dividing the goal of 400 calories burnt by the rate of 60 calories a mile. $400 \div 60 = \frac{20}{3}$, which equals $6\frac{2}{3}$.

23. a. The question asks you to rewrite the improper fraction $\frac{12}{9}$ as a mixed number. To do this, divide the numerator 12 by the denominator 9. The result is $1\frac{3}{9}$, which reduces to $1\frac{1}{3}$.

24. b. To reduce $\frac{42}{51}$, you must find a number that divides evenly into both 42 and 51. Both numbers are divisible by 3, so you can reduce $\frac{42}{51}$ to $\frac{14}{17}$.

25. d. The question tells you that 12,800 represents 40%, or $\frac{2}{5}$ of the total number of respondents. To solve, set the two fractions equal to each other, cross-multiply, and solve for x. So, $\frac{12,800}{x} = \frac{2}{5}$; $64,000 = 2x$; $32,000 = x$, the total number of respondents.

26. c. To determine the number of workers who responded to the survey, add the number of

workers who gave each response. Three workers chose 11:30 A.M., nine workers chose 12 P.M., 11 chose 12:30 P.M., ten chose 1 P.M., and two chose 1:30 P.M.; $3 + 9 + 11 + 10 + 2 = 35$, the correct answer to this question.

27. a. The range of a data set is the difference between the greatest and least values in the set. The greatest value in this set is 11 and the least value is 2, so the range of the data is 11 − 2, which equals 9.

28. b. Since there are 60 minutes are in an hour, in an eight hour work day there are a total of $60 \times 8 = 480$ minutes. The question tells us that $\frac{6}{15}$ of this number was spent reviewing reports. To solve, multiply 480 minutes by the numerator (6) and divide by the denominator (15). $480 \times 6 = 2,880$; $2,880 \div 15 = 192$ minutes.

29. c. To solve rate problems, apply the equation $rt = d$, where r equals rate, t equals time, and d equals distance. This problem provides the time (4 hours) and the distance (15 miles), allowing you to write the equation $4r = 15$. Now divide both sides of the equation by 4 to solve for r. The result is $r = 3.75$, the correct answer.

30. b. To rewrite a proportion as a percent, create an equation that allows you to rewrite the fraction with a denominator of 100. Here's the equation you should write: $\frac{3}{25} = \frac{x}{100}$. Next, cross multiply to create the equation $300 = 25x$. Finally, divide both sides of the equation by 25 to produce the result $12 = x$. Because a percent is the numerator of a fraction when it is written with a denominator of 100, this is the correct answer.

31. c. This question asks you to rewrite the mixed number $8\frac{1}{4}$ as an improper fraction. To do this, first multiply the whole number (8) by the denominator (4) to get $8 \times 4 = 32$.

Next, add 32 to the numerator (1) and set above the denominator: 32 +1 = 33, which yields $\frac{33}{4}$.

32. c. The pie chart shows that Candidate X received 45% of the votes, more than any other single candidate received. Thus, the graph supports the conclusion that Candidate X received the greatest number of votes. The graph does not mention what percent of eligible voters participated in the election, so choice **a** cannot be correct. Only one candidate received more than 40% of the vote, so choice **b** is incorrect. The graph does not mention whether voters would have chosen Candidate W if she were running, so choice **d** cannot be correct.

33. b. A total of 600 votes were cast in the election. Candidate Z received 18% of the votes; therefore, Candidate Z received 18% of 600 votes; $\frac{18}{100} \times 600 = 108$, the correct answer.

34. c. One way to solve this problem is to convert the mixed number $5\frac{2}{5}$ into an improper fraction. To do this, multiply the whole number (5) by the denominator (5) to get 25. Add 25 to the numerator (2) and set above the denominator: $\frac{27}{5}$. Next, multiply the numerator by 8 and divide by the denominator: $27 \times 8 = 216$; $216 \div 5$ is equivalent to the mixed number $43\frac{1}{5}$.

35. b. 180 of 300 consumers polled purchases household cleaning products once per week. To find out how many of 1,000 consumers would be likely to purchase household cleaning products once per week, write the proportion $\frac{180}{300} = \frac{x}{1,000}$ and solve by cross multiplying to get 300= 18,000. Divide both sides by 300 to get = 600, the solution to the problem.

36. d. To multiply fractions, multiply numerator by numerator and denominator by denominator, and then reduce if necessary. Because this problem includes a mixed number, you must first rewrite the mixed number $2\frac{1}{5}$ as the improper fraction $\frac{11}{5}$. Next, multiply $\frac{7}{10}$ and $\frac{11}{5}$ to get $\frac{77}{50}$, which equals $1\frac{22}{50}$; $\frac{22}{50}$ reduces to $\frac{11}{25}$, so the answer is $1\frac{11}{25}$.

37. c. To answer this question, find 15% of 1,660 (the number of employees in 2009). 15% of 1,660 is $.15 \times 1,660 = 249$. Now subtract 249 from 1,660: $1,660 - 249 = 1,411$.

38. a. To solve rate problems, apply the equation $rt = d$, where r equals rate, t equals time, and d equals distance. This problem provides the time (4 hours) and the rate (480 miles per hour), allowing you to write the equation $4(480) = d$; 4×480 equals 1,920, the correct answer to the problem.

39. c. To find the mean price of the DVD players shown in the table, add all the prices together and divide by the number of DVD players shown. The sum of the four prices is $320. $320 divided by 4, the number of DVD players shown, is $80, so $80 is the average price.

40. d. The range of a data set is the difference between the greatest and least values in the set. The greatest value in this set is $95 and the least value is $61.50, so the range of the data is $95 − $61.50, which equals $33.50.

Section 2: Written Communication

41. b. The main idea of the passage is that there are significant differences between the Library of Congress classification system and the Dewey decimal classification system. The details of the passage enumerate those differences. An expression of the main idea of the passage should focus on the fact that there are important differences between the two systems; of the choices, choice **b** does that best. Choices **a, c,** and **d** express opinions that the author never states, so neither can be the correct answer.

42. a. Reread the sentence, substituting each choice for the word *diverse*. Of the four choices, only choice **a** makes sense in context.

43. c. The passage points out that "Users searching for books about dogs, for example, almost always find it easier to remember the Dewey code for such books (636) than the Library of Congress code (SF427)" and also that "there is an internal logic to the entire Dewey system" while "[e]ach Library of Congress subject category . . . was developed independently of the others, so each follows its own unique set of rules." These statements all support the conclusion stated in choice **c**.

44. d. The passage states this clearly in paragraph 2. Of the incorrect choices, choice **a** covers information not mentioned in the passage, while choices **b** and **c** are directly contradicted by information in the passage.

45. a. The purpose of this passage is to describe how education can improve police effectiveness. It begins by telling the reader that many professions have recognized the importance of requiring college as a prerequisite to employment. It then informs the reader about the benefits associated with obtaining a college education.

46. d. The fourth sentence lists many of the benefits associated with a college education, but this list does not include a more authoritarian attitude among police officers. In fact, the author states that higher education produces less authoritarian attitudes.

47. c. The second sentence tells the reader that requiring a college education for police officers has been controversial for over 100 years. The other choices contain the benefits associ-

ated with education, but are not the main source of controversy.

48. d. Reread the sentence, substituting each choice for the word *myriad*. Choices **a** and **b** make no sense in context; choice **c** has the opposite meaning of *myriad*. *A great number* makes the most sense in context, so choice **d** is the best answer.

49. b. The overall subject of the passage concerns the extent to which race and ethnicity are taught to criminal justice students. Choices **a**, **c**, and **d**, are not even mentioned in the passage, so they should be eliminated.

50. c. This is a slightly tricky one, because the passage acknowledges that many students feel that their professors need to be more sensitive to issues of race. However, the passage does not suggest that students believe teaching race and ethnicity in criminal justice courses is directly important, which means choice **b** is incorrect. The first sentence of the passage states "Some scholars believe all roads in American criminology eventually lead to issues of race," so choice **c** is the best answer.

51. b. The answer is clearly stated in the first sentence of the second paragraph, "even given the importance of race and ethnicity, criminal justice educators have been reluctant to confront the issue directly."

52. a. The first paragraph establishes that race statistics show disproportionate representation of people of color at each stage of the criminal justice system. The other answer choices are not supported by the passage.

53. c. Use context clues here; the sentence tells us that the *prudent* restrictions are perhaps necessary. Could they be *optional*? No, they can't be optional and necessary, so choice **a** cannot be correct. Can they be *ill-advised* or *counterproductive* and also be necessary? No, so choices **b** and **d** must also be incorrect. The answer must be choice **c**, *sensible*.

54. a. The passage provides a summary of regulations on the political activity of federal employees. Both choices **b** and **d** suggest that the author has written a persuasive passage that argues a particular point of view; in fact, the author has written an informational passage that does not expound any opinion. Thus, choices **b** and **d** must both be incorrect. Choice **c** refers to a detail in the passage; the choice to a main idea question, however, must address the entire passage, not just one detail in it.

55. b. In paragraph 2, the passage states that "Thomas Jefferson issued an executive circular in 1801 advising federal employees to abstain from campaigning and electioneering." Choice **b** is a good paraphrase of this sentence.

56. c. This statement is supported in the final paragraph, which states that "discontent ultimately led to a 1993 amendment that allowed federal employees to participate in elections so long as their activity occurred outside their place of work. At the same time, the amendment increased penalties for those who abused the powers of their offices for political gain." Thus, the passage supports the conclusion drawn in choice **c**.

57. b. The passage discusses both the potential strengths and some of the possible problems with community policing programs; thus, choice **b** is a good summary of the entire passage. Choices **a** and **c** address specific details in the passage; the choice to a main idea question, however, must address the entire passage, not just one detail in it. Choice **d**

offers an opinion that the author never states or implies.

58. d. Consider the context; *initiative* clearly connotes something positive, so choices **a** and **b** cannot be correct. Although Brown's *initiative* may have represented a victory, that is not the clear sense of the word here; therefore, choice **c** is not the best answer. Clearly Brown made a *decision* to implement the COPS program in Houston. Thus, the choice closest in meaning to *initiative* is **d**, *decision*.

59. a. Paragraph 3 states that "Although this drop in crime rates has occurred nationwide (including areas that receive no federal assistance), the drops have been more pronounced in those locations that receive substantial COPS funding." The fact that the drops have been greater in areas that receive COPS funding suggests that COPS programs have contributed to the drop in crime rates.

60. d. The passage points out that "Brown believed that officers should be accessible to the community at the street level. If officers were assigned to the same area over a period of time, those officers would eventually build a network of trust with neighborhood residents. As a result, merchants and residents in the community would be more likely to inform officers about criminal activities in the area and support police intervention." These sentences best support choice **d**. None of the other choices is supported by information in the passage.

61. a. The correct spelling is *merchandise*.

62. c. The correct spelling is *bandanna*.

63. a. The correct spelling is *spontaneous*.

64. b. The correct spelling of choice **b** is *embellish*.

65. c. The correct spelling of choice **c** is *retaliate*.

66. b. Another word for *attest* is *verify*.

67. a. Another word for *consummate* is *expert*.

68. a. A *virtuoso* musician is a musician with great expertise. An *amateur* musician is one who plays music for the love of playing, but who lacks the experience and/or skill to be considered a *virtuoso*.

69. c. The sentence provides necessary context clues. What sort of shade could keep a hotel room nice and dark? An *opaque* shade is one that does not let light through. Therefore, *opaque* is the best choice.

70. c. *Remuneration* means *payment*. *Reprisal* and *retribution* (choices **a** and **b**) both mean *revenge*.

71. c. Choice **a** has a subject (*the onset of the cold war*) but no predicate. Likewise, choice **b** has a compound subject that is never completed with a predicate.

72. b. Choice **a** begins with a misplaced modifier, thereby incorrectly indicating that *many consumers* have been genetically modified. Choice **c** also misplaces a modifying phrase (*that consumers do not trust*), thereby inaccurately indicating that the consumers do not trust *disease*.

73. b. Every proper noun and adjective in this sentence is correctly capitalized.

74. c. The series commas in this sentence are in the correct spots.

75. c. In choices **a** and **b**, it is unclear whether the pronouns refer to the *perpetrator* or the *police officer*. Only choice **c** clearly identifies the antecedents to the pronouns.

76. a. Choice **a** uses apostrophes correctly. In choice **b**, the apostrophes are misplaced in the words *wasn't* and *couldn't*, and they are missing completely in choice **c**.

77. b. Choice **a** contains a subject-verb agreement error; *everyone* is a collective pronoun that should take the singular verb *has*, not the plural verb *have*. Also, *everyone* should take a singular pronoun such as *his* or *her*, not the plural pronoun *their*. The latter error appears in choice **c** as well.

78. a. Choice **b** contains a pronoun error; the singular pronoun *its* does not agree with its plural antecedent *benefits*. Choice **c** also contains a pronoun error; the pronoun *their* refers to *therapy*, not *benefits*, and, therefore, should be singular rather than plural.

79. b. Choices **a** and **c** both contain punctuation errors. In choice **a**, there should be a comma between *course* and *Renee*. In choice **c**, the comma after *proceeded* is confusing and ungrammatical.

80. c. Choices **a** and **b** are incorrectly punctuated; because the sentence includes no direct quotes, the quotation marks are incorrectly used. The question mark in choice **a** is also grammatically incorrect, because the sentence is a statement of fact, not a question.

Section 3: Civil Service Skills

81. c. The primary governing principle of customer service is to make things as easy and pleasant for the customer as possible. Thus, the primary reason for maintaining customer records is to minimize the need for the customer to provide redundant information. Choice **a** has nothing to do with customer service and, therefore, cannot be the correct answer to a question in this section of the test. Choice **b** falsely suggests that there is a limit to the amount of government service a citizen may receive. Choice **d** falsely suggests that citizens are not entitled to a government service if they have previously received it.

82. b. Callers should be able to find the street address of the agency via numerous accessible means (e.g., telephone book, Internet). The information mentioned in choices **a**, **c**, and **d** is not as easy to find. Furthermore, it is more immediately relevant to the needs of a person who calls an agency outside of business hours.

83. d. A recorded message providing choices to frequently asked questions should allow some callers to resolve their queries without speaking to a representative, a win for both the caller and the agency. Music, choice **a**, is a good second choice but is not as advantageous as the above-described recorded message. Choices **b** and **c** represent options likely to annoy callers.

84. a. Some customers left on hold for a long time will hang up before they get to speak with a representative. The number of total calls divided by the number of hang-ups is used to calculate the *abandonment rate*. If 5 out of every 100 calls results in a hang-up, then the abandonment rate is 1 in $\frac{100}{5}$, or 1 in 20.

85. c. This is a common-sense question. It would not be economically feasible or practical to give appointments simply because customers cannot see a representative immediately (choice **a**); a short wait is reasonable. A one-hour wait (choice **b**), however, is far beyond reasonable. Fifteen minutes (choice **c**, the correct choice) is a reasonable amount of time to expect people to wait. Choice **d** falsely suggests that it is a good idea to implement policies that discourage citizens from using government services.

86. c. Three other station names are shown, 18th and California, 30th and Downing, and Union Station.

87. b. The arrow in the photograph indicates the train will be traveling north from the Broadway Station to Union Station.

88. c. Recycling is never collected on the same day as garbage, so if you remembered that Sector 2's garbage was collected on Tuesday and Saturday, you would have been able to eliminate choices **b** and **d**.

89. a. Recycling is collected Tuesday through Saturday; Monday is not a recycling-collection day.

90. c. In Sector 2, garbage is collected on Tuesday and on Saturday, creating a four-day break between the first and second collection. Garbage in Sector 5 is collected on Monday and Friday, which also leaves a four-day break between the first and second collection.

91. c. The instructions indicate that each code is preceded by the time of the visit it represents. Eliminate choices **a**, **b**, and **d**, none of which begins with the time. The correct answer, by process of elimination, must be choice **c**.

92. d. The instructions indicate that each code is preceded by the time of the visit it represents. Eliminate choices **a** and **b**, neither of which begins with the time. Choice **c** records the visitor's actual age of 67 rather than the code for her age (4 = over age 65). Therefore, choice **d** must be the correct answer.

93. a. Eliminate choices **c** and **d**, neither of which begins with the time. Choice **b** incorrectly includes the code Z, indicating that the visitor lives outside the city. In fact, the visitor lives in the southwest quadrant of the city, as choice **a** correctly indicates.

94. b. The F in the code indicates that the visitor was female. The Y in the code indicates that she filed a complaint. The code indicates that the visitor arrived at 12:00 P.M., was a female (F) citizen (C) between the ages of 31 and 65 (3) from the southwest quadrant of the city (W) who filed a complaint (6).

95. c. The question asks for the purpose of the visit, which is represented by the final digit of the code. That digit, 7, indicates "applying for employment," meaning that choice **c** is the correct answer.

96. d. The first two letters of the code correspond to the first two letters of the recipient's county of residence. The recipient lives in Ardmore County, so her license will begin with the letters AR. Eliminate choices **b** and **c**, which begin with the letters DV (the recipient's initials). The final three characters in the license must be randomly generated letters; choice **a** omits these characters and so cannot be correct.

97. a. The first two letters of the code correspond to the first two letters of the recipient's county of residence. The recipient lives in Hazelton County, so his license will begin with the letters HA. Eliminate choices **c** and **d**, which do not begin with these letters. Choice **b** does not round the recipient's height to the nearest whole inch as required by the rules; therefore, choice **a** must be the correct answer.

98. d. The rules state that the birth date should be recorded as month-date-year. Thus, the correct coding of the recipient's birth date would be 08261980, not 26081980 as it erroneously appears on the license.

99. b. The code indicates that the recipient's initials are WE. Therefore, the license could belong to someone named Warren Evers.

100. a. The recipient of this license lives in a county that begins with the letters LA; was born on August 8, 1967; has the initials MU; and is 66 inches tall.

9

CIVIL SERVICE
PRACTICE EXAM 2

L ike the first practice exam, this test was designed to prepare you for the kinds of questions you will encounter on your civil service exam. The 100 multiple-choice questions that follow will test your knowledge of math, reading, spelling, vocabulary, grammar, civil service skills, memory, and coding.

Make sure you take the time to score your test, and then read all the answer explanations, regardless of whether you answered the question correctly. Compare your score on this test with your score on the first test. Are there areas in which you need more improvement? If so, go back to the review chapters and keep studying before you take the third practice test.

Civil Service Practice Exam 2

1.	ⓐ	ⓑ	ⓒ	ⓓ	36.	ⓐ	ⓑ	ⓒ	ⓓ	71.	ⓐ	ⓑ	ⓒ	ⓓ
2.	ⓐ	ⓑ	ⓒ	ⓓ	37.	ⓐ	ⓑ	ⓒ	ⓓ	72.	ⓐ	ⓑ	ⓒ	ⓓ
3.	ⓐ	ⓑ	ⓒ	ⓓ	38.	ⓐ	ⓑ	ⓒ	ⓓ	73.	ⓐ	ⓑ	ⓒ	ⓓ
4.	ⓐ	ⓑ	ⓒ	ⓓ	39.	ⓐ	ⓑ	ⓒ	ⓓ	74.	ⓐ	ⓑ	ⓒ	ⓓ
5.	ⓐ	ⓑ	ⓒ	ⓓ	40.	ⓐ	ⓑ	ⓒ	ⓓ	75.	ⓐ	ⓑ	ⓒ	ⓓ
6.	ⓐ	ⓑ	ⓒ	ⓓ	41.	ⓐ	ⓑ	ⓒ	ⓓ	76.	ⓐ	ⓑ	ⓒ	ⓓ
7.	ⓐ	ⓑ	ⓒ	ⓓ	42.	ⓐ	ⓑ	ⓒ	ⓓ	77.	ⓐ	ⓑ	ⓒ	ⓓ
8.	ⓐ	ⓑ	ⓒ	ⓓ	43.	ⓐ	ⓑ	ⓒ	ⓓ	78.	ⓐ	ⓑ	ⓒ	ⓓ
9.	ⓐ	ⓑ	ⓒ	ⓓ	44.	ⓐ	ⓑ	ⓒ	ⓓ	79.	ⓐ	ⓑ	ⓒ	ⓓ
10.	ⓐ	ⓑ	ⓒ	ⓓ	45.	ⓐ	ⓑ	ⓒ	ⓓ	80.	ⓐ	ⓑ	ⓒ	ⓓ
11.	ⓐ	ⓑ	ⓒ	ⓓ	46.	ⓐ	ⓑ	ⓒ	ⓓ	81.	ⓐ	ⓑ	ⓒ	ⓓ
12.	ⓐ	ⓑ	ⓒ	ⓓ	47.	ⓐ	ⓑ	ⓒ	ⓓ	82.	ⓐ	ⓑ	ⓒ	ⓓ
13.	ⓐ	ⓑ	ⓒ	ⓓ	48.	ⓐ	ⓑ	ⓒ	ⓓ	83.	ⓐ	ⓑ	ⓒ	ⓓ
14.	ⓐ	ⓑ	ⓒ	ⓓ	49.	ⓐ	ⓑ	ⓒ	ⓓ	84.	ⓐ	ⓑ	ⓒ	ⓓ
15.	ⓐ	ⓑ	ⓒ	ⓓ	50.	ⓐ	ⓑ	ⓒ	ⓓ	85.	ⓐ	ⓑ	ⓒ	ⓓ
16.	ⓐ	ⓑ	ⓒ	ⓓ	51.	ⓐ	ⓑ	ⓒ	ⓓ	86.	ⓐ	ⓑ	ⓒ	ⓓ
17.	ⓐ	ⓑ	ⓒ	ⓓ	52.	ⓐ	ⓑ	ⓒ	ⓓ	87.	ⓐ	ⓑ	ⓒ	ⓓ
18.	ⓐ	ⓑ	ⓒ	ⓓ	53.	ⓐ	ⓑ	ⓒ	ⓓ	88.	ⓐ	ⓑ	ⓒ	ⓓ
19.	ⓐ	ⓑ	ⓒ	ⓓ	54.	ⓐ	ⓑ	ⓒ	ⓓ	89.	ⓐ	ⓑ	ⓒ	ⓓ
20.	ⓐ	ⓑ	ⓒ	ⓓ	55.	ⓐ	ⓑ	ⓒ	ⓓ	90.	ⓐ	ⓑ	ⓒ	ⓓ
21.	ⓐ	ⓑ	ⓒ	ⓓ	56.	ⓐ	ⓑ	ⓒ	ⓓ	91.	ⓐ	ⓑ	ⓒ	ⓓ
22.	ⓐ	ⓑ	ⓒ	ⓓ	57.	ⓐ	ⓑ	ⓒ	ⓓ	92.	ⓐ	ⓑ	ⓒ	ⓓ
23.	ⓐ	ⓑ	ⓒ	ⓓ	58.	ⓐ	ⓑ	ⓒ	ⓓ	93.	ⓐ	ⓑ	ⓒ	ⓓ
24.	ⓐ	ⓑ	ⓒ	ⓓ	59.	ⓐ	ⓑ	ⓒ	ⓓ	94.	ⓐ	ⓑ	ⓒ	ⓓ
25.	ⓐ	ⓑ	ⓒ	ⓓ	60.	ⓐ	ⓑ	ⓒ	ⓓ	95.	ⓐ	ⓑ	ⓒ	ⓓ
26.	ⓐ	ⓑ	ⓒ	ⓓ	61.	ⓐ	ⓑ	ⓒ	ⓓ	96.	ⓐ	ⓑ	ⓒ	ⓓ
27.	ⓐ	ⓑ	ⓒ	ⓓ	62.	ⓐ	ⓑ	ⓒ	ⓓ	97.	ⓐ	ⓑ	ⓒ	ⓓ
28.	ⓐ	ⓑ	ⓒ	ⓓ	63.	ⓐ	ⓑ	ⓒ	ⓓ	98.	ⓐ	ⓑ	ⓒ	ⓓ
29.	ⓐ	ⓑ	ⓒ	ⓓ	64.	ⓐ	ⓑ	ⓒ	ⓓ	99.	ⓐ	ⓑ	ⓒ	ⓓ
30.	ⓐ	ⓑ	ⓒ	ⓓ	65.	ⓐ	ⓑ	ⓒ	ⓓ	100.	ⓐ	ⓑ	ⓒ	ⓓ
31.	ⓐ	ⓑ	ⓒ	ⓓ	66.	ⓐ	ⓑ	ⓒ	ⓓ					
32.	ⓐ	ⓑ	ⓒ	ⓓ	67.	ⓐ	ⓑ	ⓒ	ⓓ					
33.	ⓐ	ⓑ	ⓒ	ⓓ	68.	ⓐ	ⓑ	ⓒ	ⓓ					
34.	ⓐ	ⓑ	ⓒ	ⓓ	69.	ⓐ	ⓑ	ⓒ	ⓓ					
35.	ⓐ	ⓑ	ⓒ	ⓓ	70.	ⓐ	ⓑ	ⓒ	ⓓ					

Section 1: Mathematics

Select the best choice for each question.

1. Find the fraction equivalent of 45%.
   a. $\frac{4}{5}$
   b. $\frac{9}{20}$
   c. $\frac{1}{2}$
   d. $\frac{45}{10}$

2. $\frac{16}{5} =$
   a. $2\frac{1}{5}$
   b. $16\frac{1}{5}$
   c. $3\frac{1}{5}$
   d. $1\frac{5}{6}$

3. A tortoise crawls 3 feet per minute. How far does the tortoise crawl in 1 hour?
   a. 3 feet
   b. 30 feet
   c. 60 feet
   d. 180 feet

4. Almonds are sold in bulk for $5.60 per pound (16 ounces) or $3.60 for a 12-ounce package. If Pierre only needs 12 ounces for a recipe, how much would he save by purchasing the 12-ounce package instead of 12 ounces of almonds sold in bulk?
   a. $0.60
   b. $0.65
   c. $0.80
   d. $0.85

Study the following graph, and then use it to answer questions 5 to 7.

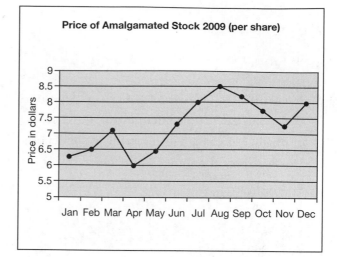

5. The graph shows the price of amalgamated stock throughout 2009. Across what two consecutive months did the largest change in price occur in 2009?
   a. February to March
   b. March to April
   c. May to June
   d. July to August

6. A person who bought one share of stock in January and sold it in December would have realized a
   a. profit of $2.25.
   b. profit of $1.75.
   c. loss of $0.50.
   d. loss of $1.25.

7. What information is displayed on the *y*-axis of the graph?
   a. the months of the year
   b. the price of the stock in dollars
   c. the number of shares sold
   d. the title of the graph

8. $10\frac{2}{3} - 3\frac{1}{8} =$

a. $7\frac{1}{5}$

b. $7\frac{11}{24}$

c. $7\frac{13}{24}$

d. $7\frac{3}{11}$

9. Jamal invests $2,000 in a certificate of deposit that yields 6% simple interest compounded annually. How much is the certificate of deposit worth 2 years after Jamal's initial investment?

a. $2,247.20

b. $2,240

c. $2,120

d. $2,060

10. Reduce $\frac{28}{45}$ to lowest terms.

a. $\frac{2}{3}$

b. $\frac{4}{7}$

c. $\frac{3}{5}$

d. The fraction cannot be reduced.

11. Belinda walked a total of 18.6 miles in 4 days. On average, how many miles did Belinda walk each day?

a. 14.6 miles

b. 4.65 miles

c. 4.6 miles

d. 4.15 miles

12. A piece of ribbon 3 feet 4 inches long was divided into 5 equal parts. How long was each part?

a. 1 foot 2 inches

b. 8 inches

c. 10 inches

d. 6 inches

13. $2\frac{2}{5} + 3\frac{1}{3} + 1\frac{1}{2} =$

a. $7\frac{7}{30}$

b. $7\frac{4}{17}$

c. $6\frac{2}{5}$

d. $6\frac{1}{15}$

14. During a 20% off sale, the price of a widescreen television is reduced by $300. What was the price of the television before the sale?

a. $1,500

b. $2,400

c. $3,000

d. $6,000

15. In Mr. Cortez's swim class, $\frac{1}{5}$ of the students are aged nine and the remaining students are eight. Once students can tread water for two minutes they reach the guppy level, and age is not a factor in this test. $\frac{1}{8}$ of all the students have reached this level. What is the best estimate of the fraction of students in this class that are eight-year-old guppies?

a. $\frac{1}{20}$

b. $\frac{2}{13}$

c. $\frac{1}{10}$

d. $\frac{5}{8}$

16. A bread recipe calls for $3\frac{1}{2}$ cups of flour during the initial mixing process and an additional $\frac{1}{4}$ cup of flour during the kneading process. How much flour is used to produce the bread?

a. $3\frac{1}{8}$ cups

b. $3\frac{3}{4}$ cups

c. $\frac{7}{8}$ cup

d. $7\frac{1}{4}$ cups

Study the following graph, and then use it to answer questions 17 to 19.

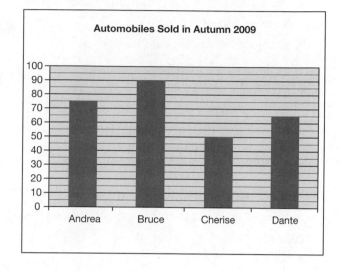

Automobiles Sold in Autumn 2009

17. Andrea, Bruce, Cherise, and Dante sell automobiles for a living. The graph above shows the number of cars sold during the autumn of 2009. Determine the average number of automobiles sold by each salesperson. Find the difference between this average and each salesperson's individual total. What is the sum of the differences between the group average and their actual totals?
  a. 40
  b. 45
  c. 50
  d. 70

18. What is the range of the data shown in the graph?
  a. 15
  b. 25
  c. 40
  d. 90

19. What information is displayed on the *x*-axis of the graph?
  a. the number of automobiles sold
  b. the names of the salespeople
  c. the title of the graph
  d. the months of autumn

20. $\frac{7}{8} - (\frac{1}{3} + \frac{1}{4}) =$
  a. $\frac{41}{56}$
  b. $\frac{19}{24}$
  c. $\frac{5}{24}$
  d. $\frac{7}{24}$

21. Find the decimal equivalent of 4%.
  a. 0.4
  b. 4.0
  c. 0.04
  d. 0.004

22. $\frac{5}{7} \div 10 =$
  a. $\frac{1}{70}$
  b. $\frac{7}{5}$
  c. $7\frac{1}{7}$
  d. $\frac{1}{14}$

23. The ratio of men to women attending a university is 5:4. If there are 7,650 students at the school, how many are men?
  a. 4,250
  b. 3,400
  c. 1,530
  d. 850

24. After receiving a 10% increase in salary, Marisol earns a salary of $55,000. What was Marisol's salary before she received the raise?
  a. $40,000
  b. $45,000
  c. $50,000
  d. $54,000

25. One day Sam spent $\frac{1}{8}$ of his workday in a meeting and $\frac{5}{6}$ of his workday doing research. The rest of the workday was spent making calls. What fraction of Sam's workday was spent not making calls?

a. $\frac{3}{7}$

b. $\frac{6}{13}$

c. $\frac{3}{4}$

d. $\frac{23}{24}$

Study the following graph, and then use it to answer questions 26 to 28.

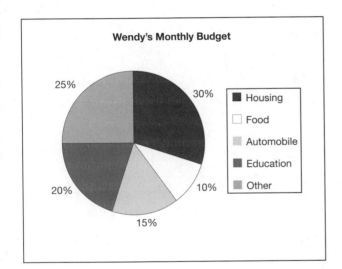

26. The legend of the graph tells you

a. how much money Wendy has to spend each month.

b. which categories correspond to which sections of the graph.

c. what type of food Wendy buys each month.

d. why type of expenses are classified under the category "other."

27. Which of the following conclusions is supported by the graph?

a. Wendy spends half her monthly budget on housing and education.

b. Automobile expenses are Wendy's single biggest monthly expense.

c. Wendy does not spend any money on entertainment.

d. If Wendy earned more money, she would spend more money on food.

28. Wendy budgets for $3,000 in expenditures each month. What is her monthly expenditure on education?

a. $300

b. $450

c. $600

d. $900

29. Over the course of a 63-mile-long bicycle ride, a cyclist averages a speed of 18 miles per hour. How long does it take the bicyclist to complete the ride?

a. 3 hours

b. 3 hours 9 minutes

c. 3 hours 30 minutes

d. 45 hours

30. A warbler that weighs 9 grams eats 80% of its body weight each day. How much food, in grams, does a warbler eat daily?

a. 7.2 grams

b. 8.0 grams

c. 8.9 grams

d. 9.8 grams

31. There are 5,280 feet in a mile. If David biked a distance of 19,800 feet how many miles did he travel?
   a. $2\frac{2}{3}$ miles
   b. $3\frac{1}{2}$ miles
   c. $3\frac{5}{8}$ miles
   d. $3\frac{3}{4}$ miles

32. $8\frac{1}{2} \times 3\frac{1}{4} =$
   a. $27\frac{5}{8}$
   b. $24\frac{1}{8}$
   c. $24\frac{3}{4}$
   d. $11\frac{3}{4}$

33. While Nicole checked tickets at a concert she would rip the tickets in half when a patron presented them, keep one half of each, and return the other half to the purchaser. If Nicole ripped 38 tickets, how many half tickets (counting portions kept by both her and the patron) would she have created?
   a. 17
   b. $38\frac{1}{2}$
   c. 76
   d. 78

34. Last Monday, 20% of the 140-member nursing staff was absent. How many nurses were absent on Monday?
   a. 14
   b. 20
   c. 28
   d. 112

35. Derek jogs for 2 hours 15 minutes at an average rate of 8 kilometers per hour. How far does Derek jog?
   a. 19 kilometers
   b. 18 kilometers
   c. 17 kilometers
   d. 16 kilometers

Study the following table, and then use it to answer questions 36 to 37.

CITY OF HULE 911 CALL FREQUENCY		
MONTH	911 CALLS	TEST SCORE
May	213	66
June	196	70
July	257	61
August	267	78
September	279	70
October	308	68

36. What was the average (arithmetic mean) of 911 calls for the six months in the table above?
   a. $248\frac{2}{5}$
   b. $253\frac{1}{3}$
   c. 257
   d. 279

37. The data in the table supports which of the following conclusions?
   a. The city of Hule has a high crime rate.
   b. October is always a high crime month.
   c. 911 call frequency tended to increase over the period range shown.
   d. The number of 911 calls can be used to predict how many times police will be dispatched.

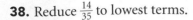

38. Reduce $\frac{14}{35}$ to lowest terms.

   a. $\frac{7}{17}$

   b. $\frac{2}{5}$

   c. $\frac{1}{21}$

   d. $\frac{2}{3}$

39. Of the 840 crimes committed last month, 42 involved petty theft. What percent of crimes committed last month involved petty theft?

   a. 5%

   b. 0.5%

   c. 0.05%

   d. 2%

40. A recipe calls for $5\frac{1}{4}$ cups of apples for six servings. How many cups of apples would be required to make nine servings?

   a. $7\frac{3}{4}$ cups

   b. $7\frac{7}{8}$ cups

   c. $8\frac{1}{4}$ cups

   d. 9 cups

Section 2: Written Communication

Reading Comprehension—Questions 41 to 60

Read the following passage. Then, answer questions 41 to 44.

Today, bicycles are elegant and simple machines that are common all over the globe. Many people ride bicycles for recreation, while others use them as a means of transportation. The first bicycle, called a draisienne, was invented in Germany in 1818 by Baron Karl de Draid de Sauerbrun. Because it was made of wood, the draisienne was not very durable, nor did it have pedals. Riders moved it by pushing their feet against the ground.

In 1839, Kirkpatrick Macmillan, a Scottish blacksmith, invented a much better bicycle. Macmillan's machine had tires with iron rims to keep them from getting worn down. He also used foot-operated cranks—similar to pedals—so that his bicycle could be ridden at a quick pace. It did not look much like a modern bicycle because its back wheel was substantially larger than its front wheel. Although Macmillan's bicycle could be ridden easily, it was never produced in large numbers. In 1861, Frenchman Pierre Michaux and his brother Ernest invented a bicycle with an improved crank mechanism. They called their bicycle a velocipede, but many people called it a bone shaker because of the jarring effect that the wood and iron frame had on the rider. Despite the unflattering nickname, the velocipede was a hit and the Michaux family made hundreds of the machines annually. Most of them were sold to fun-seeking young people.

Ten years later, James Starley, an English inventor, made several innovations that <u>revolutionized</u> bicycle design. He made the front wheel many times larger than the back wheel, put a gear on the pedals to make the bicycle more efficient, and lightened the wheels by using wire spokes. Although this bicycle was much lighter and less tiring to ride, it was still clumsy, extremely top-heavy, and ridden mostly for entertainment.

It was not until 1874 that the first truly modern bicycle appeared on the scene. Invented by another Englishman, H. J. Lawson, this safety bicycle would look familiar to today's cyclists. The safety bicycle had equalized wheels, which made it much less prone to toppling over. Lawson also attached a chain to the pedals to drive the rear wheel. By 1893, the safety bicycle had been further improved with air-filled rubber tires, a diamond-shaped frame, and an improved brake system. With the improvements made by Lawson, bicycles became extremely popular and useful for transportation. Today, bicycles are built and enjoyed all over the world.

41. There is enough information in this passage to show that
  a. several people contributed to the development of the modern bicycle.
  b. only a few velocipedes built by the Michaux family are still in existence.
  c. for most of the nineteenth century, few people rode bicycles just for fun.
  d. bicycles with wheels of different sizes cannot be ridden by today's riders.

42. The first person to use a gear system on bicycles was
  a. H. J. Lawson.
  b. Kirkpatrick Macmillan.
  c. Pierre Michaux.
  d. James Starley.

43. This passage was most likely written to
  a. persuade readers to use bicycles for transportation.
  b. describe the problems that bicycle manufacturers encounter.
  c. compare bicycles used for fun with bicycles used for transportation.
  d. tell readers a little about the history of the bicycle.

44. As used in the passage, the word *revolutionized* most nearly means
  a. canceled.
  b. transformed.
  c. maintained.
  d. preserved.

Read the following passage. Then answer questions 45 to 48.

Our fire department has always been a leader in creating positive community initiatives and providing new services to the community as they are needed. Our newest service is the Fire Assistance and Support Team (FAST). In the past, we would arrive on the scene of a residential fire, put out the fire as <u>expeditiously</u> as possible, and then leave—the homeowners would be left to deal with the aftermath on their own. With this new program, the families affected are not left alone to deal with everything that needs to be done. The FAST will stay with the victims and assist them in a variety of ways. The services provided by FAST personnel include:

- explaining what is going on at the fire scene.
- keeping the family informed as to when they will be able to re-enter their home.
- making phone calls on the family's behalf (insurance company, family members, schools, etc.).
- assisting the family with finding a place to stay for the night.
- accompanying the family as the investigator goes through their home.
- assisting with the removal of any items the family may wish to retrieve.
- providing the family with transportation.

The team works with the Red Cross, Salvation Army, and other service organizations. The team will remain in contact with the victims until their assistance is no longer required.

45. What is this passage about?

    a. cooperating with the Red Cross and similar private agencies

    b. getting insurance companies to deliver on their contracts

    c. explaining fire department operations to the general public

    d. assisting victims in dealing with the aftermath of a fire

46. The description of FAST in this passage includes all of the following duties listed EXCEPT

    a. explaining fire department actions at the fire scene.

    b. boarding up the home after the fire.

    c. finding the family a place to stay for the night.

    d. transporting the victims to a shelter.

47. What would be the best possible title for this passage?

    a. A FAST Way to Happiness

    b. A New Way to Assist and Support Fire Victims

    c. Standing Up for All Victims

    d. Providing Help for Those Without Hope

48. As used in the passage, the word *expeditiously* most nearly means

    a. furiously

    b. intensely

    c. quickly

    d. cleanly

Read the following passage. Then, answer questions 49 to 52.

This information sheet is provided courtesy of the Centers for Disease Control and Prevention (CDC). It is intended to help citizens make informed choices when deciding whether to consume raw oysters.

Nearly all oysters carry the *Vibrio vulnificus* bacteria, although in the vast majority of cases it is present in concentrations too low to affect humans adversely. The bacteria tends to be more active during the warmer months, making oysters harvested during this period substantially more dangerous. There is an old saying: "Never eat an oyster in a month that does not have an 'r' in it." The saying is grounded in fact, as there is a markedly increased danger of *Vibrio vulnificus* infection during these months.

In healthy adults, a *Vibrio vulnificus* infection usually manifests itself in symptoms commonly associated with food poisoning. These symptoms typically include stomach pain, diarrhea, and vomiting. The infection is much more dangerous to people with weakened immune systems, especially those who suffer from chronic liver disease. In such individuals, *Vibrio vulnificus* can infect the bloodstream, resulting in decreased blood pressure, fever, chills, and skin lesions. Such infections are fatal approximately half the time. Such individuals should avoid not only eating oysters, but also swimming in oyster-inhabited waters during the summer months, as infection can be transmitted in the water through open wounds.

People infected with *Vibrio vulnificus* should seek immediate help; antibiotics can be effective in reducing mortality. In the case of infection through an open wound on a limb, amputation may be necessary.

Fortunately, the incidence of *Vibrio vulnificus* is low, with only about 40 cases reported annually. Most cases occur in the Gulf Coast region. Researchers suspect that many low-grade cases of *Vibrio vulnificus*—

those that result in food-poisoning-like symptoms—go unreported, making the actual incidence of infection difficult to calculate accurately. The CDC strongly urges patients and medical professionals to report such incidents, as it allows the agency to identify potentially risky oyster beds and thus to prevent <u>subsequent</u> infections. To reduce the risk of *Vibrio vulnificus* infection, eat only shellfish that has been fully cooked and wear gloves and other protective clothing when handling raw shellfish.

49. The author's main purpose is to
   a. convince readers to avoid all seafood.
   b. warn readers about a specific danger.
   c. refute an erroneous report.
   d. describe the life cycle of an oyster.

50. According to the passage, a *Vibrio vulnificus* infection is especially dangerous to
   a. children and the elderly.
   b. people who do not live on the Gulf Coast.
   c. those with compromised immune systems.
   d. amputees.

51. It can be inferred from the passage that
   a. one does not have to eat an oyster to contract a *Vibrio vulnificus* infection.
   b. it is safer to eat oysters in the summertime than in the wintertime.
   c. a *Vibrio vulnificus* infection is usually fatal to everyone who contracts it.
   d. there is currently no effective treatment for a *Vibrio vulnificus* infection.

52. As used in the passage, the word *subsequent* most nearly means
   a. vigilant.
   b. unnecessary.
   c. more dangerous.
   d. future.

Read the following passage. Then, answer questions 53 to 56.

The "broken window" theory was originally developed to explain how minor acts of vandalism or disrespect can quickly escalate to crimes and attitudes that break down the entire social fabric of an area. This theory can easily be applied to any situation in society. The theory contends that if a broken window in an abandoned building is not replaced quickly, soon all the windows will be broken. In other words, a small violation, if condoned, leads to other similar or greater violations. Thus, after all the windows have been broken, the building is more likely to be looted and perhaps even burned down.

According to the theory, violations increase exponentially. Thus, if disrespect to a superior is tolerated, others will be tempted to be disrespectful as well. A management crisis could erupt literally overnight. For example, if one firefighter begins to disregard proper housewatch procedure by neglecting to keep up the housewatch administrative journal, and if this firefighter is not <u>reproved</u>, others will follow suit by committing similar violations of procedure. The theory is that group members begin to reason, "If he can get away with it, why can't I?" Thus, what starts out as a minor problem, such as a violation that may not seem to warrant disciplinary action, may ultimately undermine efficiency throughout the entire firehouse, putting the people the firehouse serves at risk.

There are, of course, dangers inherent to implementing the broken window theory. Many conclude that the theory mandates a zero tolerance policy toward malfeasance and even toward legal but disrespectful behavior. In practice, such a policy can quickly result in the abuse of power by authority figures, whether they be police officers patrolling a community, firefighters maintaining a firehouse, or managers supervising a team of employees. Excessive exertion of authority typically gives rise to its own set of problems, such as resentment of authority and disobedience as an act of defiance.

53. Which of the following best expresses the main idea of the passage?
  a. A theory explains how disorder can escalate under certain conditions.
  b. If order is not maintained in a firehouse, public safety can be compromised.
  c. Some bosses are too demanding, which results in employee insubordination.
  d. The housewatch administrative journal is the most important document in a firehouse.

54. As used in the passage, the word *reproved* most nearly means
  a. condoned.
  b. ostracized.
  c. fired.
  d. scolded.

55. With which of the following statements would the author most likely agree?
  a. The broken window theory is a fatally flawed concept.
  b. The broken window theory may help explain certain behavior.
  c. The broken window theory should be applied to all situations.
  d. The broken window theory really pertains to firehouses only.

56. According to the passage, the broken window theory helps explain
  a. how disciplinary problems can arise quickly seemingly from nowhere.
  b. why cities today are more successful in combating vandalism than they have been in the past.
  c. which organizations the broken window phenomenon is mostly likely to affect adversely.
  d. what personality traits drive a citizen to disrespect authority.

Read the following passage. Then, answer questions 57 to 60.

If you are looking for a new pet in your life, please consider adopting one from the county animal shelter. Every year the county takes custody of thousands of stray cats and dogs. Those pets that the county cannot find homes for, sadly, must be euthanized. By adopting a pet from the county, you'll be saving the life of an innocent animal and adding a new and wonderful member to your family.

As an <u>inducement</u> to adopt, the county provides a number of valuable services for your pet. Your dog will receive his or her first round of bordatella, parvo, parainfluenza, distemper, and hepatitis vaccinations; if your pet is old enough, he or she will also receive the first rabies shot and implantation of an identifying microchip. Your dog will also be wormed and given a full physical examination by our in-house veterinarian. Cats receive their first round of vaccinations for calici virus, chlamydia, panleukopenia, and rhinotracheitis. If he or she is old enough, your cat will also receive the first rabies shot and implantation of an identifying microchip.

The county charges a uniform adoption fee of $60 for all pets. Please note that you are required to have your pet spayed or neutered. The county does not perform these operations; however, it will provide you with a certificate that pays for the entire cost of the operation, redeemable at a number of local veterinarian hospitals. Failure to have your pet spayed or neutered will result in a $100-per-month fine, so please fulfill your obligation.

Keep in mind that owning a pet is a big responsibility. We hope that you will decide to adopt one of our animals, but only if you make the commitment to care for your pet correctly. The shelter offers regular evening seminars in pet care. You may wish to enroll in one before you adopt an animal to learn more about a pet owner's responsibilities so you can decide whether a pet is right for you.

57. The author's main purpose in this passage is to
   a. persuade all citizens to adopt at least one pet.
   b. warn citizens of fines they may face.
   c. inform citizens of the details regarding pet adoption.
   d. explain why the county shelter must put down so many animals each year.

58. It can be inferred from the passage that
   a. most people are not responsible enough to take care of a pet.
   b. the author believes the adoption fee charged by the county is too high.
   c. cats and dogs must reach a certain age before they can be implanted with a microchip.
   d. it is less expensive to care for a cat than to care for a dog.

59. According to the passage, dogs adopted from the county shelter receive vaccinations for all of the following EXCEPT
   a. parvo.
   b. distemper.
   c. bordatella.
   d. panleukopenia.

60. As used in the passage, the word *inducement* most nearly means
   a. imperative.
   b. encouragement.
   c. evasion.
   d. ultimatum.

Spelling—Questions 61 to 65
Select the choice that is spelled correctly.

61. We will be able to move forward after the planning office _____ a policy.
   a. formalates
   b. formulates
   c. formulaits

62. The _____ inspected the corpse and found no evidence of foul play.
   a. coroner
   b. corroner
   c. coronor

63. Which of the following words is spelled incorrectly?
   a. congeal
   b. sirmount
   c. personnel

64. Which of the following words is spelled incorrectly?
   a. demeanor
   b. cuncoct
   c. whimsical

65. Which of the following words is spelled incorrectly?
   a. mischievous
   b. exhilarate
   c. negoshiate

Vocabulary—Questions 66 to 70

Select the best choice for each question.

66. Find the word that is closest in meaning to the underlined word below.
    an <u>excruciating</u> experience
    a. enlightening
    b. boring
    c. painful

67. Find the word that is closest in meaning to the underlined word below.
    a <u>trite</u> saying
    a. biblical
    b. nonsensical
    c. overused

68. Find the word that is most nearly the opposite of the underlined word below.
    a <u>monotonous</u> speech
    a. annoying
    b. interesting
    c. short

69. Find the word that best completes the sentence below.
    Smoking can have a _____ effect on ones health.
    a. zealous
    b. detrimental
    c. benevolent

70. Find the word that best completes the sentence below.
    The spies arranged a secret _____ to exchange secrets.
    a. liaison
    b. confection
    c. premonition

Grammar—Questions 71 to 80

Select the best choice for each question.

71. Which of the following sentences is NOT a complete sentence?
    a. Hearing the thunder, the lifeguard ordered us out of the water.
    b. Turn off the lights.
    c. Sunday afternoon spent reading and playing computer games.

72. Select the sentence that is written most correctly
    a. A program to reduce homelessness in community is worked on by the council.
    b. The council is working on a program to reduce homelessness in the community.
    c. The counsil is working on program to reduce homelessness in the community.

73. Select the sentence that is written most correctly
    a. While visiting the zoo, Chelsea could not believe how large in size a elephant was.
    b. While visiting the zoo, Chelsea could not believe how large the elephant was.
    c. While visiting the zoo, Chelsea could not believe how large the elephant was at the zoo.

74. Select the sentence that is written most correctly
    a. Police commissioner jarrett will be retiring from the department on October 23rd.
    b. Police Commissioner Jarrett will be retiring from the Department on October 23rd.
    c. Police Commissioner Jarrett will be retiring from the department on October 23rd.

75. Select the sentence that is written most correctly.

   a. Please make sure that Mr and Mrs Anderson receive an invitation to the meeting.

   b. Please make sure that Mr. and Mrs. Anderson receive an invitation to the meeting.

   c. Please make sure that Mr. and Mrs Anderson receive an invitation to The Meeting.

76. Select the sentence that is written most correctly.

   a. Unlike other pianists, Thelonious Monk played in a style that is difficult to trace to that of an earlier musician.

   b. Unlike other pianists, the style of Thelonious Monk is difficult to trace to an earlier musician.

   c. Unlike other pianists, whose styles can be traced to an earlier musician, Thelonious Monk's cannot.

77. Select the sentence that is written most correctly.

   a. William Morrison the president of the local Chamber of Commerce will address the class next Thursday.

   b. William Morrison, the president of the local Chamber of Commerce will address the class next Thursday.

   c. William Morrison, the president of the local Chamber of Commerce, will address the class next Thursday.

78. Select the sentence that is written most correctly.

   a. The use of electronic devices, including cellular phones, are prohibited on airplanes when the aircraft is in flight.

   b. The use of electronic devices, including a cellular phone, are prohibited on airplanes when the aircraft are in flight.

   c. The use of electronic devices, including cellular phones, is prohibited on airplanes when the aircraft are in flight.

79. Select the sentence that is written most correctly.

   a. Miguel has been assigned to work on the project with Leticia and I.

   b. Miguel has been assigned to work on the project with Leticia and me.

   c. Miguel, he has been assigned to work on the project with Leticia and I.

80. Select the sentence that is written most correctly.

   a. Roberta went to the store to pick up some butter, sugar, milk, and flour.

   b. Roberta went to the store to pick up some butter sugar milk and flour.

   c. Roberta went to the store to pick up some butter, sugar, milk and, flour.

Section 3: Civil Service Skills

Customer Service— Questions 81 to 85

Select the best choice for each question.

81. Customers who complain about government service should

   a. receive a response even if they request that no response be provided.

   b. be offered a variety of outlets through which to complain (e.g., complaint desk, e-mail, website).

   c. register their complaints in person so they can receive an immediate response.

   d. be allowed to complain only if they can register the complaint in English.

CIVIL SERVICE PRACTICE EXAM 2

82. Quality-assurance agents focus primarily on
  a. citizens' level of satisfaction in their government interactions.
  b. government employees' level of satisfaction with their pay and benefits.
  c. the speed and frequency at which agencies update their websites.
  d. the punctuality of government employees.

83. An office that offers language translation services should have as its highest priority
  a. offering the greatest number of languages possible.
  b. providing accurate translation of those languages it offers.
  c. requiring non-English-speaking users to enroll in English courses.
  d. making sure that all forms are available in multiple languages.

84. When transferring a call, which of the following pieces of information is least important to provide the customer?
  a. the number of the extension to which they are being transferred
  b. the reason they are being transferred
  c. the number to call in case they are disconnected
  d. the name of your supervisor

85. The term *web chat* refers to
  a. a list of frequently asked questions and choices posted on a website.
  b. a telephone line dedicated to customer queries about how to navigate a website.
  c. a training program designed to teach government employees how to use the Internet.
  d. live interactive online help from an agency representative.

Memory—Questions 86 to 90

Take five minutes to study the following picture. Then, answer questions 86 to 87 without looking back at the picture.

© Corbis

86. The automobile on the right-hand side of the photograph is a
   a. two-door sedan.
   b. station wagon.
   c. sport-utility vehicle.
   d. motorcycle.

87. The skateboarder is wearing
   a. a large hat.
   b. a jacket.
   c. Bermuda shorts.
   d. a cape.

Take five minutes to study the following text. Then, answer questions 88 through 90 without looking back at the text.

You are about to begin a meeting with siprofessional peers you have never met before. Their images and names follow.

Sylvia Martinez

Victor Dinapoli

Janet Barnes

Arthur Jones

Maureen Cho

Carlos Domingo

88. Sylvia Martinez's hair
   a. is worn in an afro style.
   b. is blonde.
   c. is shoulder-length.
   d. covers her ears.

89. Arthur Jones is distinguished from all the other people by all of the following details EXCEPT for which?
   a. He is the only one with dark hair.
   b. He is the only one wearing a hat.
   c. He is the only one with a beard and moustache.
   d. He is the only one wearing sunglasses.

90. Which is a complete list of all the people who are wearing glasses?
   a. Sylvia Martinez, Victor Dinapoli
   b. Victor Dinapoli, Arthur Jones, Maureen Cho
   c. Victor Dinapoli, Janet Barnes, Carlos Domingo
   d. Arthur Jones, Carlos Domingo

Coding—Questions 91 to 100

To answer questions 91 through 95, refer to the following scenario.

A record of all correspondences sent from a particular government office must be entered into a log. The following code is used to record the information.

letters = first four letters of the recipient's last name and the first letter of the recipient's first name

2 digits = first two digits of the recipient's street address; if the address is one digit long, precede that digit with a zero (0)

1 letter = I if the correspondence represents an inquiry originating in the government office;

R if the correspondence represents a response to an inquiry from the recipient

1 digit = 0 if the letter is high priority; 1 if the letter is medium priority; 2 if the letter is low priority

3 letters and 2 digits = First three letters of the month and date correspondence was sent (e.g., July 6 = JUL06)

91. In response to an inquiry from Denise Fong of 3724 Haywood Boulevard, the office sends a letter graded medium priority on November 15. How should this correspondence be entered into the log?
   a. RFONGD37241NOV15
   b. FONGD37R1NOV15
   c. FONG3724RNOV15
   d. 37R1NOV15FONG

92. The office originated an inquiry to Martin Ramirez of 8 Elm Court on June 2. The office graded the letter high priority. How should this correspondence be entered into the log?
   a. MARTR8I0JUN2
   b. MARTR08I0JUN02
   c. RAMIM8I0JUN2
   d. RAMIM08I0JUN02

93. In response to a letter from John Davis of 1277 Highland Road on October 15, the office sent a low priority letter on October 23. How should the office's response be entered into the log?

   a. JOHND12R2OCT15
   b. DAVIJ12R2OCT15
   c. JOHND12R2OCT23
   d. DAVIJ12R2OCT23

94. A log entry reading BERNM35I0FEB05 could represent

    a. a reply sent to Martin Bernstein of 3 Fifth Avenue on February 5.

    b. an inquiry sent to Bernard Moskowitz of 3 Fifth Avenue on February 5.

    c. an inquiry sent to Martin Bernstein of 35 Michigan Drive on February 5.

    d. a reply sent to Bernard Moskowitz of 35 Michigan Drive on February 5.

95. The following log entry for a response to Harold McCarthy of 5 Stevenson Road, sent high priority on March 6, was coded MCCAH5R0MAR06. It contains which of the following errors?

    a. It omits a zero (0) that should appear between H and 5.

    b. It incorrectly codes the recipient's name.

    c. The date on which the letter was sent is recorded incorrectly.

    d. The priority level of the letter is miscoded.

To answer questions 96 through 100, refer to the following scenario.

A city health department inspects salad bars in grocery stores as well as the areas in which foods for the salad bars are prepared. It logs violations of the health code according to the following rules:

Major Infraction (subtract 5 points for each incident; infraction must be remedied immediately)

A—Cooked foods not cooked through
B—Cooked foods stored under 140° F
C—Cold food stored above 41° F
D—Raw and cooked foods stored together, allowing for cross-contamination
E—Improper cleaning of knives and other utensils

F—Employee with contagious condition (e.g., flu) preparing food
G—Employee fails to wash hands thoroughly
H—Presence of animal droppings detected

Minor infraction (subtract 3 points for each incident; infraction must be remedied within two business days)

j—Hand-washing facilities not immediately accessible to food preparers
k—Lack of soap or towels at hand-washing facility
m—Improper temperature or water pressure in automatic dishwasher or washing machine
n—Inaccurate labeling of food items
p—Inaccurate labeling or improper storage of toxic cleaning materials
r—Consumer advisories (e.g., notices about safety of shellfish) improperly displayed
s—Smoking in the food preparation area

Multiple infractions are logged multiple times (e.g., an inspector who observes three incidents of under-cooked food would log the code AAA). A health code score is tabulated by adding the value of all infractions and subtracting the sum from 100.

96. An inspector visits Wilson's Supermarket to observe its salad bar and preparation areas. During her visit, she notes one incident of cold food stored at too high a temperature. She also finds animal droppings in two separate areas of the store. Finally, she notes that one food item is improperly labeled. What code does the inspector record for this visit?

    a. CCHp

    b. CHp

    c. CHHp

    d. CHHppp

97. An inspector visits Hungry Bob's Mini-Mart to inspect its salad bar and preparation areas. The inspector observes three incidents of improper storage of toxic cleaning materials. He also notes that a consumer advisory that should be posted clearly is not posted. What code should he assign for his visit?
   a. pppr
   b. EEEn
   c. En
   d. pr

98. An inspector visits Hungry Bob's Mini-Mart to inspect its salad bar and preparation areas. The inspector observes three incidents of improper storage of toxic cleaning materials. He also notes that a consumer advisory that should be posted clearly is not posted. What score should the inspector assign for this visit?
   a. 88
   b. 80
   c. 90
   d. 94

99. An inspector visits Mega-Mart and logs the following code:
   EGkss
   The inspector observed more than one incident of
   a. poor cleaning of utensils.
   b. poor hand-washing technique.
   c. insufficient amount of soap or towels.
   d. smoking where food is prepared.

100. An inspector visits Mega-Mart and logs the following code:
   EGkss
   What score should the inspector assign for the report?
   a. 75
   b. 81
   c. 79
   d. 85

Civil Service Practice Exam 2 Answers

Section 1: Mathematics

1. **b.** To find the fraction equivalent of a percent, rewrite the percent as a fraction with 100 in the denominator and reduce. $45\% = \frac{45}{100}$. Divide numerator and denominator by 5 to produce the result $\frac{9}{20}$, the correct answer.

2. **c.** The question asks you to rewrite the improper fraction $\frac{16}{5}$ as a mixed number. To do this, divide the numerator 16 by the denominator 5. The result is $3\frac{1}{5}$.

3. **d.** It is easiest to solve this as a proportion problem. Write a proportion with *feet* in the numerator and *minutes* in the denominator. Don't get fooled by the fact that the question asks you about both minutes AND hours; just convert 1 hour to 60 minutes so that your time units remain constant throughout your calculations. Write the following proportion: $\frac{3}{1} = \frac{x}{60}$. Now cross multiply to solve; $x = 180$, so 180 is the answer to the question.

4. **a.** Begin to solve this problem by finding the price per ounce of both options. Do this by dividing the price per number of ounces gotten for that price. For bulk, it is $\$5.60 \div 16 = \$0.35$; for the package it is $\$3.60 \div 12 = \$0.30$. Therefore, bulk almonds cost $\$0.05$ more per ounce. Since Pierre buys 12 ounces of almonds in a package he saves $12 \times \$0.05 = \$0.60$ by purchasing the package instead of in bulk.

5. **b.** The question asks for the greatest change seen in consecutive months. This change is in absolute terms and could be either negative or positive. The change from February to March was +.5, from March to April it was −1.0, from May to June it was about +.80, and from July to August it was +.5. Therefore, among the four options given the change from March to April (−1.0) was the greatest.

6. **b.** To answer this question, first determine whether the stock price in December was higher or lower than it was in January. Because it was higher, you know that the stock showed a profit for 2009. Eliminate choices **c** and **d**, because they say the stock took a loss. Next, subtract the December price from the January price. $\$8.00 − \$6.25$ equals $\$1.75$, so the stock showed a $\$1.75$ per share profit between January and December.

7. **b.** The y-axis is the vertical axis of a graph.

8. **c.** To solve this problem, rewrite each mixed number as a fraction. Rewrite $10\frac{2}{3}$ as $\frac{32}{3}$ and $3\frac{1}{8}$ as $\frac{25}{8}$. Next, find a common denominator by multiplying the two denominators. 3×8 equals 24, so rewrite each fraction with 24 in its denominator. $\frac{32}{3} \times \frac{8}{8}$ equals $\frac{256}{24}$; $\frac{25}{8} \times \frac{3}{3} = \frac{75}{24}$. Now you can subtract. $\frac{256}{24} − \frac{75}{24} = \frac{181}{24}$. Divide 181 by 24 to get the result $7\frac{13}{24}$.

9. **a.** To solve this problem, first determine the value of Jamal's certificate of deposit after one year. The certificate of deposit is worth $\$2,000$ and it earns 6% interest, so it increases in value by 6% of $\$2,000$, which is $\$120$. After one year, then, the certificate of deposit is worth $\$2,120$. In the second year, the certificate of deposit earns 6% interest on its entire value of $\$2,120$. Therefore, it earns another $\$127.20$, meaning that after two years, its value is $\$2,247.20$.

10. **d.** In order to reduce a fraction, the numerator and the denominator must be divisible by a common factor. 28 and 45 have no common factors; therefore, $\frac{28}{45}$ cannot be reduced.

11. d. To solve rate problems, apply the equation $rt = d$, where r equals rate, t equals time, and d equals distance. This question provides the time (4 days) and the distance (18.6) miles, so you can write the equation $4r = 18.6$. Next, divide both sides by 4 to get $r = 4.15$. Therefore, Belinda walks 4.15 miles per day.

12. b. When solving problems that include two different units, convert to one of the units. In this problem, both feet and inches are included. Convert 3 feet 4 inches to 40 inches by converting 3 feet to 36 inches. Next, divide 40 inches by 5 to determine that each of the five pieces of ribbon is 8 inches long.

13. a. To add mixed numbers with uncommon denominators, first convert all mixed numbers to improper fractions. Convert $2\frac{2}{5}$ to $\frac{12}{5}$, $3\frac{1}{3}$ to $\frac{10}{3}$, and $1\frac{1}{2}$ to $\frac{3}{2}$. Next, multiply the denominators 2, 3, and 5 to find a common denominator of 30. Now, rewrite all three fractions so that 30 is in the denominator of each; $\frac{12}{5} \times \frac{6}{6} = \frac{72}{30}$; $\frac{10}{3} \times \frac{10}{10} = \frac{100}{30}$; $\frac{3}{2} \times \frac{15}{15} = \frac{45}{30}$. Now you can add the fractions: $\frac{72}{30} + \frac{100}{30} + \frac{45}{30} = \frac{217}{30}$. Finally, divide 217 by 30 to produce the result $7\frac{7}{30}$.

14. a. Use the equation translation technique to write an equation for this problem. 20% of the price of the television equals $300; translate that sentence into the equation $\frac{20}{100} = 300$. Now solve by multiplying both sides by 100 to get $20 = 30,000$, and then divide both sides by 20 to get $= \$1,500$.

15. c. Because the class is exclusively populated by eight and nine-year-olds, and nine-year-olds represent $\frac{1}{5}$ of the class, it can be determined that eight-year-olds represent the remaining $\frac{4}{5}$ of the class. To estimate the fraction of guppies that are eight-year-olds, you must multiply $\frac{4}{5}$ by the fraction of students that are guppies ($\frac{1}{8}$). To multiply fractions, multiply

numerators and then denominators, and reduce if necessary. $\frac{4}{5} \times \frac{1}{8} = \frac{4}{40}$, which reduces to $\frac{1}{10}$.

16. b. This question asks you to add $3\frac{1}{2}$ and $\frac{1}{4}$. Fractions can be added together only if they have a common denominator, so rewrite $\frac{1}{2}$ as $\frac{2}{4}$. Now you can add $3\frac{2}{4}$ and $\frac{1}{4}$ to get $3\frac{3}{4}$, the correct answer. If you chose choice **a**, you probably tried to add the fractions without first finding a common denominator. If you chose choice **c**, you probably multiplied the two numbers.

17. c. To find the average number of cars sold by each salesperson, add up all the cars sold by each and then divide by the total number of salespeople. The total number of cars sold was $75 + 90 + 50 + 65 = 280$. Now divide: $280 \div 4 = 70$, which is the mean for each salesperson. Next, find the absolute difference between the mean (70) and each salesperson's total and add them together. $75 - 70 = 5$; $90 - 70 = 20$; $50 - 70 = -20$, and $65 - 70 = -5$. We are looking for absolute numbers so we can disregard the signs and add these numbers to arrive at the correct answer: $5 + 20 + 20 + 5 = 50$.

18. c. The range of a data set is the difference between the greatest and least values in the set. The greatest value in this set is 90 and the least value is 50, so the range of the data is $90 - 50$, which equals 40.

19. b. The x-axis is the horizontal axis of a graph.

20. d. To add and subtract fractions, first rewrite the fractions over a common denominator. The parentheses in the problem tell you that you must first add $\frac{1}{3}$ and $\frac{1}{4}$, so rewrite them over the common denominator 12 to get $\frac{4}{12} + \frac{3}{12}$, which equals $\frac{7}{12}$. Next, rewrite $\frac{7}{8}$ and $\frac{7}{12}$ over the common denominator 24 to get $\frac{21}{24} - \frac{14}{24} = \frac{7}{24}$.

21. c. One way to find the decimal equivalent of a percent is to rewrite the percent as a fraction: 4% equals $\frac{4}{100}$. Now, write $\frac{4}{100}$ as a decimal. If seeing the fraction "four hundredths" isn't enough to help you write the correct decimal, simply divide the numerator by the denominator to get the correct answer, 0.04.

22. d. To divide fractions, multiply the dividend (the first fraction in the equation) by the reciprocal of the divisor (the second fraction in the equation). Thus, $\frac{5}{7} \div 10$ should be rewritten as $\frac{5}{7} \times \frac{1}{10}$, which equals $\frac{5}{70}$. Divide both numerator and denominator by 5 to reduce $\frac{5}{70}$ to $\frac{1}{14}$.

23. a. To solve this problem, deduce a fraction from the ratio provided. The ratio of men to women at the school is 5:4, which means that 5 out of every 9, or $\frac{5}{9}$, of all students are men. Next, calculate $\frac{5}{9}$ of 7,650 by multiplying to get 4,250.

24. c. You can solve this problem algebraically by setting Marisol's original salary equal to x. After receiving a 10% raise, Marisol's salary will be $1.1x$. Set 1.1 equal to $55,000 and divide both sides by 1.1 to determine that equals $50,000. Another way to solve this problem is to look at the choices and work backward. Which choice, when increased by 10%, would result in a salary of $55,000? 10% of $50,000 is $5,000, so someone with a $50,000 salary who receives a 10% raise would earn a new salary of $55,000.

25. d. To determine the fraction of Sam's time spent not making calls you must add together the portions of Sam's day spent not making telephone calls. Fractions can only be added together if they have a common denominator, so rewrite $\frac{1}{8}$ and $\frac{5}{6}$ using the common denominator 24; $\frac{1}{8} = \frac{3}{24}$ and $\frac{5}{6} = \frac{20}{24}$; $\frac{3}{24} + \frac{20}{24} = \frac{23}{24}$.

26. b. The legend of a circle graph shows which sections represents which set of data.

27. a. Add the sections of the pie that represent housing and education. Wendy spends 30% of her budget on housing and 20% on education; therefore, she spends 50%, or half, her monthly budget on housing and education. Because housing is Wendy's biggest single expense, choice **b** is incorrect. Because entertainment spending could be included in the "other" category, choice **c** is not necessarily true. The graph includes no information about what Wendy would do if she had more money, so choice **d** cannot be correct.

28. c. Wendy spends 20% of her budget on education, so if her total monthly budget is $3,000, then her education spending is 20% of $3,000. Calculate 20% of $3,000 by translating the question into the equation $\frac{20}{100} \times 3,000$ and solving to get $600.

29. c. To solve rate problems, apply the equation $rt = d$, where r equals rate, t equals time, and d equals distance. This question provides the rate (18 miles per hour) and the distance (63 miles), so you can write the equation $18t = 63$. To solve, divide both sides of the equation by 18 to get $t = 3\frac{1}{2}$. Remember that there are 60 minutes in an hour; therefore, $\frac{1}{2}$ an hour equals 30 minutes; 3 hours 30 minutes is the correct answer.

30. a. Use the percent equation translation technique to write an equation for this question. The problem states that a warbler weighs 9 grams and eats an amount equal to 80% of its body weight. This means that the warbler eats $\frac{80}{100} \times 9$, which equals $\frac{720}{100}$. In decimal form, $\frac{720}{100}$ equals 7.2.

31. d. To solve this problem, divide the distance (19,800 feet) by the amount of feet in a mile (5,280). $19,800 \div 5,280 = 3.75$ or $3\frac{3}{4}$ miles.

32. a. To multiply mixed numbers, first rewrite them as improper fractions; $8\frac{1}{2}$ should be rewritten as $\frac{17}{2}$, and $3\frac{1}{4}$ should be rewritten as $\frac{13}{4}$. Next, multiply numerator by numerator and denominator by denominator; $\frac{17 \times 13}{2 \times 4} = \frac{221}{8}$. Next, rewrite the product as a mixed number by dividing the numerator by the denominator. The result is 27 with a remainder of 5, so $27\frac{5}{8}$.

33. c. There are several ways to answer this problem. One way is to multiply the number of tickets by 2; $38 \times 2 = 76$. Another way would be to divide the number of tickets by $\frac{1}{2}$; $38 \div \frac{1}{2}$ can be rewritten $38 \times \frac{2}{1} = 76$.

34. c. 20% of 140 equals 28.

35. b. To solve rate problems, apply the equation $rt = d$, where r equals rate, t equals time, and d equals distance. This question provides the time (2 hours 15 minutes) and the rate (8 kilometers per hour). Before plugging these numbers into the equation, rewrite the time as a mixed number. 2 hours 15 minutes equals $2\frac{1}{4}$ hours, so use the mixed number $2\frac{1}{4}$; $8 \times 2\frac{1}{4} = d$; $8 \times 2\frac{1}{4}$ equals $8 \times \frac{9}{4}$, which equals $\frac{72}{4}$, which reduces to 18.

36. b. To find the average number of 911 calls placed each month, add up the 911 calls for every month, and then divide by the total number of months. The total number of calls was $213 + 196 + 257 + 267 + 279 + 308 = 1,520$; $1,520 \div 6 = 253.33$ or $253\frac{1}{3}$.

37. c. The number of 911 calls per month in chronological order was 213, 196, 257, 267, 279, and 308. With the exception of the second month, the frequency of calls had increased with every month in question.

Thus, the data supports the conclusion that the frequency of 911 calls tended to increase during the period range shown.

38. b. Reduce fractions by dividing numerator and denominator by a common factor. 14 and 35 are both divisible by 7, so $\frac{14}{35}$ can be reduced to $\frac{2}{5}$.

39. a. According to the problem, last month 42 out of 840 crimes involved petty theft. You can convert this proportion to a percent using the equation $\frac{42}{840} = \frac{x}{100}$. Cross multiply to get $4,200 = 840x$, and then divide both sides of the equation by 840 to get $x = 5$. The correct answer is 5%.

40. d. One way to solve this problem is to convert the mixed number $5\frac{1}{4}$ into an improper fraction. To do this, multiply the whole number (5) by the denominator (4); $5 \times 4 = 20$. Add 20 to the numerator (1) to get $\frac{21}{4}$. Notice we are increasing the size from 6 to 9—this is $\frac{9}{6}$ the size we needed before, which can be reduced to $\frac{3}{2}$. Next, multiply the numerator of $\frac{21}{4}$ by $\frac{3}{2}$ and divide by the denominator; $21 \times \frac{3}{2} = 31\frac{1}{2}$; $31\frac{1}{2} \div 4$ is equivalent to the mixed number $7\frac{7}{8}$.

Section 2: Written Communication

41. a. Each paragraph of the passage describes an inventor whose innovations improved upon the bicycle. There is no evidence to support choice **b**. Choices **c** and **d** are incorrect because they both make statements that, according to the passage, are untrue.

42. d. The fourth paragraph states that James Starley added a gear to the pedals.

43. d. The passage gives a brief history of the bicycle. Choice **a** is incorrect because few opinions are included in the passage. There is no support for choices **b** and **c** within the passage.

44. b. Based on the passage, this is the only possible choice. Starley *revolutionized—transformed—* the bicycle.

45. d. The passage does mention the Red Cross and other agencies, and aiding victims when contacting their insurance companies, but the main focus of the passage is the role FAST plays in assisting victims dealing with the aftermath of a fire.

46. b. The team may help a victim to arrange for boarding up the fire-damaged home, but they do not do it themselves.

47. b. Among all the possible titles, choice **b** is the one that best captures the passage's main point.

48. c. Try replacing the word *expeditiously* with each answer choice. The choice that makes the most sense is **c**, *quickly*.

49. b. The passage is an information sheet about a particular food-borne illness. The main purpose of the passage is to warn readers about the dangers of contracting *Vibrio vulnificus* bacteria from oysters. Of the incorrect choices, choice **a** is too strongly worded; the passage suggests cooking all seafood but does not advise readers to avoid all seafood. No erroneous report is referenced in the passage, so choice **c** cannot be correct. Similarly, the life cycle of oysters is not discussed, so choice **d** cannot be correct.

50. c. In paragraph 2, the passage states: "The infection is much more dangerous to people with weakened immune systems, especially those who suffer from chronic liver disease."

51. a. Choice **a** is supported by the following statement from the passage: "Such individuals should avoid not only eating oysters, but also swimming in oyster-inhabited waters during the summer months, as infection can be transmitted in the water through open wounds." Choices **b**, **c**, and **d** are all contradicted by information in the passage.

52. d. Reread the sentence, substituting each choice for the word *subsequent*. In the context, only choice **d** makes sense.

53. a. The main purpose of the passage is to describe the "broken window" theory, which explains how disorder escalates if it is not checked early. Choices **b** and **d** refer to conditions in a firehouse; the example of the firehouse, however, is offered as a detail in support of the main idea. The answer to a main idea question must summarize the entire passage, not just one part of the passage. Choice **c** summarizes an idea presented in the final paragraph; however, this idea is not the main idea of the entire passage, so this cannot be the correct answer.

54. d. This is a tricky question because several of the choices are potentially challenging vocabulary words. *Condoned* (choice **a**) means *approved*, making it the opposite of *reproved*. *Ostracized* (choice **b**) means *to be outcast*, which like *reproved* has a negative connotation but is not the right word for the context; the passage suggests that the firefighter should be disciplined, not that he or she should be kicked off the fire department. For this reason, choice **c** is also incorrect.

55. b. Use process of elimination to get rid of answers that cannot be correct. The author discusses the merits of the broken window theory throughout the first two paragraphs of the passage; therefore, it is inaccurate to say that the author finds the theory "fatally flawed," so choice **a** cannot be correct. The author devotes paragraph 3 to situations in which the broken window theory causes as many problems as it addresses; therefore, choice **c** cannot be correct. Because the author describes the broken window theory as one "that can easily be applied to any situation in society," choice **d** cannot be correct.

56. a. The author makes this point most clearly at the beginning of paragraph 2: "...if disrespect to a superior is tolerated, others will be tempted to be disrespectful as well. A management crisis could erupt literally overnight."

57. c. The main purpose of the passage is to outline the procedure for adopting a pet. Because the passage warns that not all citizens make good pet owners, choice **a** cannot be correct. Choices **b** and **d** refer to details in the passage; neither of these details, though important, can be described as the main idea of the passage.

58. c. The passage states that adopted dogs and cats receive implantation of an identifying microchip if they are old enough. Therefore, it can be assumed that some animals are too young to be implanted with a microchip; thus, the passage supports the statement in choice **c**.

59. d. According to the passage, cats receive vaccination for panleukopenia. Dogs do not receive that vaccination.

60. b. This is a tricky question because several of the choices are potentially challenging vocabulary words. The word *imperative* (choice **a**) means *order* or *command*. Neither makes sense in the context of the sentence, so choice **a** cannot be correct. *Evasion* (choice **c**) means *the act of trying to avoid*. This also makes no sense in the context of the sentence. The word *ultimatum* (choice **d**) means *challenge*,

which again does not fit the context of the sentence. An *inducement* is a type of *encouragement* (choice **b**).

61. b. The correct spelling is *formulates*.

62. a. The correct spelling is *coroner*.

63. b. The correct spelling is *surmount*.

64. b. The correct spelling is *concoct*.

65. c. The correct spelling is *negotiate*.

66. c. *Painful* is the word that is closest in meaning to *excruciating*.

67. c. *Overused* is the word that is closest in meaning to *trite*.

68. b. The word *monotonous* means *boring*, so the word most nearly its opposite is *interesting*.

69. b. Choices **a** and **c** can be eliminated because neither makes sense in the context of this sentence. The word *zealous* means *passionate* and *benevolent* means *charitable*. Smoking can have a damaging effect on ones health, and *detrimental* and *damaging* are synonyms.

70. a. The word *liaison* means *meeting*; a *liaison* is usually held in secret. Choice **b**, *confection*, means *candy*. Choice **c**, *premonition*, means *hunch* or *suspicion*.

71. c. This is a sentence fragment and is missing the helping verb *was* that would make it a complete sentence.

72. b. Choice **a** uses the passive voice when a better alternative written in the active voice—choice **b**—is available. Choice **c** uses the incorrect spelling of the word *council*.

73. b. Sentences **a** contains the redundant phrase *in size*, and choice **c** does not need the words *at the zoo*.

74. c. Choices **a** and **b** contain capitalization errors. In choice **a**, the words *Commissioner* and *Jarrett* should be capitalized. In choice **b**, the word *department* should not be capitalized.

75. b. Choice **a** is incorrectly punctuated; there should be periods after *Mr.* and *Mrs.* Choice **c** incorrectly capitalizes the words *the meeting.*

76. a. Choice **b** contains an apples and oranges error, comparing *other pianists* to *the style of Thelonious Monk.* A properly formulated sentence must either compare one pianist to another or one pianist's style to another's style. Choice **c** is awkwardly and confusingly worded; choice **a** is a much better formulation of the same idea, so it is the better answer.

77. c. In choice **a**, the phrase *the president of the local Chamber of Commerce* is an appositive that should be set apart with commas. Choice **b** makes a similar error, failing to conclude the appositive phrase *the president of the local Chamber of Commerce* with a comma.

78. c. Choices **a** and **b** contain a subject-verb agreement error; the subject *use* requires a singular verb, not the plural verb *are.*

79. b. Choices **a** and **c** incorrectly use *I* where they should use *me.* Omit *Leticia* from the sentence to see why; would you say *Miguel has been assigned to work on the project with me* or *Miguel has been assigned to work on the project with I*? Because the sentence calls for an indirect object, the word *me* should be used, not *I.*

80. a. When you write a list of items, separate each item on the list with a comma, including the item preceding the word *and.* There should be no comma after the word *and*, as there is in the incorrect choice **c.**

Section 3: Civil Service Skills

81. b. The primary governing principle of customer service is to make things as easy and pleasant for the customer as possible. Choice **b** makes things easier for customers by offering them a variety of means by which to register their complaints. Choice **a** incorrectly suggests that it is good to offer services customers do not want. Choices **c** and **d** make it more difficult and inconvenient for customers to register complaints.

82. a. Once again, the focus of this exam is customer service, so choose the answer that indicates that customer service is the primary priority. Of the choices, only choice **a** focuses on customer satisfaction, so it is the best answer.

83. b. Inaccurate translation creates unnecessary problems and can, in certain circumstances, be even less desirable than no translation service at all (because inaccurate translation typically results in the transmission of incorrect information). Offering the greatest number of languages possible (choice **a**) would be extremely desirable in large diverse communities like New York City, but in most areas the availability of many languages is not that important; translating the most common foreign languages accurately would certainly be more important. Choice **c** would discourage non-English speakers from using government services. Choice **d** represents an important priority but not as important as the one presented in choice **b** because many forms have extremely limited applicability and because all forms, regardless of the language in which they are written, can be filled out with the assistance of an able and accurate translator.

84. d. Choices **a**, **b**, and **c** all provide information that will help the customer resume his or her query should he or she be disconnected during the transfer. Knowing the name of your supervisor will not help the customer continue his or her query, so it is the least important of the four.

85. d. The term *web chat* is used to describe live help provided via the Internet. Web chat is delivered via text in a chat window.

86. a. The only automobile visible in its entirety is a two-door sedan.

87. b. The skateboarder is wearing a jacket. He is hatless and is wearing long trousers. He is not wearing a cape.

88. c. Sylvia Martinez has dark shoulder-length hair. Janet Barnes is the only person whose hair is in an afro style (choice **a**).

89. a. Arthur Jones is the only person wearing a hat, the only one with a beard and moustache, and the only one wearing sunglasses. Sylvia Martinez and Janet Barnes also have dark hair.

90. b. Victor Dinapoli, Arthur Jones, and Maureen Cho all wear glasses. Carlos Domingo wears an eye patch but does not wear glasses.

91. b. The first four letters of the code must be the first four letters of the recipient's last name; therefore, the code for this entry should begin with the letters FONG. Choices **a** and **d** do not start with the letters FONG and, therefore, can be eliminated. The fifth letter in the code must be the recipient's first initial; therefore, the fifth letter of the code should be D. Only choice **b** has D as its fifth letter, so it must be the correct answer.

92. d. The first four letters of the code must be the first four letters of the recipient's last name; therefore, the code for this entry should begin with the letters RAMI. This information allows you to eliminate choices **a** and **b**. Study choices **c** and **d** to detect differences. You should see that choice **c** records the date of the correspondence JUN2, while choice **d** records the date JUN02. Check the rules to see that JUN02 is the proper format; the correct answer is choice **d**.

93. d. The code for this response should be: the first four letters of the recipient's last name (DAVI); the recipient's first initial (J); the first two digits of the recipient's street address (12); response (R); low priority (2); on October 23 (OCT23). The correct code is DAVIJ12R2OCT23.

94. c. This letter was sent to a recipient whose last name begins with the letters BERN; therefore, only choices **a** and **c** can be correct. Eliminate choices **b** and **d**. The first two digits of the recipient's address are 35; therefore, choice **a** cannot be correct. By process of elimination, the answer must be choice **c**.

95. a. The code states that two digits are to be used to indicate the recipient's street address; if the address is only one digit long, that digit should be preceded by a zero (0).

96. c. One incident of cold food stored at too high a temperature should be coded C. Two incidents of animal droppings should be coded HH. One incident of improperly labeled food should be coded p. The correct code for this set of violations is CHHp.

97. a. Three incidents of improper storage of toxic cleaning materials should be coded ppp. One incident of a misplaced consumer advisory should be coded r. The correct code for this set of violations is pppr.

98. a. All four of the incidents described earn a three-point deduction from 100, a perfect score: 4×3 equals 12; $100 - 12$ equals 88.

99. d. The inspector observed multiple incidents of the violation coded *s*. The letter *s* is the code for smoking in the food preparation area.

100. b. Each of the violations coded with a capital letter results in a five-point deduction; each of the violations coded with a lower-case letter results in a three-point deduction: 2×5 equals 10 and 3×3 equals 9; $10 + 9$ equals 19, and $100 - 19$ equals 81.

10 ▶ CIVIL SERVICE PRACTICE EXAM 3

This is the last practice exam in this book, but it is not designed to be any harder than the other two. It is simply another representation of the kinds of questions you might expect to see on your civil service exam.

For this exam, pull together all the tips you've been practicing since the first practice exam. Give yourself the time and space to work. Because you won't be taking the real test in your living room, you might want to take this one in an unfamiliar location, such as a library. Make sure you have plenty of time to complete the exam in one sitting. In addition, use what you have learned from reading the answer explanations on the previous practice exams. Remember the types of questions that have caused problems for you in the past, and when you are unsure, try to consider how those answers were explained.

Once again, use the answer explanations at the end of the exam to understand questions you may have missed.

A version of this practice test is available through the LearningExpress online link if you prefer to take it on a computer. See the back of this book for complete details.

Civil Service Practice Exam 3

1.	ⓐ	ⓑ	ⓒ	ⓓ
2.	ⓐ	ⓑ	ⓒ	ⓓ
3.	ⓐ	ⓑ	ⓒ	ⓓ
4.	ⓐ	ⓑ	ⓒ	ⓓ
5.	ⓐ	ⓑ	ⓒ	ⓓ
6.	ⓐ	ⓑ	ⓒ	ⓓ
7.	ⓐ	ⓑ	ⓒ	ⓓ
8.	ⓐ	ⓑ	ⓒ	ⓓ
9.	ⓐ	ⓑ	ⓒ	ⓓ
10.	ⓐ	ⓑ	ⓒ	ⓓ
11.	ⓐ	ⓑ	ⓒ	ⓓ
12.	ⓐ	ⓑ	ⓒ	ⓓ
13.	ⓐ	ⓑ	ⓒ	ⓓ
14.	ⓐ	ⓑ	ⓒ	ⓓ
15.	ⓐ	ⓑ	ⓒ	ⓓ
16.	ⓐ	ⓑ	ⓒ	ⓓ
17.	ⓐ	ⓑ	ⓒ	ⓓ
18.	ⓐ	ⓑ	ⓒ	ⓓ
19.	ⓐ	ⓑ	ⓒ	ⓓ
20.	ⓐ	ⓑ	ⓒ	ⓓ
21.	ⓐ	ⓑ	ⓒ	ⓓ
22.	ⓐ	ⓑ	ⓒ	ⓓ
23.	ⓐ	ⓑ	ⓒ	ⓓ
24.	ⓐ	ⓑ	ⓒ	ⓓ
25.	ⓐ	ⓑ	ⓒ	ⓓ
26.	ⓐ	ⓑ	ⓒ	ⓓ
27.	ⓐ	ⓑ	ⓒ	ⓓ
28.	ⓐ	ⓑ	ⓒ	ⓓ
29.	ⓐ	ⓑ	ⓒ	ⓓ
30.	ⓐ	ⓑ	ⓒ	ⓓ
31.	ⓐ	ⓑ	ⓒ	ⓓ
32.	ⓐ	ⓑ	ⓒ	ⓓ
33.	ⓐ	ⓑ	ⓒ	ⓓ
34.	ⓐ	ⓑ	ⓒ	ⓓ
35.	ⓐ	ⓑ	ⓒ	ⓓ

36.	ⓐ	ⓑ	ⓒ	ⓓ
37.	ⓐ	ⓑ	ⓒ	ⓓ
38.	ⓐ	ⓑ	ⓒ	ⓓ
39.	ⓐ	ⓑ	ⓒ	ⓓ
40.	ⓐ	ⓑ	ⓒ	ⓓ
41.	ⓐ	ⓑ	ⓒ	ⓓ
42.	ⓐ	ⓑ	ⓒ	ⓓ
43.	ⓐ	ⓑ	ⓒ	ⓓ
44.	ⓐ	ⓑ	ⓒ	ⓓ
45.	ⓐ	ⓑ	ⓒ	ⓓ
46.	ⓐ	ⓑ	ⓒ	ⓓ
47.	ⓐ	ⓑ	ⓒ	ⓓ
48.	ⓐ	ⓑ	ⓒ	ⓓ
49.	ⓐ	ⓑ	ⓒ	ⓓ
50.	ⓐ	ⓑ	ⓒ	ⓓ
51.	ⓐ	ⓑ	ⓒ	ⓓ
52.	ⓐ	ⓑ	ⓒ	ⓓ
53.	ⓐ	ⓑ	ⓒ	ⓓ
54.	ⓐ	ⓑ	ⓒ	ⓓ
55.	ⓐ	ⓑ	ⓒ	ⓓ
56.	ⓐ	ⓑ	ⓒ	ⓓ
57.	ⓐ	ⓑ	ⓒ	ⓓ
58.	ⓐ	ⓑ	ⓒ	ⓓ
59.	ⓐ	ⓑ	ⓒ	ⓓ
60.	ⓐ	ⓑ	ⓒ	ⓓ
61.	ⓐ	ⓑ	ⓒ	ⓓ
62.	ⓐ	ⓑ	ⓒ	ⓓ
63.	ⓐ	ⓑ	ⓒ	ⓓ
64.	ⓐ	ⓑ	ⓒ	ⓓ
65.	ⓐ	ⓑ	ⓒ	ⓓ
66.	ⓐ	ⓑ	ⓒ	ⓓ
67.	ⓐ	ⓑ	ⓒ	ⓓ
68.	ⓐ	ⓑ	ⓒ	ⓓ
69.	ⓐ	ⓑ	ⓒ	ⓓ
70.	ⓐ	ⓑ	ⓒ	ⓓ

71.	ⓐ	ⓑ	ⓒ	ⓓ
72.	ⓐ	ⓑ	ⓒ	ⓓ
73.	ⓐ	ⓑ	ⓒ	ⓓ
74.	ⓐ	ⓑ	ⓒ	ⓓ
75.	ⓐ	ⓑ	ⓒ	ⓓ
76.	ⓐ	ⓑ	ⓒ	ⓓ
77.	ⓐ	ⓑ	ⓒ	ⓓ
78.	ⓐ	ⓑ	ⓒ	ⓓ
79.	ⓐ	ⓑ	ⓒ	ⓓ
80.	ⓐ	ⓑ	ⓒ	ⓓ
81.	ⓐ	ⓑ	ⓒ	ⓓ
82.	ⓐ	ⓑ	ⓒ	ⓓ
83.	ⓐ	ⓑ	ⓒ	ⓓ
84.	ⓐ	ⓑ	ⓒ	ⓓ
85.	ⓐ	ⓑ	ⓒ	ⓓ
86.	ⓐ	ⓑ	ⓒ	ⓓ
87.	ⓐ	ⓑ	ⓒ	ⓓ
88.	ⓐ	ⓑ	ⓒ	ⓓ
89.	ⓐ	ⓑ	ⓒ	ⓓ
90.	ⓐ	ⓑ	ⓒ	ⓓ
91.	ⓐ	ⓑ	ⓒ	ⓓ
92.	ⓐ	ⓑ	ⓒ	ⓓ
93.	ⓐ	ⓑ	ⓒ	ⓓ
94.	ⓐ	ⓑ	ⓒ	ⓓ
95.	ⓐ	ⓑ	ⓒ	ⓓ
96.	ⓐ	ⓑ	ⓒ	ⓓ
97.	ⓐ	ⓑ	ⓒ	ⓓ
98.	ⓐ	ⓑ	ⓒ	ⓓ
99.	ⓐ	ⓑ	ⓒ	ⓓ
100.	ⓐ	ⓑ	ⓒ	ⓓ

Section 1: Mathematics

Select the best answer for each question.

1. Patrolman Peterson drove $3\frac{1}{2}$ miles to the police station. Then he drove $4\frac{3}{4}$ miles to his first assignment. Next, he drove $3\frac{2}{3}$ miles back to the police station for a meeting. Finally, he drove $3\frac{1}{2}$ miles home. How many miles did Patrolman Peterson drive?
   a. $15\frac{5}{12}$
   b. $14\frac{5}{12}$
   c. $14\frac{1}{4}$
   d. $13\frac{11}{12}$

2. Martine made a pie and cut it into eight equal slices. He kept two slices for himself and gave the rest of the pie to April. April gave Mae $\frac{1}{3}$ of her share of the pie and ate the rest of what she had gotten from Martine. How many slices of pie did April eat?
   a. 2
   b. $2\frac{1}{3}$
   c. 3
   d. 4

3. $\frac{9}{10} - \frac{2}{5} =$
   a. $\frac{1}{2}$
   b. $\frac{7}{5}$
   c. $\frac{5}{7}$
   d. $1\frac{3}{10}$

4. A bus travels along a highway at a constant rate of 55 miles per hour. How far does the bus travel in 3 hours 24 minutes?
   a. 165 miles
   b. 178.2 miles
   c. 187 miles
   d. 192.5 miles

5. A certain state charges sales tax of $\frac{1}{9}$ of the purchase price on all entertainment services. What is the percentage of sales tax charged in this state on entertainment services?
   a. 9%
   b. 9.19%
   c. 10%
   d. 11.11%

Study the following graph, and then use it to answer questions 6 to 8.

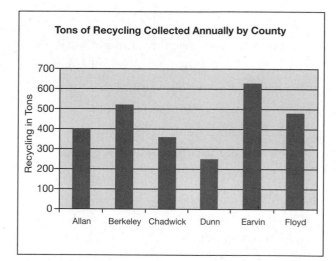

6. The data on the *x*-axis represents the
   a. amount of recycling collected, in tons.
   b. names of the counties.
   c. time period during which the data was collected.
   d. names of the companies hired to collect recycling.

7. The data on the *y*-axis represents the
   a. amount of recycling collected in tons.
   b. names of the counties.
   c. time period during which the data was collected.
   d. names of the companies hired to collect recycling.

8. The graph best supports which of the following conclusions?

   a. The population of Berkeley County is greater than the population of Floyd County.

   b. Of all the state's residents, the people of Berkeley County are most enthusiastic about recycling.

   c. Dunn County does not need to collect its recycling as frequently as does Earvin County.

   d. The people of Floyd County are more avid newspaper readers than are the people of Chadwick County.

9. Joanne must complete three tasks at work. She estimates that the first two tasks will each take her 45 minutes to complete and that the third task will take her 2 hours 10 minutes to complete. If Joanne's estimate is correct, how long will it take her to complete all three tasks?

   a. 2 hours 40 minutes

   b. 3 hours

   c. 3 hours 20 minutes

   d. 3 hours 40 minutes

10. The Gleason Theater seats 296 people and was sold out for the premier of a new play, *Captain Coffee*. Friends and family of the cast accounted for $\frac{5}{8}$ of all the seats. VIP tickets were given away on the radio and winners accounted for 37 of the seats. The general public bought the remaining tickets. What portion of the total seats was taken by the general public?

   a. $\frac{1}{4}$

   b. $\frac{3}{8}$

   c. $\frac{2}{5}$

   d. $\frac{1}{2}$

11. $\frac{4}{5} + \frac{1}{6} =$

   a. $\frac{29}{30}$

   b. $\frac{5}{11}$

   c. $\frac{2}{15}$

   d. $\frac{5}{6}$

12. Reduce $\frac{33}{121}$ to lowest terms.

   a. $\frac{1}{4}$

   b. $\frac{3}{11}$

   c. $\frac{1}{3}$

   d. The fraction cannot be reduced.

13. Ken earns a bonus when he works on Saturdays. The bonus is $1\frac{1}{2}$ times his standard hourly pay for the first four hours, and 2 times his standard pay on any additional hours he works. If his standard hourly pay is $12.50, how much bonus pay does Ken earn when he works six hours on a Saturday?

   a. $75

   b. $100

   c. $112.50

   d. $125

14. $\frac{72}{10} =$

   a. $7\frac{1}{10}$

   b. $\frac{10}{72}$

   c. $\frac{5}{36}$

   d. $7\frac{1}{5}$

Study the following graph, and then use it to answer questions 15 to 17.

PRICE AND MILES PER GALLON BY MAKE OF AUTOMOBILE		
MAKE	RETAIL PRICE (STICKER)	MILES PER GALLON (CITY/ HIGHWAY)
Voltero	$16,600	31/38
Accellator	$22,100	22/28
Montannic	$27,800	16/20
GXC 501	$31,500	27/32

15. Which conclusion is best supported by the data in the table?

a. There is no correlation between the price of a car and its gas mileage.

b. The more an automobile costs, the poorer its gas mileage.

c. The chief factors in determining the price of an automobile are its size and weight.

d. Most people pay considerably less than retail price for a new car.

16. What is the range of highway mileage shown in the table?

a. 38

b. 15

c. 10

d. 18

17. Compare the price of the different automobiles as a function of miles per gallon each is able to drive in the city. Which is the most expensive in this comparison?

a. Voltero

b. Accellator

c. Montannic

d. GXC 501

18. The star of a baseball team earns a salary of $8.5 million per year. A second-string player on the team earns a salary equal to 5% of the star's salary. What is the second-string player's salary?

a. $50,000

b. $425,000

c. $850,000

d. $8 million

19. $7\frac{1}{5} - 4\frac{4}{5} =$

a. $2\frac{2}{5}$

b. $3\frac{2}{5}$

c. $1\frac{3}{5}$

d. 0

20. Find the percent equivalent of 0.7.

a. 7%

b. 70%

c. 0.7%

d. 700%

21. Mr. Wallace is writing a budget request to upgrade his personal computer system. He wants to purchase 256 mb of SDRAM, which costs $80; two new software programs that cost $350 each; a 2 GB flash memory card for $65; and a new scanner for $165. What is the total amount Mr. Wallace should write on his budget request?

a. $660

b. $1,010

c. $1,356

d. $1,366

22. A migrating bird flies 12 hours per day. If the bird flies at an average speed of 20 miles per hour, how far does the bird fly in one day?

a. 400 miles

b. 240 miles

c. 200 miles

d. 32 miles

23. $\frac{2}{5} \div \frac{4}{7} =$

a. $\frac{8}{35}$

b. 1

c. $\frac{1}{2}$

d. $\frac{7}{10}$

24. Frank wants a pair of jeans that are priced at $86.00. He has a coupon for 20% off that price. What price would Frank pay if he used his coupon to buy this pair of jeans?

a. $64.50

b. $66.00

c. $68.00

d. $68.80

25. $2\frac{3}{8} =$

a. $\frac{19}{3}$

b. $\frac{19}{8}$

c. $\frac{13}{8}$

d. $\frac{5}{8}$

26. Find the fraction equivalent of 0.0034.

a. $\frac{34}{100}$

b. $\frac{34}{1,000}$

c. $\frac{34}{10,000}$

d. $\frac{34}{100,000}$

Study the following graph, and then use it to answer questions 27 to 28.

Causes of Household Fires in Percentages

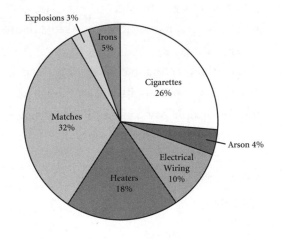

27. According to the circle graph, the most common cause of household fires is

a. matches.

b. cigarettes.

c. heaters.

d. arson.

28. The city of Grandee had 500 household fires last year. Based on the information in the graph, how many of those fires were most likely caused by explosions?

a. 3
b. 5
c. 15
d. 30

29. A community service organization has a staff of 40 people. At any given time, six members of the staff are on duty. What percent of the staff is on duty at the organization?

a. 6%
b. 8%
c. 12%
d. 15%

30. A lottery jackpot of $30,000 was split between four co-workers. Will and David each received 20% of the jackpot and the rest was split between June and Karen. If Karen is given a portion of the jackpot that is 3 times the size of the portion given to June, how much was given to Karen?

a. $4,500
b. $6,000
c. $12,000
d. $13,000

31. Bill leaves his house and walks directly toward Melissa's house at a rate of 110 yards per minute. Melissa leaves her house at the same time and walks directly toward Bill's house at a rate of 95 yards per minute. Bill and Melissa's houses are exactly 2,870 yards apart. In how many minutes will Bill and Melissa meet?

a. 11 minutes
b. 14 minutes
c. 26 minutes
d. 30 minutes

32. Thirty percent of The Parking Authority's employees are over the age of 50. If The Parking Authority has 150 employees, how many are over the age of 50?

a. 45
b. 50
c. 105
d. 120

33. At the grocery store, Erica purchased bread for $4.80, eggs for $2.65, and juice for $3.95. There was no tax on the purchase and she paid for the items with a twenty dollar bill. What amount of change will Erica receive?

a. $8.40
b. $8.60
c. $11.40
d. $11.60

34. $5\frac{1}{3} \div 1\frac{5}{9} =$

a. $3\frac{3}{7}$
b. $3\frac{7}{9}$
c. $6\frac{8}{9}$
d. $4\frac{289}{42}$

35. An empty swimming pool is filled by two inlet pipes. One pipe can fill $\frac{1}{10}$ of the swimming pool in one hour. The other can fill $\frac{1}{8}$ of the swimming pool in one hour. If both inlet pipes are used to fill the pool, how many hours will it take to fill the empty pool?
- **a.** 8 hours
- **b.** 6 hours
- **c.** 4 hours 6 minutes
- **d.** 2 hours 45 minutes

36. 200 marbles weigh 5 pounds. If 5% of the marbles are red, how much do just the red marbles weigh?
- **a.** $\frac{1}{40}$ pound
- **b.** $\frac{1}{20}$ pound
- **c.** $\frac{1}{4}$ pound
- **d.** $\frac{2}{5}$ pound

37. $6\frac{1}{5} \times 75 =$
- **a.** 450
- **b.** $71\frac{1}{5}$
- **c.** 465
- **d.** $522\frac{3}{5}$

Study the following graph, and then use it to answer questions 38 to 40.

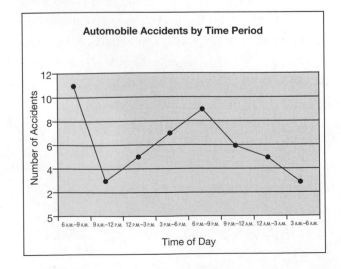

Automobile Accidents by Time Period

38. What is the range of the data shown in the graph?
- **a.** 3
- **b.** 8
- **c.** 11
- **d.** 14

39. The average (arithmetic mean) number of accidents per three-hour time period is
- **a.** between 3 and 4.
- **b.** between 4 and 5.
- **c.** between 5 and 6.
- **d.** between 6 and 7.

40. The number of accidents per time period is represented by the
- **a.** scale.
- **b.** x-axis.
- **c.** y-axis.
- **d.** legend.

Section 2: Written Communication

Reading Comprehensions—Questions 41 to 60

Read the following passage. Then, answer questions 41 to 44.

Federal, state, and local courts produce a mountain of documents every day. Those documents need to be recorded and stored accurately in order for the various legal systems to function. The person who maintains these records is called the clerk of the court.

The parameters of the clerk of the court's job is defined by statute and so varies somewhat from <u>jurisdiction</u> to jurisdiction, but most clerks share a number of responsibilities in common. First and foremost, the clerk maintains the court's clerical records. Everything from the court's seal to the contracts and the orders it approves, to the judgments it issues to the verdicts it hands down must be accurately recorded and filed. The clerk also maintains official records of all marriages, leases, mortgages, deeds, and other property transfers.

Most localities assign additional responsibilities to the clerk of the court. In many jurisdictions, the clerk is empowered to perform marriages; the clerk of the court in St. Mary's County, Maryland, for example, conducts more than 3,000 marriages per year. Many clerks are responsible for issuing passports and jury summons, distributing jurors' pay, and overseeing the collection and distribution of court fines and court-ordered child support and alimony. As if those jobs weren't enough to keep a clerk busy, in some jurisdictions the clerk is also the chief financial officer of the court, responsible for making sure that budgets are met, that paychecks are issued, and that court expenditures all conform with the law.

With such a formidable list of tasks, it's no wonder that most clerks' offices are busy places. The operation of the clerk's duties requires a well-trained, dedicated, and efficient staff. Organizational skill is obviously required of anyone working for the clerk, but people skills are also important; the clerk's office deals with the public on a regular basis, often under stressful circumstances. Although demanding, work in a clerk's office brings with it the satisfaction of knowing that one has performed an essential role in allowing our court system to function properly.

41. The author's primary purpose in writing this passage is to
   a. argue that most clerks of the court deserve salary increases.
   b. inform people of the number of marriages performed annually in the United States.
   c. describe the many functions of the clerk of the court.
   d. define the term *clerical records*.

42. The final paragraph of the passage suggests that
   a. very few people are qualified to work in the clerk of the court's office.
   b. the clerk of the court's office is a satisfying place to work.
   c. all one needs to succeed in the clerk of the court's office is good people skills.
   d. the court's seal is an extremely important document.

43. As used in the passage, the word *jurisdiction* most nearly means
   a. domain.
   b. nation.
   c. individual.
   d. political party.

44. According to the passage, the clerk of courts
   a. decides verdicts in criminal cases.
   b. determines alimony levels in divorce cases.
   c. exists only in the state of Maryland.
   d. maintains the court's records.

Read the following passage. Then, answer questions 45 to 48.

State and local governments are almost always underfunded, a situation that compels them to constantly seek new ways to cut costs. Of course, the same governments are run by elected officials who, as a consequence of the conditions of their employment, must concern themselves with their constituents' satisfaction with government services. Thus, government leaders face a near-impossible challenge: reduce costs while improving—or at least, not diminishing—the quality of service.

In recent years, governments have increasingly turned to outsourcing as a solution to their problems. Working on the belief that the private sector operates more efficiently than does the government, state and local governments have started contracting private companies to perform jobs previously managed publicly. The results have been mixed.

One of the great success stories of government outsourcing is found in New York City. The city owns 13 public golf courses, which, under city management, fell into disrepair. The courses were not only poorly kept, they were dangerous; one course in the Bronx became a notorious dumping ground for garbage and the occasional corpse. Making matters worse, the city lost an average of $2 million per year on the golf courses. Since contracting out operations, the city has reversed that $2 million loss, instead realizing an annual profit of $2 million; best of all, they've done it without significantly increasing course income. Furthermore, conditions on the courses have greatly improved, as the private operators have invested substantially in material upgrades.

Texas has not been quite as fortunate, however, in its effort to privatize management of welfare benefits. With its caseload increasing and federal funding shrinking, the state naturally looked for a way to reduce costs. Privatization seemed the best choice: Contract bids suggested that the states could save hundreds of millions of dollars by shifting benefits administration services to a private company. The relationship started promisingly: The company replaced the state's <u>antiquated</u> computer program with a modern database, and then opened four new call centers to handle client queries. Unfortunately, the quality of service was initially poor, with many clients complaining that the call centers were difficult to reach and that the information they provided was often inaccurate. As a result, clients quickly grew to distrust the new system. The state and its contractor are now attempting to address the problems; it is too early to know whether they will succeed.

Outsourcing offers some benefits to governments eyeing the bottom line. It is by no means a guaranteed panacea, however, and public officials must consider

each situation closely before deciding whether outsourcing is an appropriate solution.

45. The author's main idea is best summarized by which of the following?
   a. The municipal golf courses of New York have both grown more profitable and improved in quality since their management was outsourced.
   b. The state of Texas may never be able to undo the damage caused by its experiment in outsourcing social services.
   c. State and local governments always save money and improve services when they outsource.
   d. Outsourcing of government services can be successful, but by no means is it guaranteed to solve more problems than it causes.

46. As used in the passage, the word *antiquated* most nearly means
   a. outdated.
   b. broken.
   c. slow.
   d. uncertain.

47. According to the passage, clients of Texas's outsourced social service programs complained that
   a. call center operators did not speak Spanish.
   b. benefits checks were slow in arriving.
   c. clients were often given incorrect information.
   d. user fees discouraged them from taking advantage of the programs.

48. The passage suggests that the contractors who took control of New York City's golf courses
  a. had little previous experience in golf course management.
  b. used course income more efficiently than did the city.
  c. charged golfers much higher user fees than did the city.
  d. were difficult to reach by telephone.

Read the following passage. Then, answer questions 49 to 52.

Most criminals do not suffer from antisocial personality disorder; however, nearly all persons with this disorder have been in trouble with the law at some point in their lives. Sometimes labeled sociopaths, they are often a grim problem for society. Their crimes often range from con games to murder, and they are set apart by what appears to be a complete lack of conscience. Often attractive and charming, and always inordinately self-confident, they nevertheless demonstrate a disturbing emotional shallowness, as if they had been born without a faculty as vital as sight or hearing. These individuals are not legally insane, nor do they suffer from the distortions of thought associated with mental illness; however, some experts believe they are mentally ill. If so, it is an illness that is exceptionally resistant to treatment, particularly since these individuals have a marked inability to learn from their past actions. It is this latter trait that makes them a special problem for law enforcement officials. Their ability to mimic true emotion enables them to convince prison officials, judges, and psychiatrists that they feel remorse. However, when released from incarceration they go back to their old tricks, impulsive destructiveness, and sometimes lethal deceptions.

49. Based on the passage, which of the following is likely not a characteristic of a person with antisocial personality disorder?
  a. delusions of persecution
  b. feelings of superiority
  c. inability to suffer deeply
  d. inability to feel joy

50. Which of the following careers would probably best suit a person with antisocial personality disorder?
  a. soldier with ambition to make officer
  b. warden of a large penitentiary
  c. loan officer in a bank
  d. salesperson dealing in nonexistent real estate

51. Based on the passage, which of the following words best sums up the inner emotional life of a person with antisocial personality?
  a. angry
  b. empty
  c. anxious
  d. repressed

52. According to the passage, which of the following characteristics is most helpful to a person with an antisocial personality in terms of getting out of trouble with the law?
  a. inability to learn from the past.
  b. ability to mimic the emotions of others
  c. attractiveness and charm
  d. indifference to the suffering of others

Read the following passage. Then, answer questions 53 to 56.

Did you ever wonder how the U.S. Postal Service chooses the images that appear on postage stamps? Nearly all the subjects of stamps originate with a suggestion from the public. The Citizens' Stamp Advisory Committee (CSAC), a 15-member board appointed by the Postmaster General, is charged with reviewing suggestions and selecting approximately 25 <u>commemorative</u> stamps each year.

Upon receiving a suggestion, the CSAC first determines whether the stamp meets the 12 major criteria for selection. Among the qualifying characteristics: The subject must be American or related to America; the subject must be of national, rather than regional or local, interest; if human, the subject must been deceased for at least ten years (except for former presidents, who can be honored immediately after their deaths); and, if commemorating an historic event, the stamp must be released on an anniversary that is a multiple of 50. Prohibited subjects include individual towns, cities, elementary and secondary schools, hospitals, and libraries; fraternal, political, sectarian, and service organizations; and religious groups.

If a nominee meets all the qualifications, it is added to the roster for consideration at the upcoming meeting of the CSAC, which meets four times each year. The committee may decide to reject the nominee, or it may set it aside for consideration of future issuance. All stamps in the latter category must undergo a second round of review before they can be scheduled for design and their subsequent release.

If you've submitted a suggestion to the CSAC, don't expect to be notified of the committee's decision; the committee has no staff, and announcements of upcoming stamp subjects are made by press release only. In other words, if you want to see whether your stamp has been chosen, you'll have to read the newspaper or check the U.S. Postal Service website. You should also be aware that the entire selection process typically takes three years. If you're the impatient type, suggesting subjects for stamps is probably not the right hobby for you!

53. As used in the passage, the word *commemorative* most nearly means
   a. funereal.
   b. mnemonic.
   c. celebratory.
   d. exclusive.

54. The author's purpose in writing this passage is to
   a. explain a process.
   b. define terms.
   c. persuade an audience.
   d. propose a new idea.

55. According to the passage, the Citizens' Stamp Advisory Committee
   a. determines the rules for selecting stamps.
   b. meets four times each year.
   c. is made up of former Postmaster Generals of the United States.
   d. contacts everyone who suggests a subject for a stamp.

56. Based on information in the passage, which of the following is the subject most likely to be honored with a U.S. postage stamp?
   a. the city of Chicago
   b. the current president of the United States
   c. the Republican Party
   d. Yellowstone National Park

Read the following passage. Then, answer questions 57 to 60.

Although many companies offer tuition reimbursement, most reimburse employees only for classes that are relevant to their position. This is a very limiting policy. A company that reimburses employees for all college courses—whether job related or not—offers a service not only to the employees, but to the entire company and greater community as well.

One good reason for giving employees unconditional tuition reimbursement is that it shows the company's dedication to its employees. In today's economy, where job security is a thing of the past and employees feel more and more <u>expendable</u>, it is important for a company to demonstrate to its employees that it cares. The best way to do this is with concrete investments in its employees and their futures.

In turn, this dedication will create greater employee loyalty. A company that releases funds to pay for the education of its employees will get its money back by having employees stay with the company longer. Employee turnover will be reduced because even the employees who do not take advantage of the tuition reimbursement program will be more loyal—just knowing that their company cares enough to pay for their education invokes loyalty. Most importantly, the company that has an unrestricted tuition reimbursement program will have higher quality employees.

Although these companies do indeed run the risk of losing money on an employee who goes on to another job at a different company as soon as he or she gets a degree, more often than not the employee will stay with the company. And even if employees do leave after graduation, it generally takes several years to complete any degree program. If the employee leaves upon graduation, the employer will have had a more sophisticated, more intelligent, and therefore more valuable and productive employee during that employee's tenure. If the employee stays, that education will doubly benefit the company. Not only is the employee more educated, but now that employee is in a better position to be promoted, and the company does not have the challenge of filling a high-level vacancy from the outside. Though unconditional tuition reimbursement requires a significant investment on the employer's part, it is perhaps one of the wisest investments a company can make.

57. According to the passage, unconditional tuition reimbursement is good for which of the following reasons?
　a. employees get a cheaper education
　b. employees become more valuable
　c. employees can find better jobs
　d. employers lose a great deal of money

58. The author's reason for writing this passage was to
　a. entertain the reader.
　b. narrate a story.
　c. explain tuition reimbursement.
　d. persuade the reader.

59. The writer most likely uses the word *wisest* in the last sentence, rather than words such as *profitable*, *practical*, or *beneficial*, because
　a. wisdom is associated with education, the subject of the passage.
　b. the writer is trying to appeal to people who are already highly educated.
　c. education could not be considered practical.
　d. the word *beneficial* is too abstract for readers to comprehend.

60. In paragraph two, the word *expendable* most nearly means
a. expensive.
b. flexible.
c. replaceable.
d. extraneous.

Spelling—Questions 61 to 65
Select the choice that is spelled correctly.

61. Mrs. Ramirez agrees that the effectiveness of her new hiring policy is _____
a. debatible
b. debateable
c. debatable

62. The archaeologist strained the sand through a_____ to see if it contained any small artifacts.
a. sieve
b. sive
c. seive

63. Which of the following words is spelled incorrectly?
a. subside
b. feesable
c. impersonal

64. Which of the following words is spelled incorrectly?
a. recktify
b. narrate
c. transcribe

65. Which of the following words is spelled incorrectly?
a. atrocious
b. infernal
c. detearierating

Vocabulary—Questions 66 to 70
Select the best choice for each question.

66. Find the word that is closest in meaning to the underlined word below.
an <u>opulent</u> home
a. luxurious
b. shabby
c. occasional

67. Find the word that is closest in meaning to the underlined word below.
a <u>laborious</u> task
a. profitable
b. simple
c. difficult

68. Find the word that is most nearly the opposite of the underlined word below.
the <u>pompous</u> professor
a. uneducated
b. humble
c. strict

69. Find the word that best completes the sentence below.
If you collect my mail while I am on vacation, I will _____ by mowing your lawn when I return.
a. renege
b. reciprocate
c. rejuvenate

70. Find the word that best completes the sentence below.

The defendant's fingerprints on the murder weapon provided the most

_____ evidence against her.

a. incriminating

b. exonerating

c. dubious

Grammar—Questions 71 to 80

Select the best choice for each question.

71. Which of the following is a complete sentence?

a. Because of the worsening weather conditions, the cancellation of tonight's event.

b. The worsening of weather conditions has caused the cancellation of tonight's event.

c. The cancellation of tonight's event on account of there being worsening weather conditions.

72. Select the sentence that is written most correctly.

a. "Would you prefer sugar or artificial sweetener with your coffee?" Humphrey inquired.

b. Would you prefer sugar or artificial sweetener with your coffee, Humphrey inquired?

c. "Would you prefer sugar or artificial sweetener with your coffee?" Humphrey inquired?

73. Select the sentence that is written most correctly.

a. Located along the railroad tracks, the noise of passing trains disrupted performances at the community theater.

b. Located along the railroad tracks, the community theater had, by the noise of passing trains, its performances disrupted.

c. Because it was located along the railroad tracks, the community theater had its performances disrupted by the noise of passing trains.

74. Select the sentence that is written most correctly.

a. Mr. and Mrs. Harrison decided to have a picnic to celebrate Labor Day.

b. Mr. and mrs. Harrison decided to have a picnic to celebrate Labor day.

c. Mr. and Mrs. Harrison decided to have a Picnic to celebrate Labor day.

75. Select the sentence that is written most correctly.

a. Each member of the Jameson family holds an advanced degree in either science or mathematics.

b. Each member of the Jameson family hold an advanced degree in either science or mathematics.

c. Each and every member of the Jameson family hold an advanced degree in either science or mathematics.

76. Select the sentence that is written most correctly.

a. Dr. Richard K Brown, CEO of the company, will speak to the scientists at Brookhaven National Laboratory on Wed at 9:00 A.M.

b. Dr Richard K Brown, C.E.O. of the company, will speak to the scientists at the Brookhaven National Laboratory on Wed. at 9:00 A.M.

c. Dr. Richard K. Brown, C.E.O. of the company, will speak to the scientists at the Brookhaven National Laboratory on Wed. at 9:00 A.M.

77. Select the sentence that is written most correctly.

a. A decision was made by the manager and will be followed by her subordinates.

b. A decision was made by the manager her subordinates will follow it.

c. The manager made a decision and her subordinates will follow it.

78. Select the sentence that is written most correctly.

　a. The committee did their work very effectively.

　b. The committee did their work very effective.

　c. The committee did its work very effectively.

79. Select the sentence that is written most correctly.

　a. The bands performance has greatly bettered since they increased the length of their practice sessions.

　b. The band's performance has greatly improved since they increased the length of their practice sessions.

　c. The bands performance has greatly improved since they increased the length of their practice session's.

80. Select the sentence that is written most correctly.

　a. The consensus of opinion among the advertisers was that customers would be enticed by a free gift.

　b. The consensus of opinion among the advertisers was that customers would be enticed by a gift.

　c. The consensus among the advertisers was that customers would be enticed by a gift.

Section 3: Civil Service Skills

Customer Service— Questions 81 to 85

Select the best choice for each question.

81. Government offices strive to address customers' queries during a single visit or exchange whenever possible, a principle known as

　a. self-service communication.

　b. first contact resolution.

　c. interactive voice response.

　d. the abandonment rate.

82. Responses to citizen complaints should be

　a. processed twice annually to ensure uniformity of response.

　b. approved by a supervisor before they are delivered.

　c. delivered as quickly and accurately as possible.

　d. withheld until the citizen completes a customer satisfaction evaluation.

83. When scheduling an agency's office hours, a supervisor's primary consideration should be

　a. employees' personal commitments outside work.

　b. the schedules of other agencies with which the agency sometimes interacts.

　c. the time of year and its effect on electricity usage.

　d. the schedules of citizens who most often contact the agency.

84. Customers who request to speak to a supervisor should be

　a. allowed to do so in a timely manner whenever possible.

　b. informed that the help of a supervisor is not necessary to resolve their situation.

　c. prevented from distracting the supervisor from his or her duties.

　d. given an appointment at a later date to meet the supervisor.

85. Customers who contact an office by telephone and are put on hold more than one minute should

　a. not be informed of the projected wait time because inaccurate estimates anger customers.

　b. be informed of the projected wait time so they can make an informed decision about whether to wait.

　c. hear a recorded message encouraging them to resolve their matter via mail or in person.

　d. be offered a face-to-face appointment on the following day if their call is not handled within five minutes.

Memory—Questions 86 to 90

Take five minutes to study the following picture. Then, answer question 86 without looking back at the picture.

© Corbis

86. Who is holding a cellular telephone in the
photograph?
   a. only the woman on the left
   b. only the woman in the middle
   c. only the woman on the right
   d. all three women

Take five minutes to study the following picture. Then answer questions 87 to 88 without looking back at the picture.

© Corbis

87. There are two women in the photograph. Which woman has hair long enough to cover her shoulder?
a. only the woman on the left
b. only the woman on the right
c. both women
d. neither woman

88. Which type of vehicle is visible in the photograph?
a. a city bus
b. a cable car
c. a locomotive
d. an airplane

Take five minutes to study the text that follows. Then, answer questions 89 through 90 without looking back at the text.

The following is the text of a notice posted in a government office. It instructs employees on the proper procedure for evacuating the office during a fire.

- Know the location of all stairwells, emergency exits, and fire extinguishers. Learn how to operate a fire extinguisher.
- If you see a fire, activate the nearest fire alarm. If you have a cell phone or are near a public telephone, call 911 to alert the fire department.
- If you do not have access to an alarm or a phone, inform other building occupants that they should vacate the building.
- If possible, assist others in evacuating the building.
- If the fire is small, use a fire extinguisher to extinguish the fire. Remember that you should never attempt to extinguish a fire when:

—you do not know what is fueling the fire (e.g., chemicals)
—you cannot keep a clear path between yourself and a fire exit
—the fire might block your path of escape
—the fire has spread to many locations
—the fire is spreading rapidly
—the fire is producing copious amounts of smoke

- Evacuate the building. If possible, close windows and doors if you are the last one to leave.
- Exit the building by stairwells. Do not use elevators.
- If you have not yet done so, notify the fire department. Report the location and nature of the fire.
- Do not reenter the building without the permission of the fire department.

89. According to the notice, people should not try to extinguish a fire on their own if they
a. can detect the color blue in the burning flames.
b. do not have the assistance of at least one other person.
c. cannot maintain ready access to a fire exit.
d. can contain the fire to a contained location.

90. According to the notice, why should people not use elevators during a fire?
a. The fire might interrupt electrical service, rendering elevators inoperative.
b. It is impossible to determine the fire conditions in an elevator shaft.
c. An elevator is not always the quickest way to leave a building.
d. The notice does not provide a reason people should not use elevators.

Coding—Questions 91 to 100

To answer questions 91 through 95, refer to the following scenario.

Each employee at a government office is assigned a unique identification code. The code is created according to the following rules:

4 digits = the first two digits represent an employee's last name; the second two digits represent the employee's first name. Digits are assigned accordingly:

0 = ABC

1 = DEF

2 = GHI

3 = JKL

4 = MNO

5 = PQR

6 = STU

7 = VWX

8 = YZ

1 letter = job grade. Jobs are graded 1 through 19; letters are assigned based on the numerical equivalent of the letter (i.e., A = 1, B = 2, C = 3, D = 4, etc.)

4 digits = month and date of birth (e.g., April 7 = 0407)

91. Marlene Romanoff is a grade 12 employee. Her birthday is December 24. What is her identification code?
   a. 4053AB2412
   b. 4053M2412
   c. 5440M1224
   d. 5440AB1224

92. Abdul Qoph is a grade 5 employee. His birthday is July 8. What is his identification code?
   a. 5400E0708
   b. 5400E78
   c. 0054E0708
   d. 0054E78

93. To whom might the identification code 6521R1115 belong?
   a. Barry Felton
   b. Spencer Henderson
   c. William Trieste
   d. Gerald Springer

94. Which of the following statements about the employee with identification code 0524D1102 must be true?
   a. The employee's birthday is May 24.
   b. The employee's birthday is November 2.
   c. The employee's last name begins with the letter D.
   d. The employee is a grade 8 employee.

95. Create an identification code for the following employee:
   Name: Rodriguez, Alexis
   Date of Birth: September 22
   Job Grade: 8
   a. 03540922H
   b. 03542209H
   c. 5403H0922
   d. 54032209H

To answer questions 96 through 100, refer to the following scenario.

A county animal control uses a code to log all complaints it receives. Each call receives a single code even if it includes multiple complaints. The code follows the rules below:

Subject of complaint

C = cat
D = dog
H = horse
R = reptile
Z = none of the above

Nature of complaint (record all that apply)

0 = noise
1 = animal not properly restrained (e.g., no leash, not contained in enclosed area)
2 = animal improperly fed, watered, or sheltered
3 = animal not properly licensed
4 = animal behaves menacingly toward human or other animal
5 = abandoned animal
6 = illegal animal breeding

The nature of complaint or complaints directly follows the code for the animal that is the subject of the complaint.

96. A citizen called animal control to complain that a neighbor's dog was barking and that the same neighbor owns a horse that is not properly fenced in. How should this complaint be coded?
  a. D0H1
  b. DH01
  c. 0DH1
  d. H10D

97. An animal control officer is flagged down by a citizen who directs the officer to a neighbor's house. There, the citizen points out that the neighbor owns a dog and a cat; he further notes that the dog is not receiving food or water and that neither the dog nor cat is properly licensed. How should this complaint be coded?
  a. DC23
  b. D3C23
  c. D23C3
  d. D2C3

98. Animal control receives a complaint of an abandoned horse that is not properly fed or watered. How should this complaint be coded?
  a. 25
  b. H5
  c. H2
  d. H25

99. The code Z5 could refer to
  a. a barking dog.
  b. an underfed horse.
  c. an abandoned pig.
  d. a menacing reptile.

100. An inspector discovers an illegal breeding facility at which the owner is breeding dogs, cats, horses, and ferrets. How should the inspector code this discovery?
  a. CDHZ6
  b. C6D6H6Z6
  c. CDHZ6666
  d. C6DHZ

Civil Service Practice Exam 3 Answers

Section 1: Mathematics

1. a. To add mixed numbers with uncommon denominators, first convert all mixed numbers to improper fractions. First, convert $3\frac{1}{2}$ to $\frac{7}{2}$, $4\frac{3}{4}$ to $\frac{19}{4}$, $3\frac{2}{3}$ to $\frac{11}{3}$, and $3\frac{1}{2}$ to $\frac{7}{2}$. Next, rewrite $\frac{7}{2}$, $\frac{19}{4}$, $\frac{11}{3}$, and $\frac{7}{2}$ over a common denominator. Use 12 because it is evenly divisibly by 2, 3, and 4; $\frac{7}{2} \times \frac{6}{6} = \frac{42}{12}$, $\frac{19}{4} \times \frac{3}{3} = \frac{57}{12}$, $\frac{11}{3} \times \frac{4}{4} = \frac{44}{12}$, and $\frac{7}{2} \times \frac{6}{6} = \frac{42}{12}$. Now, add the fractions: $\frac{42 + 57 + 44 + 42}{12} = \frac{185}{12}$. Finally, divide 185 by 12 to produce the result, $15\frac{5}{12}$.

2. d. Martine kept 2 of 8 equal slices, which can be represented by the fraction $\frac{2}{8}$. This reduces to $\frac{1}{4}$, which would mean he gave April the remaining $\frac{3}{4}$ of the pie. Mae took $\frac{1}{3}$ of April's portion. To determine the fraction of pie Mae took you must multiply the $\frac{1}{3}$ she took from April by the $\frac{3}{4}$ of the total that April got. To multiply fractions, multiply numerators, then denominators, and then reduce if necessary. $\frac{1}{3} \times \frac{3}{4} = \frac{3}{12}$, which reduces to $\frac{1}{4}$. Mae and Martine both had $\frac{1}{4}$ of the pie or 2 slices each for a total of 4 slices. With 8 original slices less the 4 that Mae and Martine ate, April must have eaten 4 slices.

3. a. To add and subtract fractions, first rewrite the fractions over a common denominator. Rewrite this problem as $\frac{9}{10} - \frac{4}{10}$, then subtract to get $\frac{5}{10}$, which reduces to $\frac{1}{2}$.

4. c. To solve rate problems, apply the equation $rt = d$, where r equals rate, t equals time, and d equals distance. This problem provides the rate (55 miles per hour) and the time (3 hours 24 minutes). Before plugging numbers into the formula, rewrite 3 hours 24 minutes as a decimal. $\frac{24}{60}$ equals $\frac{2}{5}$, so 3 hours 24 minutes equals $3\frac{2}{5}$ hours, which equals 3.4 hours. Now plug values into the formula: $55(3.4) = d$. Multiply 55 and 3.4 to get 187.

5. d. To find the decimal equivalent of a fraction, divide the numerator by the denominator; $1 \div 9 = 0.1111$. To arrive at the percentage of sales tax this represents you must multiply the product by 100, or move the decimal point two spaces to the right, resulting in 11.11%.

6. b. The x-axis is the horizontal axis of a graph, which in this graph shows the names of the counties.

7. a. The y-axis is the vertical axis of a graph, which in this graph shows the amount of recycling collected.

8. c. According to the graph, Dunn County produces less than half as much recycling as does Earvin County. Therefore, the data in the graph supports the conclusion that Dunn County does not need to collect its recycling as frequently as does Earvin County. Choice **a** relies on faulty reasoning; just because Berkeley County produces more recycling than does Floyd County does not mean that the former has a larger population. It is possible that Berkeley residents simply produce more recycling per capita. Because the graph includes no information about citizens' attitudes toward recycling, choice **b** cannot be correct. Because the graph does not break out the different types of items that are recycled, it is impossible to draw any conclusions about the amount of newspaper recycled, and therefore, choice **d** cannot be correct.

9. d. Joanne takes 45 minutes to complete *each* of two tasks; therefore, the two tasks take a total of 90 minutes, or 1 hour 30 minutes to complete. The third task takes 2 hours 10 minutes, meaning all 30 tasks take a total of 3 hours 40 minutes to complete.

10. a. The portion of seats on sale to the general public can be found by subtracting from the total the number of seats taken by friends and family of the cast and those given away on the radio. To arrive at how many seat are left after those taken by friends and family, multiply the total number of seats (296) by the portion of that amount that they did not take ($\frac{3}{8}$); $296 \times \frac{3}{8} = 111$. Next, subtract the number of VIP tickets given away on the radio from this amount to arrive at the number of seats taken by the general public; $111 - 37 = 74$. Lastly, divide this number by the total number of seats to determine the portion taken by the general public; $74 \div 296 = \frac{1}{4}$.

11. a. To add fractions, rewrite them over a common denominator. The least common multiple of 5 and 6 is 30, so rewrite each fraction over the denominator 30; $\frac{4}{5} \times \frac{6}{6} = \frac{24}{30}$; $\frac{1}{6} \times \frac{5}{5} = \frac{5}{30}$. $\frac{24 + 5}{30} = \frac{29}{30}$. If you selected choice **b**, you probably added numerator to numerator and denominator to denominator; you should review the rules for adding fractions.

12. b. Both 33 and 121 are divisible by 11. Divide each by 11 to reduce $\frac{33}{121}$ to $\frac{3}{11}$.

13. d. There are a number of ways to arrive at the answer to this question. One way is to say Ken's bonus pay is $1\frac{1}{2}$ times his regular pay of $12.50 for the first four hours and 2 times that amount for hours worked over four hours. $\frac{1}{2}$ of Ken's regular pay would be $6.25, which when added to his regular pay equals a rate of $18.75. Ken's regular pay multiplied by 2 is $12.50 × 2 = $25.00 an hour. For the six hour shift described, Ken would get paid four hours at $18.75 an hour and two hours at $25.00 an hour; $18.75 × 4 = $75.00 and $25.00 × 2 = $50.00; $75.00 + $50.00 = $125.

14. d. Divide 72 by 10 to get 7 remainder 2, or $7\frac{2}{10}$. Reduce $\frac{2}{10}$ to $\frac{1}{5}$ to reach the final choice of $7\frac{1}{5}$.

15. a. Study the relationship between cost and gas mileage shown in the table. The data show neither an increase nor a decrease in gas mileage of an automobile as its cost increases. Therefore, the data show no relationship between cost and gas mileage. Choice **b** is contradicted by the data, as explained previously. Choice **c** cannot be correct because the table provides no data on the size and weight of the different automobiles listed. Because no data on actual sale price is provided, choice **d** also cannot be correct.

16. d. The range of a data set is the difference between the greatest and least values in the set. The greatest value in this set is 38 and the least value is 20, so the range of the data is 38 – 20, which equals 18. Note that the question asks about highway mileage, so you must use only the second of the two numbers provided in the right-hand column of the table. Using the first number, which represents city mileage, produces an incorrect answer.

17. c. To answer this question, take the retail price of each car and divide it by the number of miles per gallon it is able to drive in the city. In order from top to bottom: $16,600 ÷ 31 = $535.48; $22,100 ÷ 22 = $1,004.54; $27,800 ÷ 16 = $1,737.50; and $31,500 ÷ 27 = $1,166.66. The greatest of these results is $1,737.50, belonging to the Montannic.

18. b. To answer this question, you must calculate 5% of $8.5 million. One way to do this quickly and efficiently is to calculate 10% of $8.5 million by moving the decimal one place to the left. Thus, 10% of $8.5 million is $0.85 million; 5% is half of 10%, so 5% of $8.5 million is half of $0.85 million, which is $0.425 million, or $425,000.

19. a. To subtract mixed numbers, convert them to improper fractions. Rewrite $7\frac{1}{5}$ as $\frac{36}{5}$ and $4\frac{4}{5}$ as $\frac{24}{5}$. Now subtract: $\frac{36-24}{5} = \frac{12}{5}$, which equals $2\frac{2}{5}$.

20. b. The decimal 0.7 is equal to the fraction $\frac{7}{10}$, which can be rewritten as $\frac{70}{100}$. Because a percent is the numerator of a fraction with a denominator of 100, 0.7 equals 70%.

21. b. Mr. Wallace wants to spend $80 on SDRAM, $700 on software (two programs costing $350 each), $65 on flash memory, and $165 on a scanner; $80 + $700 + $65 + $165 equals $1,010. If you selected choice **a**, you probably forgot to double $350 to account for the fact that Mr. Wallace plans to buy two software programs that cost $350 each.

22. b. To solve rate problems, apply the equation $rt = d$, where r equals rate, t equals time, and d equals distance. The problem provides time (12 hours) and rate (20 miles per hour). Plug these values into the formula and solve; $12 \times 20 = d$, so $d = 240$.

23. d. To divide fractions, multiply the dividend (the first fraction in the equation) by the reciprocal of the divisor (the second fraction in the equation). Thus, $\frac{2}{5} \div \frac{4}{7}$ should be rewritten as $\frac{2}{5} \times \frac{7}{4}$, which equals $\frac{14}{20}$. Divide numerator and denominator by 2 to reduce $\frac{14}{20}$ to $\frac{7}{10}$.

24. d. If Frank paid with his coupon he would pay 80% or $\frac{4}{5}$ of the total price of the jeans, which is $86. To arrive at the new price, multiply the original price by the fraction of that price he will be paying ($\frac{4}{5}$); $86.00 \times \frac{4}{5} = $68.80.

25. b. This question asks you to rewrite the mixed number $2\frac{3}{8}$ as an improper fraction. To do this, multiply the whole number 2 by the denominator 8 to get the product 16. Add 16 to the numerator 3. The correct answer is $\frac{19}{8}$.

26. c. To rewrite a decimal as a fraction, count the number of places in the decimal. The denominator of the fraction will be the digit 1 with as many zeros as the number of places you counted following it. In this case, the decimal 0.0034 has four places, so the denominator of the fraction will be a 1 and 4 zeros, i.e., 10,000. The numerator of the fraction is the decimal itself, less the decimal point and all consecutive zeros to the immediate right of the decimal point. Thus, the numerator of this fraction is 34, and the fraction is $\frac{34}{10,000}$.

27. a. The graph shows that 32% of household fires are caused by matches, more than any other single cause.

28. c. The question asks you to find 3% of 500; 3% of 100 is 3, so 3% of 500 is 5×3 (because 500 is 5×100). Thus, the answer to the question is 15.

29. d. The question asks you to determine what percentage of 40 is represented by 6. Use the translation technique to write an equation that asks "6 is what % of 40" as follows: $6 = \frac{x}{100} \times 40$. Next, divide both sides of the equation by 40 to get $\frac{6}{40} = \frac{x}{100}$. Now you can cross multiply to get $40x = 6,000$ and divide both sides by 40 to get $x = 15$.

30. a. To answer this question, you must first determine how much of the jackpot was given to each of Will, David, and June, and then take the sum of those subscriptions and subtract it from the total of $30,000 to determine how many Karen sold. Will and David each received 20% of the total of $30,000 which equals $6,000 each, or $12,000 when added together. Subtract $12,000 from the total of $30,000 to arrive at $18,000, the portion split by June and Karen. You can look at the fact that Karen receives 3 times the portion June gets as creating four equal parts with Karen receiving 3 of the 4 parts or $\frac{3}{4}$. To arrive at how much Karen was given, multiply the $18,000 she and June split by her portion of that amount ($\frac{3}{4}$); $18,000 \times \frac{3}{4} = $13,500.

31. b. To solve rate problems, apply the equation $rt = d$, where r equals rate, t equals time, and d equals distance. This problem is a little tricky because it provides two rates, Bill's (110 yards per minute) and Melissa's (95 yards per minute). However, because Bill and Melissa are walking directly toward each other, they approach each other at a rate equal to the sum of their two rates. That is, for every minute they walk, Bill and Melissa get 100 + 95, or 205, yards closer to each other. They approach each other at a rate of 205 yards per minute. Now, plug the rate and the distance (2,870 yards) into the formula and solve. $205t = 2,870$; to solve, divide both sides by 205. The result is 14.

32. a. Thirty percent is equivalent to the fraction $\frac{3}{10}$. To determine the number of employees over the age of 50 you must multiply $\frac{3}{10}$ by 150, the total number of employees. $\frac{3}{10} \times \frac{150}{1} = \frac{450}{10}$, which reduces to 45.

33. b. To answer this question, sum the prices of the three items together, and subtract the total from $20.00; $4.80 + $2.65 + $3.95 = $11.40. $20.00 − $11.40 = $8.60.

34. a. To divide mixed numbers, first rewrite the mixed numbers as fractions. Rewrite $5\frac{1}{3}$ as $\frac{16}{3}$

and $1\frac{5}{9}$ as $\frac{14}{9}$. Next, multiply the dividend (the first fraction in the equation) by the reciprocal of the divisor (the second fraction in the equation). Thus, $\frac{16}{3} \div \frac{14}{9}$ should be rewritten as $\frac{16}{3} \times \frac{9}{14}$, which equals $\frac{144}{42}$. Rewrite $\frac{144}{42}$ as $3\frac{18}{42}$, and then reduce $\frac{18}{42}$ to $\frac{3}{7}$ by dividing numerator and denominator by 6. The correct answer is $3\frac{3}{7}$.

35. c. When both pipes are used to fill the pool, they fill the pool at a rate of $\frac{1}{10} + \frac{1}{8}$ per hour; $\frac{1}{10} + \frac{1}{8}$ equals $\frac{4}{40} + \frac{5}{40}$, or $\frac{9}{40}$, per hour. That means that the pipes fill slightly less than one-quarter of the pool each hour; therefore, the job takes a little more than four hours to complete. Use process of elimination to determine that choice **c** is the only possible answer.

36. c. The number of marbles is irrelevant, red marbles account for 5% or $\frac{1}{20}$ of the total weight. The total weight is 5 pounds, so to solve multiply 5 by the numerator and divide the product by the denominator; $5 \times 1 = \frac{5}{20}$, which reduces to $\frac{1}{4}$ pound.

37. c. First, rewrite $6\frac{1}{5}$ as an improper fraction by multiplying the whole number 6 by the denominator 5 and adding the product to the numerator 1 to get $\frac{31}{5}$. Next, multiply $\frac{31}{5}$ and $\frac{75}{1}$ to get $\frac{2,325}{5}$. Finally, divide 2,325 by 5 to get 465.

38. b. The range of a data set is the difference between the greatest and least values in the set. The greatest value in this set is 11 and the least value is 3, so the range of the data is 11 − 3, which equals 8.

39. d. To find the mean number of accidents per time period, add the different data points, and then divide by the number of time periods shown. The data is 11, 3, 5, 7, 9, 6, 5, and 3. The sum of the data is 49. Divide 49 by 8, the number of time periods shown, to get $6\frac{1}{8}$.

Thus, the mean number of accidents per time period is between 6 and 7.

40. c. The *y*-axis is the vertical scale of the graph.

Section 2: Written Communication

41. c. The purpose of this passage is to explain the clerk of the court's job. The passage is informational, not persuasive, so choice **a** cannot be correct. Choices **b** and **d** refer to details of one paragraph of the passage; the correct answer to a main idea question must describe the entire passage, not just one small part of it.

42. b. The final paragraph states, "Although demanding, work in a clerk's office brings with it the satisfaction of knowing that one has performed an essential role in allowing our court system to function properly." This sentence suggests that the clerk of the court's office is a satisfying place to work. Choice **a** draws too strong a conclusion; although working in the clerk of the court's office requires special skills, that does not mean that "very few people are qualified" to work there. Choice **c** is contradicted by the statement "Organizational skill is obviously required of anyone working for the clerk." The court's seal is not even mentioned in the final paragraph, so choice **d** cannot be correct.

43. a. *Domain* means "area under control of a particular government, court, etc." It is the best choice. The clerk of the court works for federal, state, or local courts whose jurisdiction is local or regional, not national; therefore, choice **b** cannot be correct. The clerk of the court functions in a system governed by the rule of law, not by an individual or a political party, so choices **c** and **d** cannot be correct.

44. d. In the second paragraph, the passages states, "First and foremost, the clerk maintains the court's clerical records."

45. d. Use process of elimination to find the answer to this question. Choices **a** and **b** refer to specific details of the passage. They do not summarize the entire passage and, therefore, cannot sum up the author's main idea. Choice **c** is contradicted by the example of Texas's outsourcing of welfare benefits, which the author tells us has *not* improved services.

46. a. This is a tricky question, because choices **b** and **c** make sense in context; the state's computer system may indeed have been *broken* or *slow*. However, the word *antiquated* means *old* or *obsolete*. The word shares a root with the word *antique*, which should have helped you figure out that the word *antiquated* has something to do with age.

47. c. The passage states, "Unfortunately, the quality of service was initially poor, with many clients complaining that the call centers were difficult to reach *and that the information they provided was often inaccurate*." This statement supports choice **c**. None of the other choices are supported by information in the passage.

48. b. The passage states, "Since contracting out operations, the city has reversed that $2 million loss, instead realizing an annual profit of $2 million; best of all, they've done it without significantly increasing course income." This statement supports the conclusion that the contractors who took control of New York City's golf courses used course income more efficiently than did the city, because they have increased profits and improved services without increasing income.

49. a. The discussion of the traits of a person with antisocial personality disorder in the middle of the passage specifies that such a person does not have distortions of thought, such as delusions of persecution. The passage speaks of the antisocial person as being inordinately self-confident (choice **b**) and of the person's emotional shallowness (choices **c** and **d**).

50. d. The third sentence of the passage speaks of con games. None of the other professions would suit an impulsive, shallow person who has been in trouble with the law.

51. b. The passage mentions emotional shallowness. The other choices hint at the ability to feel meaningful emotion.

52. b. The passage says that a person with antisocial personality disorder can mimic real emotion, thereby conning prison officials, judges, and psychiatrists. The other choices are mentioned in the passage, but not in connection with getting out of trouble with the law.

53. c. *Commemorative* means *preserving or honoring the memory of.* Thus, *celebratory* is closest in meaning to *commemorative. Funereal* (choice **a**) means *sad* or *somber; mnemonic* means *promoting memory;* and *exclusive* means *available to a select group only.*

54. a. The passage explains the process by which subjects for U.S. stamps are selected.

55. b. In paragraph 3, the passage states that the committee meets four times each year. The passage does not say how the rules for selecting a stamp were established, so choice **a** cannot be correct. The committee is appointed by the Postmaster General, but the passage does not say whether it is made up of former Postmasters General, so choice **c** cannot be correct. Choice **d** is contradicted in the first sentence of the final paragraph.

56. d. The final sentence of paragraph 2 states, "Prohibited subjects include individual towns, cities, elementary and secondary schools, hospitals, and libraries; fraternal, political, sectarian, and service organizations; and religious groups." Chicago (choice **a**) is an individual city, so it cannot be honored in a stamp. Likewise, the Republican Party (choice **c**) is a political organization, and so it cannot be honored on a stamp. The passage also points out that stamps may not depict living human beings; therefore, choice **b** cannot be correct.

57. b. The idea that employees will become more valuable if they take courses is stated in the fourth paragraph, which argues that the employer will have had a more sophisticated, more intelligent, and therefore more valuable and productive employee.

58. d. The writer of this passage states the opinion that a company that reimburses employees for all college courses, whether job related or not, offers a service to its employees, the entire company, and the greater community. The writer then proceeds to give reasons to persuade the reader of the validity of this statement.

59. a. By using a word associated with education, the writer is able to reinforce the importance of education and tuition reimbursement.

60. c. As used in the passage, *expendable* means *replaceable.* The writer uses the word immediately after saying that job security is a thing of the past. This clue tells you that workers do not feel they are important or valuable to a company that can fire them on a moment's notice.

61. c. The correct spelling is *debatable*.

62. a. The correct spelling is *sieve*.

63. b. The correct spelling is *feasible*.

64. a. The correct spelling is *rectify*.

65. c. The correct spelling is *deteriorating*.

66. a. *Opulent* means *luxurious*.

67. c. Take a look at the word *laborious*. You may notice that it includes the word *labor*, which means *hard work*.

68. b. *Pompous* means *stuck up* and *snobbish*, so *humble* is its opposite.

69. b. *Reciprocate* means *to repay*. The speaker in the sentence offers to repay a favor with a similar favor, so *reciprocate* is the best word for the blank. *Renege* (choice **a**) means *to go back on your work*. *Rejuvenate* (choice **c**) means *to modernize*.

70. a. *Incriminating* means *suggesting guilt*. Fingerprints on a murder weapon are definitely *incriminating* evidence. *Exonerating* (choice **b**) means *suggesting innocence*, which is the opposite of *incriminating*. *Dubious* (choice **c**) means *doubtful*.

71. b. Choices **a** and **c** consist of dependent clauses only, so they are not complete sentences.

72. a. Because the statement *Would you prefer sugar or artificial sweetener in your coffee* is a direct quote, it must be in quotation marks. Thus, choice **b** is incorrect. Because this statement is a question, it must end in a question mark. The entire sentence, however, is not a question; it is a statement of fact reporting what Humphrey asked. Thus, the sentence should not end in a question mark. Choice **c** ends in a question mark and is, therefore, incorrect.

73. c. The phrase *located along the railroad tracks* is a modifier describing *the community theater*. Choice **a** incorrectly states that it is *the noise of passing trains* rather than *the community theater* that is located along the tracks. Choice **b** is awkwardly and confusingly constructed; choice **c**, the correct answer, demonstrates how to express the same ideas much more clearly.

74. a. Choices **b** and **c** contain capitalization errors. In both, the word *Day* should be capitalized. In choice **b**, the word *Mrs.* should be capitalized. In choice **c**, the word *picnic* should not be capitalized.

75. a. The subject of the sentence is *each member*, which takes a singular verb. Therefore, choices **b** and **c**, in which the subject takes the plural verb *hold*, are incorrect.

76. c. Periods are correctly placed after all abbreviations in this sentence.

77. c. Each of the incorrect answers is written in the passive voice; the correct answer is written in the active voice, which is preferred.

78. c. *Committee* is a collective noun that takes a singular pronoun. Both incorrect choices use the plural pronoun *their* to refer to the committee.

79. b. Choice **a** is incorrect because *bands* should have an apostrophe and *bettered* is not an appropriate word choice. Choice **c** is incorrect because the word *sessions* contains an unnecessary apostrophe.

80. c. The phrase *consensus of opinion* is redundant; the word *consensus* means *unity of opinion*. Therefore, choices **a** and **b** are redundant. The term *free gift* in choice **a** is also redundant, because all gifts are free.

Section 3: Civil Service Skills

81. b. The correct term for this principle is *first contact resolution.*

82. c. The primary governing principle of customer service is to make things as easy and pleasant for the customer as possible. Choice **c** best articulates this principle. Each of the incorrect answers would result in an unnecessary delay in delivering service to the customer.

83. d. Once again, the correct answer reflects the need to place primary importance on the needs of citizens, the users of government services.

84. a. Choices **b** and **c** will almost certainly antagonize the customer, never a good idea when satisfying customer service is the goal. Choice **d** adds an unnecessary inconvenience and, therefore, will also probably annoy the customer. Only choice **a** reflects a "customer service first" attitude.

85. b. In general, the more accurate information you provide a customer, the better the customer's assessment of service will be. By informing customers of the approximate wait to speak with a representative, you allay their fears that they have been forgotten, that the call has been routed to a dead end, etc. Of course, some customers will be annoyed if the estimate turns out to be inaccurate, but not as annoyed as customers become when left on hold indefinitely with no idea of when they will ultimately be served.

86. a. Only one woman—the woman on the left—is holding a cell phone.

87. c. Both women have shoulder-length hair.

88. b. The vehicle is a cable car.

89. c. The notice states that "you should never attempt to extinguish a fire when . . . you cannot keep a clear path between yourself and the fire exit."

90. d. The notice simply states that people should not use the elevators; it does not explain the reasoning for this advice.

91. c. The first pair of digits in the code represent the employee's last name; the second pair represent the employee's first name. Marlene Romanoff's identification number should begin 54 (for the RO in Romanoff) 40 (for the MA in Marlene). Only choices **c** and **d** begin 5440; eliminate choices **a** and **b**. Job codes are a single letter; therefore, the two-letter job code AB that appears in choice **d** is incorrect. Choice **c** must be the correct answer by process of elimination.

92. a. Abdul Qoph's identification number should begin 54 (QO in Qoph) 00 (AB in Abdul). Eliminate choices **c** and **d**, which begin 0054. The code uses four digits to represent birthdays; therefore, choice **b** is incorrect. Choice **a** must be the correct answer by process of elimination.

93. d. This identification belongs to someone whose last name begins with the letter S, T, or U; the second letter in his last name is P, Q, or R. Only choices **c** and **d** meet this requirement; eliminate choices **a** and **b**. The employee's first name begins with the letter G, H, or I; this information allows you to eliminate choice **c**. The correct answer must be choice **d**.

94. b. The final four digits of the identification code represent the holder's birthday. The figures 1102 tell you that this employee's birthday is November 2.

95. c. The RO in Rodriguez is coded 54; the AL in Alexis is coded 03; the job grade 8 is coded H, because H is the eighth letter in the alphabet; the birthday September 22 is coded 0922. The correct identification number for Alexis Rodriguez is 5403H0922.

96. a. The rules of the code state, "The nature of complaint or complaints directly follows the code for the animal that is the subject of the complaint." Therefore, the code for a barking dog is D0 and the code for an improperly restrained horse is H1. The correct code for the incident described in the question is D0H1.

97. c. The code for a dog that is improperly fed and is not licensed is D23; the code for a cat that is not licensed is C3. The correct code for this incident is D23C3.

98. d. The code for a horse is H. The code for an abandoned animal is 5, and the code for improper food and water is 2. The code for this incident is H25.

99. c. The code Z refers to any animal other than a cat, dog, horse, or reptile. The code 5 refers to an abandoned animal. Thus, Z5 could refer to an abandoned pig.

100. b. The rules of the code state, "The nature of complaint or complaints directly follows the code for the animal that is the subject of the complaint." Therefore, the code for improper breeding of cats is C6; the code for improper breeding of dogs is D6, etc. The correct code for this incident is C6D6H6Z6.

ADDITIONAL ONLINE PRACTICE ▶

Whether you need help building basic skills or preparing for an exam, visit the LearningExpress Practice Center! On this site, you can access additional practice materials. Using the code below, you'll be able to log in and take a practice Civil Service exam. This online practice exam will also provide you with:

- **Immediate Scoring**
- **Detailed answer explanations**
- **Personalized recommendations for further practice and study**

Log on to the LearningExpress Practice Center by using the URL: **www.learnatest.com/practice**

This is your Access Code: **7441**

Follow the steps online to redeem your access code. After you've used your access code to register with the site, you will be prompted to create a username and password. For easy reference, record them here:

Username: _____ **Password:** _____

With your username and password, you can log in and answer these practice questions as many times as you like. If you have any questions or problems, please contact LearningExpress customer service at 1-800-295-9556 ext. 2, or e-mail us at **customerservice@learningexpressllc.com**

NOTES